UNRAVELLING HOUSING FINANCE

UNRAVELLING HOUSING FINANCE

Subsidies, Benefits, and Taxation

JOHN HILLS

CLARENDON PRESS · OXFORD

Oxford University Press, Walton Street, Oxford OX2 6DP

Oxford New York Toronto
Delhi Bombay Calcutta Madras Karachi
Kuala Lumpur Singapore Hong Kong Tokyo
Nairobi Dar es Salaam Cape Town
Melbourne Auckland Madrid
and associated companies in
Berlin Ibadan

Oxford is a trade mark of Oxford University Press

Published in the United States by
Oxford University Press Inc., New York

First published 1991
First issued in paperback 1992

British Library Cataloguing in Publication Data
Hills, John
Unravelling housing finance : subsidies, benefits and taxation.
1. Great Britain. Housing. Subsidies by government
I. Title
363.58
ISBN 0-19-877303-X

Library of Congress Cataloging in Publication Data
Hills, John.
Unravelling housing finance : subsidies, benefits, and taxation
John Hills.
p. cm.
Includes bibliographical references and index.
1. Housing—Great Britain—Finance. 2. Housing subsidies—Great
Britain. 3. Real property and taxation—Great Britain. 4. Housing
policy—Great Britain. I. Title.
HD7333.A4H55 1991 363.5'82-dc20 90-20613
ISBN 0-19-877303-X

1 3 5 7 9 10 8 6 4 2

Printed in Great Britain by
Biddles Ltd., Guildford and King's Lynn

To Anne

Preface

The debts which I owe to those who have helped me produce this book are many. First, its writing and the research behind substantial parts of it were made possible by generous support from the Joseph Rowntree Foundation as part of its Housing Finance Initiative. The Economic and Social Research Council funded the research underlying Chapter 13 (as part of its Public Expenditure Research Programme) and Chapter 14 (as part of the Welfare Research Programme at the LSE, Programme Grant X 206 32 2001). The author is also grateful to Suntory Limited for its support for the LSE Welfare State Programme, under which earlier versions of material included in Chapters 4, 5, 6, 8, 15, and 16 were written.

Parts of the taxation chapters draw on a University of Birmingham Master's Degree dissertation supervised and inspired by Mervyn King a decade ago, while the chapter on housing benefits draws on joint work with Richard Hemming at the Institute for Fiscal Studies in 1983. Several of the chapters started life as lectures for the LSE's Diploma in Housing, and I am very grateful to the students on that course both for acting as sounding boards for some of the material, and for their responses, which have helped me identify the parts which needed most clarification.

During the course of the research behind the book I was greatly assisted by many including: Tony Atkinson, Richard Berthoud, Richard Best, Roger Brayshaw, Hilary Chipping, Ralph Connelly, Peter Englund, Howard Glennerster, Chris Gordon, Sue Goss, Alan Holmans, Stephanie Holmans, Gordon Hughes, Estelle James, Julian Le Grand, Duncan Maclennan, Peter Malpass, David Page, David Piachaud, John Posnett, Steven Preston, Euan Ramsay, Nick Raynsford, Nick Stern, Tony Travers, David Treanor, and Christine Whitehead. Colleagues with the Welfare State Programme at the LSE have helped in a variety of different ways—not least forbearance while the book was completed—especially Jane Dickson, Stephen Edward, Maria Evandrou, Karen Gardiner, Gervas Huxley, Beverley Mullings, Holly Sutherland, Brian Warren, and David Winter. Earlier drafts of particular parts have been greatly improved by comments kindly made by Glen Bramley, Stephen Duckworth, Peter Kemp, Anne Power, and John

Stevens, and especially by Mark Kleinman, and Judy Yates, who uncomplainingly read the entire manuscript, making numerous suggestions for improvements. While none of these bears responsibility for any errors which remain, the book could not have been completed without their assistance, and I am most grateful to all of them.

J.H.

London School of Economics
May 1990

Contents

Figures

Tables

Abbreviations

ACL	Admissible Cost Limits
BES	Business Expansion Scheme
BSM	Building Society Mortgages (Survey)
CIT	Comprehensive Income Tax
FES	Family Expenditure Survey
GDP	Gross Domestic Product
GFC	General Fund Contribution
GGE	General Government Expenditure
GHS	General Household Survey
GIA	General Improvement Area
GLC	Greater London Council
GNI	Generalised Needs Index
GRE	Grant Related Expenditure
GRF	Grant Redemption Fund
GRP	Grant Related Poundage
HAA	Housing Action Area
HAG	Housing Association Grant
HATs	Housing Action Trusts
HBS	Housing Benefit Supplement
HDG	Hostel Deficit Grant
HIP	Housing Investment Programme
HMA	Higher Management Allowance
HMOs	Houses in Multiple Occupation
HRA	Housing Revenue Account

HSG	Housing Support Grant (Scotland)
IS	Income Support
LIT	Local Income Tax
MIRAS	Mortgage Interest Relief at Source
NFHA	National Federation of Housing Associations
PESC	Public Expenditure Survey Committee
RDG	Revenue Deficit Grant
RFC	Rate Fund Contribution
RSF	Rent Surplus Fund
SB	Supplementary Benefit
SBC	Supplementary Benefits Commission
SHAC	The London Housing Aid Centre
TCI	Total Cost Indicator
TIC	Total Indicative Cost
VAT	Value Added Tax

PART I
BACKGROUND

1

Introduction

Housing in Britain is the subject of a web of subsidies, benefits, and tax concessions which has grown steadily more tangled as the years have gone by. Faced with this, drastic action has been advocated, with some would-be reformers wanting to pull the strings of abolishing mortgage interest relief overnight, others those of raising council rents to 'market' levels. Experience suggests, however, that the very worst thing one can do when faced with a cat's cradle of this kind is to grab the nearest loose end and give it a hard tug. The most likely result is an even tighter knot, making the tangle even worse. A better strategy is to try to work out how the whole thing is tied together and then patiently to try to disentangle it bit by bit, keeping in mind the whole time what it should all eventually look like. The main aim in this book is to contribute to such a process by describing how the various parts of the system work, and to analyse their effects and interactions. In the final part I also look at the proposals which have been made for untangling the system and add some of my own.

The start of the 1990s is an appropriate moment for a study of this kind. In the last two years virtually every aspect of housing policy examined in this book has been changed in one way or another. The Housing Benefit system was radically changed in April 1988, along with the social security system as a whole. New tax concessions to private landlords through the Business Expansion Scheme were introduced in the 1988 Budget, which also made substantial changes to the capital gains tax system, which affects the position of housing relative to other assets. Under the 1988 Housing Act subsidies to housing associations were reformed (from 1989) and the rents of new private-sector lettings decontrolled. The same Act established new provisions for ownership of local authority estates to be transferred to new landlords. Subsidies to local authority housing in England and Wales were reformed in April 1990, with a 'ring fence' put around Housing Revenue Accounts, ending the ability of authorities to make contributions into them from their general funds. At the same time, the whole structure of local government finance was

TABLE 1.1 *Housing subsidies, taxation and benefits: a summary*[a]

Local authorities	Housing associations	Private rented sector	Owner-occupiers
Recurrent subsidy from central government (7)	Capital grants (HAG) (8)	Taxation of landlord (12)	Taxation of owner-occupiers (12)
Rate Fund Contributions and Block Grant (until 1990) (6)	Recurrent subsidies (RDG/HDG) (8)	– Rents taxable – Interest deductible – Capital gains taxed – No depreciation allowance	– Tax relief on first £30,000 of mortgage – No capital gains tax – No tax on imputed rents
Rent pooling within HRAs (5)	Surplus 'tax' (GRF/RSF) (8)	– Business Expansion Scheme concessions – Stamp duty	– Stamp duty
Right to Buy discounts (9)	Right to Buy discounts (non-charitable HAs) (9)		
Terms for estate transfers (9)	Effective tax exemption (12)		

Improvement grants (9)

Housing Benefit for tenants' rents (rent rebates/allowances) (10)

Domestic rates net of rate rebates (until 1990) (12)
Exemption from VAT (except repairs and improvements) (12)

[a] Numbers in brackets give reference to main chapter where topic is discussed.

changed with the replacement of domestic rates with the Poll Tax (or Community Charge). The abolition of domestic rates itself has major implications for the overall tax burden levied on housing. Improvement grants were simplified and means-tested from July 1990. The 'composite' rate of tax on building society (and other) accounts is to be abolished from April 1991, with likely effects on the cost of mortgages. Even the change which has *not* been made—to the £30,000 limit for mortgages eligible for tax relief—represents an important if gradual shift in the balance of housing policy; in 1988, for the first time, the average new mortgage exceeded the limit.

What is perhaps most disappointing is that there is little evidence of a coherent goal for this flurry of changes. The steadfastness of the Treasury in defence of the mortgage relief limit may eventually result in a significant reduction in the tax advantages of owner-occupation. At the same time, the abolition of domestic rates mass-ively increases the tax privilege of housing as a whole, and of the most valuable (generally owner-occupied) housing in particular. The new subsidy systems for local authorities and housing associa-tions are intended to result in rents which at least embody differen-tials which look more like those of the market than they used to. Yet at the same time, the new Housing Benefit system entirely isolates its recipients from the effects of any changes in gross rents. The new grants to housing associations are designed to give them new incent-ives to control their capital costs, while the new local authority subsidy system removes equivalent incentives. Even if the reader does not agree with the direction of change suggested in the final chapter, it is to be hoped that the rest of the book will provide the background for designing a consistent alternative.

AN OVERVIEW OF THE SYSTEM

Table 1.1 provides a summary of the main components of the system examined in this book. The focus here is on explicit subsidies from central and local government, on income-related benefits tied to housing costs, and on the tax system as it affects housing. Even this list is not exhaustive in terms of the levers of policy by which govern-ment can affect the price which people pay for their housing. Despite their importance, the macroeconomic determinants of interest rates, regulation of financial institutions providing finance for housing, and planning policy lie outside the scope of what is already a long

TABLE 1.2 *Housing tenure since 1939* (% stock)

	Owner-occupiers	Local authority or new town	Housing association	Private rented and other	Total stock (million)
(a) England and Wales					
1939	33.0	10.3	56.7		11.5
1953	34.5	18.8	46.6		12.7
1961	44.4	24.3	31.3		14.5
1971	52.1	28.2	0.9	18.8	17.0
1978	56.2	29.2	1.9[a]	12.8[a]	18.6
1988	67.0	22.5	2.7	7.9	20.3
(b) United Kingdom					
1978	54.1	31.7	1.8[a]	12.4[a]	21.0
1983	59.3	28.7	2.3	9.7	21.9
1988	64.9	24.9	2.6	7.6	23.0

[a] Estimated.

Sources: Holmans (1987), table V.I and DoE (1989a), table 9.3. 1961 and 1971 figures are for April; 1978, 1983 and 1988 figures are for December.

enough book. Nor is rent regulation discussed in any great detail. For an introduction to housing finance as a whole, see Garnett, Reid, and Riley (1990).

Issues of housing tenure dominate discussion of housing policy in Britain. Table 1.2 recapitulates what will be a familiar story to many readers, showing the doubling of the share of the stock owned by its occupiers over the last fifty years, the rise until 1978 and subsequent fall of local authority housing, the continuing attenuation of the private rented sector, and the relatively small—but growing—role of housing associations. The differences between the tenure shares in England and Wales and in the UK as a whole mainly result from the substantial share of local authority housing in Scotland—reaching a peak of 54.3 per cent at the end of 1978 and, at 46.3 per cent, still just above that of owner-occupation ten years later. The overall tenure breakdown is important in interpreting the relative importance of policy towards the different sectors; what it shows is also in many (but not all) respects a result of the differences in treatment accorded to each tenure.

Table 1.3 shows the important differences between tenures in the incomes of the households which they contain. A measure of the polarisation which has occurred is given by the proportion of households in each group with incomes of less than £10,000 in 1987, putting them in the bottom half of the overall income distribution. This was only 17 per cent for mortgagers, but 60 per cent for outright owners and private furnished tenants, and more than 70 per cent for other tenants. Differences in the treatment of the various tenures therefore have very important distributional effects.

THE STRUCTURE OF THE BOOK

This book has been written for a variety of audiences. Some readers may simply want a description of how the current system works and how it has evolved. Others may be more interested in an economic analysis of the effects of the system than of its detailed rules. Another group, familiar with the current system and its shortcomings, may want to get on with the proposals which have been made for reform. Readers may also vary in the extent to which they feel comfortable with technical material. The way the chapters have been divided up attempts to cater for these different needs.

The book is intended to be as free from technicalities as the material will allow. In particular, algebra has been avoided except where it is needed to give a precise definition of part of the analysis presented, in which case it has been kept to notes at the end of chapters. The separation of the chapters is also intended to allow readers to avoid the more technical material if they want to, the more analytical chapters being Chapters 5, 11, 13, 14, and 15.

The first part of the book sets out the background in which the subsidy, benefit, and taxation systems operate. Chapter 2 explores the varied reasons why there is such extensive government intervention in the housing market, drawing out the links between particular instruments of policy and reasons for intervention. Chapter 3 looks at trends in recent years in the figures conventionally used to measure public spending on housing and tax concessions to it, looking at and explaining the various ways of making such measurements and their limitations. Chapter 4 examines how the costs of local authority and housing association tenants and of owner-occupiers have changed over the same period, and presents figures for costs in relation to net incomes in all tenures.

TABLE 1.3 *Tenure by income group, 1987 (GB Households, %)*

Household income range (£/year)	Owner-occupiers		Local authority tenants	Housing association tenants	Private tenants		All[a] households
	With mortgage	Outright owners			Unfur-nished	Fur-nished	
Under 3,000	1	13	27	30	22	21	13
3,000–3,999	1	10	13	17	13	8	7
4,000–5,999	4	14	17	14	17	11	11
6,000–7,999	4	13	11	10	12	10	9
8,000–9,999	7	10	8	7	6	10	8
10,000–11,999	10	8	8	7	6	11	9
12,000–14,999	18	10	6	5	9	11	12
15,000–19,999	24	9	6	6	7	8	14
20,000 and over	32	13	3	5	9	11	17
ALL INCOMES	100	100	100	100	100	100	100
Mean income (£'000)	18.6	10.8	7.0	6.9	8.7	10.0	12.7
Median income (£'000)	16.0	7.8	4.9	4.5	5.7	8.2	10.4
Percentage of all households	39	23	26	2	4	3	100

[a] Includes 2 per cent of households living rent free.

Source: DoE (1989*a*), table 12.1 (derived from Family Expenditure Survey).

The second part of the book describes subsidies to housing providers. Chapter 5 examines the general problems associated with the design of subsidy systems and the reasons for the forms they take, in particular looking at the distorting 'front-loading' effect of inflation on conventional loan repayments and the problems this causes. It also introduces the idea of an 'economic rent' as a benchmark for measuring the value of subsidies in economic, rather than accounting, terms. Chapter 6 describes the general system of grants from central to local government and the ways in which central government has steadily tightened its control of local authority spending, culminating in the reforms of local authority finances associated with the introduction of the Poll Tax in England and Wales in 1990, and the new capital control system. Chapter 7 looks at specific subsidies to local authority housing, in particular the introduction of 'ring fencing' and the new HRA Subsidy system in 1990. Chapter 8 describes the system of subsidies to housing associations and the changes made to it in 1989. Finally in this part of the book, Chapter 9 examines the implications of the financial terms set for the transfer of local authority estates to new landlords, the subsidies implicit in the 'Right to Buy' for council (and some housing association) tenants, and the system of improvement grants for owner-occupiers (and some private landlords).

The next part of the book consists of a single chapter, on the system of Housing Benefit, in particular payments towards the rents of public and private tenants. As well as describing the way in which the current benefit structure has evolved, it looks at three particular problems associated with it—take-up, the 'poverty trap', and the 'up-marketing' problem—and at proposals which have been put forward for alternatives to it.

Part IV is concerned with taxation. Chapter 11 discusses general principles of taxation and how they relate to housing in particular, setting out a 'Comprehensive Income Tax' (on real income) as a consistent benchmark against which to measure the tax advantages of housing. Chapter 12 then describes how housing is actually taxed in Britain, and explores the implications of this for one of the key components of owner-occupiers' housing costs—the net 'capital cost of housing services' to them.

The next part contains analysis of three different aspects of the systems described in earlier chapters. Chapter 13 presents different measures of the real rate of return which has been generated on local authority housing assets (and hence the effective level of subsidy enjoyed by tenants), both at a national level and, using detailed information for individual local authorities, on a regional basis. Chapter 14 looks at the distributional effects of subsidies to local authority tenants and tax concessions to owner-occupiers, measuring these against the benchmarks of economic rent and 'neutral' taxation developed in earlier chapters. It also examines the way in which local authority domestic rates acted as an offset to these advantages until their abolition in 1990, and discusses the impact of subsidies to the different tenures over the life cycle. Chapter 15 draws together the different ways in which housing subsidies are affected by the actual behaviour of local authorities and housing associations and discusses the implications of this pattern for incentives to them and for the risks which they carry.

The final part of the book discusses possibilities for reform of the system as a whole. Chapter 16 compares nineteen different packages of reform proposals advanced in the last decade, summarising the main points of each and setting them out in a broad political spectrum running from advocates of the unfettered free market to those who put very little weight on market considerations. The final chapter draws out the key problems identified elsewhere in the book, suggests the main aims for policies which would contribute to reducing them while remaining consistent with political practicality, and suggests which specific measures would best meet these aims.

2

Why is Housing Subsidised?

Britain today has starkly visible housing problems ranging from young people sleeping rough on city streets, through the bed and breakfast hotels used for families waiting for council housing, over-crowded and unsafe houses in multiple occupation in the private sector, and system-built council estates of the 1960s where con-ditions sometimes rival those they were built to replace, to house prices and mortgage costs which have put home ownership out of reach and moving between regions out of the question for many with otherwise reasonable incomes. Given all this, it may seem obvious that continuation of subsidies and tax concessions is necessary to keep down the cost of housing, and so at least prevent these prob-lems worsening.

Some would not even see the argument as being about the need for subsidy or other intervention in a housing *market*, but rather as the need to establish a social service, distributed according to need. Back in 1937 the Minority Report of the Ridley Committee stated that: 'We cannot agree that housing is a fit subject of commodity economics, but rather hold the view that ... its management should be subject to public utility principles' (quoted in DoE 1977*b*, Part III, pp. 66–7). Fifty years later, a similar view was being upheld: 'The greatest indictment of housing policy in Britain is its failure to provide decent housing as a basic right.... There is a parallel between the right to housing and the right to health care. We have a National Health Service which is expected to provide decent health care to everyone, regardless of income' (Kelly 1986, p. 24).

By contrast, others question any interference with the prices which would be produced by a free market. For writers such as Stafford (1978), Minford, Peel, and Ashton (1987), Black and Stafford (1988), and Coleman (1989), the very process of subsidy, public provision, regulation, and tax privilege has stopped the market doing the job it performs perfectly adequately for other com-modities, thereby exacerbating problems of access to housing and removing individuals' freedom to choose their own housing.

Furthermore, most of the problems just described afflict people on low incomes. If the problem of poor housing is, in fact, just one manifestation of the wider problem of poverty, surely a better solution would be to ensure that people had adequate incomes, and leave them to make their own choice as to how much of those incomes to spend on housing? If some still prefer to spend that income on other things and little on housing, and to live in what the rest of us might regard as squalor, why should we interfere with their choice? If some assistance still has to relate to housing costs, this should be done through means-tested Housing Benefit payments, not through generalised subsidy. Thus, for Minford, Peel, and Ashton, 'Clearly ... the rental sector should be freed from regulation entirely.... For council tenants, we need only follow existing policy to raise council rents to market levels ... so that by 1992 these rents too would be at market levels' (1987, p. 117).

Between the polar positions of 'housing as a social service' and 'free the market' there is a wide range of opinion—shared by this author—which would argue that the market can be used to allocate much of the housing stock, but that there are particular problems which do justify public intervention in that market in one way or another. These reasons are grouped below under the headings of redistribution, equity, externalities, other market failure, producer interests and macroeconomics, and wider political or social aims. Listing them does not, of course, imply that they are necessarily convincing.

REDISTRIBUTION

A fundamental reason for housing subsidy has been as a means of redistribution towards the poor. Without intervention bad housing conditions would be a consequence of poverty; providing or subsidising 'decent' housing can remove at least one of poverty's effects. However, the question posed above immediately appears: why not use cash? Cash payments through the Income Support system cover items like food and clothing which are just as much 'basic needs' as housing. If they can be covered by cash rather than 'in kind', why should housing be different?

A first reason may follow from society's reasons for promoting redistribution. Certain forms of consumption may be regarded as essential parts of a minimum standard of living, but others not, even if the beneficiaries themselves would prefer them. Housing is what economists call a 'merit good', whose consumption it is politically acceptable to promote, in contrast to an equivalent cash transfer which might be spent on drinking or smoking. A connected reason identified by Rosen in the US context (1987, p. 379) lies in worries about 'welfare fiaud'. Providing transfers not only in kind, but of a bare minimum which would only appeal to the 'truly needy', may act as a targeting mechanism or a reinforcement of means-testing.

A second reason for special treatment of housing is that poor housing exacerbates other personal problems, as suggested by the Inquiry into British Housing chaired by the Duke of Edinburgh: 'The negative aspects of our lives—ill health, vandalism and crime, racial prejudice, loneliness, mental illness, family break-up—are multiplied and exaggerated by housing shortages and bad housing conditions. The cost of curing these social ills is correspondingly increased' (1985*b*, p. 3). Again, for this to justify particular treatment of housing as opposed to a general assault on poverty requires that, perhaps as a result of lack of information or understanding about the consequences of poor housing, people would make a choice which was not in their—or their family's—long-run interests if left to themselves. (It also suggests that there are external effects on the wider interests of society, as discussed below.)

These are arguments (perhaps paternalistic ones) for subsidising the housing costs of those with low incomes. But this does not have to be done through general provision in kind, for instance of subsidised council housing. An alternative is to make means-tested payments which depend on *actual* housing costs, such as Housing Benefit (see Chapter 10). Again, there is a contrast with the treatment of other items, for which a standard cash allowance is given through Income Support. However, as the Government's 1985 *Housing Benefit Review* put it, any proposal that the same should be done for housing, 'would fail to take account of the very wide variations that exist in the cost of similar housing throughout the country. It would also fail to recognise that for a number of reasons many households on low incomes have unavoidably high housing costs in proportion to their disposable income' (DHSS 1985*a*, p.v). In other words, as John Kay argued to the Inquiry into British Housing (1986), 'there [is] a case for treating help with housing differently from other kinds of social provision: because it [is] a characteristic of the housing market, unlike markets for other consumer durables, that people [pay] different amounts for the same thing' (p. 13). Against this it could be argued that one of the main reasons why people pay different prices for the same thing is precisely because of the effects of intervention in the housing market. Basing Housing Benefit on actual costs is therefore coping with a symptom, not a cause, of the problem. However, if it is not practical politics to make the changes which would equalise prices, the argument stands.

This leads to a key issue. Surely a means-tested benefit must be a more efficient means of redistribution than general housing subsidies given regardless of the occupants' incomes? This was the argument behind the introduction of the national rent rebate scheme in the 1972 Housing Finance Act at the same time as an attempt to raise gross (unrebated) local authority rents, and behind much of the direction of housing policy since 1979.

There are, however, three problems with greater reliance on Housing Benefit and less on general subsidies (for more detail, see Chapter Ten). First, there is the problem of 'take-up'. Many entitled to means-tested benefits fail to claim; such people—with low incomes—would lose from higher gross rents. Means-tested benefits may be 'targeted', but they miss some of their targets. Second, the withdrawal of Housing Benefit as income rises contributes to the 'poverty trap', under which people on low incomes can find themselves hardly any better off (allowing for tax and benefit changes) even if their earnings rise substantially. The higher the gross rents, the further the poverty trap extends, with possible problems both for economic efficiency (through disincentive effects) and for notions of fairness. Third, a feature of the current structure of Housing Benefit is that those who receive it are unaffected by changes in their gross rents: Housing Benefit adjusts by the whole of any change. An ironic effect of a move towards higher rents—perhaps in an attempt to move the price of housing nearer to its cost of provision—would be to increase the numbers for whom gross housing costs were immaterial.

Although some of these problems could be moderated (but not eliminated) by a redesign of Housing Benefit, they suggest that sole reliance on means-testing is not necessarily the most 'economically efficient' form of redistribution, a point emphasised by Whitehead (1987). The distortions it introduces may be as bad as those introduced by more general subsidies.

EQUITY

Redistribution towards those on low incomes depends on notions of 'vertical' equity between rich and poor. Housing policy is also greatly affected by notions of 'horizontal' equity—fairness between those with, for instance, similar incomes but in otherwise different circumstances. There is a powerful argument that if people in one situation receive an advantage—for instance, owner-occupiers through their tax advantages—it is only fair that others should receive an equivalent benefit in some way. In other words, policy should achieve what has been called 'tenure neutrality' (or, of course, the relative advantage of the favoured group could be removed, but there may be political problems with this).

It may also be that some people's housing costs are raised by other aspects of policy. The cost of housing in general is raised by the existence of tax concessions to owner-occupiers. Those in other tenures need compensation for this if they are not to end up not just relatively, but absolutely, worse off as a result. Similarly, planning restrictions and policies towards the Green Belt may be in the environmental interests of the whole community, but impose costs on people trying to live in or near affected areas, who face higher house prices as a result. An equity case could be made for subsidising their housing in some way—for instance, through grants to rural housing associations for local families (perhaps even financed by taxation of the capital gains of those whose property values have risen because of the restrictions).

A different equity argument for subsidies and tax concessions is that we already have them and people expect them to continue. The Housing Policy Review was set up by the Labour Government in 1975 by the then Secretary of State, Anthony Crosland, 'to get back to fundamentals, to get beyond a policy of "ad hoc"-ery and crisis management' (Kilroy 1978, p. 5), but concluded that, 'we certainly do not believe that the household budgets of millions of families— which have been planned in good faith in the reasonable expectation that present arrangements would broadly continue—should be overturned, in pursuit of some theoretical or academic dogma' (DoE 1977a, p. iv).

Taken to its logical conclusion, this could be thought to imply that nothing should ever change, however slowly. There are, none the less, reasons why this kind of argument has some force when

related to housing. In particular, the 'incidence'—the true benefit—
of existing housing subsidies and tax advantages may not be on those
now formally receiving them. House prices may be higher than they
would have been without the existence of mortgage interest tax relief—its advantages may have been 'capitalised'. Recent purchasers
pay high prices which offset the tax relief. Withdrawal of relief
would both raise their outgoings and reduce the capital value of
their houses, leaving them *worse* off than if the relief had never
existed (as a result of the capital loss which they would face without
any fall in their debts). Similarly wages in particular parts of the
country may be lower than they would have been if workers had not
been able to find subsidised housing there. Removal of subsidy
would hit rents immediately, but it might take a long time before
local wages adjusted upwards to compensate. In the meantime the
workers would suffer from the loss of a subsidy whose true benefi-
ciary had been their employers.

A final equity argument for subsidy to particular forms of housing
relates to those who have special needs. Providing housing adapta-
tions, supported, or sheltered housing helps to put those with
special needs in a position closer to that of the rest of the population
(again raising the question of whether this help should be in kind or
through cash benefits).

EXTERNALITIES
Left to itself the market may produce undesirable results because
individual decisions fail to allow for the interests of others—there
may be 'externalities'. One house in poor condition may affect its
whole neighbourhood, and may even cause structural problems for
its immediate neighbours. Poor housing may promote disease or
exacerbate social problems (and raise spending to cope with them)
affecting the whole community.

This suggests two kinds of intervention—setting of minimum
standards (with penalties for those who fail to comply) and provision of subsidies to enable those who would not otherwise be able
to afford such standards to pay for them (and possibly to encourage
others who would not choose them, even if they could afford it).
Such arguments have more force in relation to particular instruments aimed at, say, improving property in poor condition or
achieving certain minimum standards, than as a justification of
across-the-board housing subsidies.

The 'spillover' effects of improving one house on its neighbours also provide the rationale for area improvement policies (for instance, targeting grants on properties in certain designated areas): the value of the sum of improvements to a number of properties may be much greater than that of the individual parts carried out in isolation.

OTHER FORMS OF MARKET FAILURE

The market may fail to achieve an efficient result for other reasons. The Inquiry into British Housing argued, 'housing lasts a long time. It follows that development decisions made in the past will still have a powerful impact on lives many years from now' (1985*b*, p. 3). Houses have a long life and are expensive to change once built, so it may be in the interests of future generations (unrepresented in today's markets) to build to a higher standard than would otherwise be chosen given today's incomes, an argument suggested by the very title of the 1961 report which set the 'Parker Morris' standards for council housing—*Homes for Today and Tomorrow* (Central Housing Advisory Committee 1961). Again, those with low incomes may require subsidy to allow them to afford such standards.

Given the cost and the long life of housing, it has to be financed over a long period, for instance by borrowing. But it may be hard to borrow against possibly uncertain future income. The particular form of borrowing available may be too great a strain in early years (as a result of the 'front-loading problem' discussed in Chapter 5). There may be wide fluctuations in borrowing costs from year to year. One way of coping with such problems is to subsidise borrowing costs directly or indirectly. Alternatives include systems for providing guarantees for borrowers, the promotion of 'low-start' mortgages, 'equity sharing', or arrangements for extending repayment periods when interest rates rise.

A further factor is the large size of the existing stock in relation to new supply. If demand rises for some reason, the stock may take a long time to adjust. In the meantime landlords may be able to exploit the shortage and increase rents to levels which give returns above those in the rest of the economy, perhaps causing hardship to tenants. This is the classic rationale for public provision and/or introducing rent controls. Rent controls and security of tenure legislation can be justified as a response to the 'local monopoly' which landlords would otherwise have over sitting tenants, who would find it expensive or difficult to move again. The difficulty lies in setting rent ceilings at a level where new supply is still encouraged—if the ceilings are too low, the stock never adjusts (unless landlords receive enough subsidy to compensate).

PRODUCER INTERESTS AND MACROECONOMICS

In-kind provision is sometimes preferred to cash transfers as a form of redistribution because of the interests of producers—construction may be a more effective lobby than other industries, or there may be concern to protect building jobs. A particular problem for the construction industry is caused by the large fluctuations of the house price cycle; at times of low prices and falling output, calls come for measures to stabilise demand. Similarly, boosting construction output is often suggested as a desirable component of reflation of the whole economy at times of recession, on the grounds that construction is less import-intensive than other activities (although with import penetration of building materials supply during the 1980s, this argument has lost some force).

Concerns for mobility of labour have also prompted calls for intervention—or for the removal of existing intervention. A main objective of the Labour Government's 1977 *Housing Policy* Green Paper was stated thus: 'We must increase the scope for mobility in housing. It is essential, in a period of industrial change, that workers should be able to move house to change their job' (DoE 1977*a*, p. 8). Access to subsidised housing for 'key workers' in high-cost areas is one kind of way to cope with this problem. By contrast, the effects of rent controls on the supply of private rented accommodation and of subsidised council rents on labour mobility are major reasons why Minford, Peel, and Ashton (1987) and others call for deregulation and removal of subsidies.

Finally, rent control and subsidy policy have been used as elements of counter-inflation policy in the past, as were policies to prevent mortgage interest rates rising (or at least fluctuating). More recently the reverse policies of cuts in subsidy to council housing to reduce public spending and increases in interest rates, including mortgage rates, have been part of government policy intended to reduce inflationary pressures in the economy as a whole, although they have the immediate perverse effect of raising housing costs.

TABLE 2.1 *Reasons for intervention in the housing market: summary*

Rationale	Possible instruments
(a) Redistribution	
Improve welfare of poor; raise housing consumption to minimum levels (housing as 'merit good'; lack of information; targeting).	General measures to alleviate poverty; subsidies to low-income housing; housing benefits.
(b) Equity (horizontal)	
'Tenure neutrality'.	Raise subsidies in all sectors to match most favoured (or remove advantages of favoured tenure).
Compensation for effects of intervention elsewhere (e.g. on house prices; effects of Green Belt).	Offsetting subsidies to those affected (or removal of intervention).
Expectations/market already adjusted to current situation (e.g. capitalisation, wages).	Maintain status quo (or only adjust slowly).
Special needs (e.g. need for housing adaptations, sheltered housing, supported housing).	Subsidised specialised provision or special cash benefits.
(c) Externalities	
Effects of house condition on neighbours/neighbourhood ('spillover effects').	Regulations for minimum standards; subsidies to those who cannot (or would not) pay for them (e.g. improvement grants/area improvement policies).
(d) Other market failure	
Long life of housing/future generations.	Higher building standards; subsidies to allow achievement.
Capital market problems (e.g. 'front-loading' of repayments; difficulties in borrowing against future income).	Subsidies, tax concessions, or guarantees for borrowing; promote alternative ways of lending (e.g. low-start mortgages, equity sharing).
Slow adjustment to changes in demand/supply; 'local monopoly' of landlords.	Rent control; direct provision.

table continued overleaf

TABLE 2.1 (*continued*)

Rationale	Possible instruments
(*e*) **Producer interests and macroeconomics**	
Interests of construction industry/workers. Component of general reflation.	Subsidise new construction.
Promote mobility of labour.	Access to subsidised housing for job movers; remove policies causing immobility.
Counter-inflation policy.	Rent control, subsidised rents, stabilisation of mortgage rates (1970s); or lower public spending (and higher rents) and higher interest rates (1980s).
(*f*) **Wider political or social aims**	
Promote social mix; avoid ghetto areas or regions.	Area improvement policy; subsidies to allow those with low incomes to live in high-cost areas.
Promote 'property-owning democracy'.	Subsidies/tax concessions to owner-occupiers, particularly marginal owners (e.g. first-time buyers schemes; Right to Buy; 'rent to mortgage').

WIDER POLITICAL OR SOCIAL AIMS

Reasons for intervention in the housing market are not simply economic. Aneurin Bevan hoped that council housing would have 'the lovely feature of English and Welsh villages, where the doctor, the grocer, the butcher and the farm labourer all lived in the same street' (quoted in Power 1987*b*). One of the Inquiry into British Housing's five objectives was, 'to avoid the creation of "ghettos" of poor and disadvantaged people concentrated on specific estates or in particular areas' (1985*b*, p. 8). Directing subsidy to make particular areas more attractive is therefore justifiable 'in terms of the health and well-being of society as a whole'. On a larger scale, it might be most cost-effective to provide subsidised housing only in low-cost regions and to expect its beneficiaries to move there, but such a policy, with its undertones of 'bantustans', would be rejected on social grounds.

A different social aim, the promotion of the 'property-owning democracy', has been one of the factors behind the promotion of owner-occupation, both through policies aimed at helping marginal owners—such as help to first-time buyers or the discounts available under the Right to Buy—and through general concessions to the sector. This is, of course, the reverse of 'tenure neutrality'; there would not be much point in favouring the one tenure if this was matched for others.

TARGETS AND INSTRUMENTS

For some, none of these arguments is persuasive:

The main efficiency argument for subsidizing housing is the existence of externalities. However, the mechanisms through which these externalities work are not well understood and there is little evidence that they are quantitatively important. The redistributive argument is equally weak ... subsidies to owner-occupation are perverse.... The in-kind subsidies involved in low income public housing are inefficient in the sense that the poor could be made better-off if the transfers were made directly in cash'. (Rosen 1987, p. 380).

This seems unduly sweeping, particularly if one takes account of the practical politics of the point from which we start. None the less, the suggested justifications for intervention have to be matched by appropriate instruments. Table 2.1 summarises the arguments described above and the choice of instruments which might be appropriate to them. Examination of the list suggests that it is unlikely that many (apart from those who put sole weight on preservation of the status quo) would have selected the particular structure described elsewhere in this book. At the same time, the proponents of reform have to bear in mind the multiplicity of objectives as they try to untangle that structure.

3

Public Spending on Housing

To set this book's discussion of subsidies, benefits, and taxation in perspective, this chapter examines what has happened to public spending since 1976/7, the key totals for which are shown in Table 3.1 (for more detailed discussion and figures from 1973/4, see Hills and Mullings 1990).

PLANNING AND MEASURING PUBLIC SPENDING

The main source for such figures is the annual Public Expenditure White Paper (e.g. HM Treasury 1990), the key result of the annual 'PESC' (Public Expenditure Survey Committee) process (see Likierman 1988 for a more detailed description). Negotiations take place throughout the summer, with any decisions unresolved in bilateral discussions between spending departments and the Treasury being taken in the autumn to the 'Star Chamber' committee of senior ministers and officials. The outline of agreed plans for the following financial year is then published in the Treasury's Autumn Statement to Parliament (usually in November). The White Paper, published early in the calendar year, contains more detailed plans for the financial year starting in April, as well as indicative plans for the next two years. The Budget in March then sets out the taxation system for the financial year, sometimes with some minor changes to the spending plans. (This separation in timing of decisions on spending and taxation is a British peculiarity: in most other countries spending and revenue plans are decided, presented, and debated at the same time.)

This timetable means that local authorities hear the key decisions about grants towards their general spending (what is now 'Revenue Support Grant' in England and Wales) and the key guidelines for housing subsidies in November and December. They then make their own budgets for the financial year and set what is now the Poll Tax (or 'Community Charge') to raise the revenue they need over and above government grants and their share of rates on business properties by March. Rents are set at the same time. Benefit rates for the next financial year are announced in November, with the Autumn Statement, which gives time for local benefit offices and local authorities to prepare for the changes in April; this does not prevent the government from making last-minute changes which are much more difficult to implement on time.

The White Paper has grown from being a document of a few pages in the early 1960s to become a two-inch-deep twenty-one volume pile containing a wealth of data on each department's spending plans and statistics relating to government policy (in the future the responsibility for the individual volumes of the White Paper is being shifted from the Treasury to the particular departments).

The increase in the volume of information published does not necessarily make it easier to make sense of what is happening to public spending. A first problem is the meaning of the published figures themselves. Since 1982, spending in recent and future years has been shown in *cash* terms. This has advantages for accounting— and sometimes as political propaganda—but is not very useful as a way of illuminating what is going on at a time of inflation. The meaning of an increase in spending from £100 million to £200 million will be very different depending on whether prices have stayed the same or have doubled.

The figures presented in Table 3.1 and in many other tables in this book are therefore adjusted to *real* (sometimes called 'cost') terms. For example, prices in the economy as a whole (as measured by the 'GDP deflator', a wider measure of inflation than the Retail Price Index) rose by 177 per cent between 1976/7 and 1988/9. Public spending on housing totalling £5.4 billion in cash in 1976/7 was thus equivalent to £14.8 billion at 1988/9 prices.

Real figures are the most useful way of measuring the resources being put *into* different areas, removing the distorting effects of general inflation. They do not necessarily give an accurate guide to what might be expected as an *output* from different levels of spending. For instance, prices in general may rise by 10 per cent, but construction costs by 25 per cent, so that a 10 per cent increase in real spending may not be enough to prevent the number of units built from falling. Adjusting cash figures by a specific price index for what the resources are being spent on gives spending in *volume* terms (as for instance shown in Table 3.6). Until 1981, public spending was planned in volume terms, with the spending figures presented in

24 *Background*

TABLE 3.1 *Public spending on housing 1976/7–1989/90* (£bn. at 1988/9 prices)[a]

	Current (GB)	Net capital (GB)	Current plus net capital (UK)	Housing benefit[b] (UK)	Total public spending (UK)	Mortgage interest relief[c] (UK)
1976/7	3.9	8.3	12.7	2.2	14.8	3.4
1977/8	3.5	6.5	10.4	2.2	12.6	2.9
1978/9	3.8	5.7	9.9	2.1	12.0	2.7
1979/80	4.3	6.0	10.7	1.9	12.1	3.1
1980/1	4.1	4.5	9.0	2.0	11.1	3.5
1981/2	2.9	2.8	6.1	3.0	9.0	3.4
1982/3	2.2	2.6	5.1	3.5	8.7	3.3
1983/4	1.8	3.5	5.6	3.4	9.1	3.6
1984/5	1.7	3.3	5.4	3.8	9.2	4.4
1985/6	1.7	2.7	4.7	3.9	8.7	5.5
1986/7	1.7	2.4	4.4	4.1	8.6	5.3
1987/8	1.6	2.3	4.3	4.2	8.5	5.2
1988/9	1.4	1.2	3.0	4.1	7.0	5.5
1989/90	1.5	1.5	3.3	4.2	7.5	6.5

[a] Adjusted by GDP deflator.
[b] On current definitions.
[c] Including Option Mortgage Subsidy until 1983/4.

Sources: HM Treasury (1990), tables 8.1, 8.2, 15.1, 15.2, 16.1, 16.2, 17.1, 21.2.1, 21.2.9, F1, and earlier equivalents;
Welsh Office (1989), table 9.1 and earlier equivalents;
Scottish Development Department (1990), table 15.5 and earlier equivalents;
Board of Inland Revenue (1989), table 5.1; *Official Report* 12 March 1990, cols. WA 93–6.

what were called 'survey prices'. This was useful as a guide to, say, how much construction work was planned or how many doctors were to be employed, but it gave poor control over the use of resources (as it gave little indication of the effects of a change in the relative prices of public purchases). Finally, it may be useful to show spending figures in relation to the number of beneficiaries (as is done in Table 3.4) or the level of need for a particular programme. None of these measures of public spending is 'right' or 'wrong'; different measures are useful depending on the question being asked.

TABLE 3.2 *Current and Capital Spending on Housing by Territory* (£ bn. at 1988/9 prices)[a]

	England	Scotland	Wales	Northern Ireland	United Kingdom
1976/7	10.17	1.49	0.52	0.49	12.66
1977/8	8.32	1.30	0.39	0.42	10.43
1978/9	7.85	1.28	0.37	0.40	9.90
1979/80	8.52	1.38	0.39	0.40	10.69
1980/1	7.08	1.24	0.33	0.38	9.03
1981/2	4.54	1.04	0.18	0.34	6.09
1982/3	3.66	0.93	0.17	0.37	5.14
1983/4	4.07	0.93	0.25	0.39	5.64
1984/5	4.02	0.81	0.17	0.41	5.41
1985/6	3.46	0.72	0.15	0.40	4.73
1986/7	3.17	0.72	0.18	0.38	4.45
1987/8	2.98	0.74	0.22	0.36	4.30
1988/9	1.85	0.63	0.17	0.33	2.98
1989/90	2.28	0.58	0.16	0.25	3.27

[a] Adjusted by GDP deflator.

Sources: As Table 3.1.

Interpreting spending figures is made more difficult by other factors. First, geographical coverage varies. Figures published by the Department of the Environment often cover only England and figures for Wales, Scotland, and Northern Ireland have to be found elsewhere. Sometimes these are not available in the same detail. As a result, the 'territorial' basis of the tables in this book varies. While, as can be seen from Table 3.2, England takes the dominant share of spending, there are differences between English and overall trends—the English share of UK public current and capital spending on housing fell from 80 per cent in 1976/7 to 70 per cent in 1989/90, for instance, and spending in Northern Ireland has fallen less rapidly than elsewhere.

Second, definitions change from year to year. So far as possible the tables presented here are on a consistent basis. Thus Table 3.1 shows what is now counted as spending on Housing Benefit—benefit towards the rents of public and private tenants both receiving Income Support and those receiving 'standard' benefit (see Chapter 10). Before the reform in 1982/3, the figures were presented on a different basis, so those here are estimates of what the cost would have been on current definitions. This kind of problem will become more acute in the future because in 1990 the Government changed the definition of its main 'public spending planning total' to exclude 'self-financed' spending by local authorities (that is, local authority spending in excess of government grants, 'credit approvals'—see Chapter 6—and the revenue from business rates). Many of the detailed figures in the White Paper now leave out part of local spending; to construct the totals for public spending, information has to be gleaned from many other sources as well.

Even with adjustment to consistent definitions and to constant prices, 'public spending' on housing still represents a rather unsatisfactory total. It includes current subsidies to local authority Housing Revenue Accounts (HRAs), improvement grants to the private sector, capital expenditure by local authorities financed by loans, and the total of net loans and grants paid to housing associations for capital development. Even in conventional accounting terms, totalling these items involves much adding together of apples and pears, with current spending added to capital items fully covered by borrowing and future debt repayment.

The conventional totals are net of receipts from rents (for current spending) and from sales of assets (for capital). While these net figures are of interest in terms of the new public resources being channelled into housing, they can—as is explained below—be seriously misleading as a guide to how much is actually being spent on public housing. In addition, the cost of Housing Benefit—intimately related to the level of rents and hence to that of general subsidies—has in the past been counted as part of the social security programme. With the amalgamation of rent rebate and general subsidies to local authorities in England and Wales described in Chapter 7 from 1990/1, the cost of English and Welsh rent rebates—but not allowances to private tenants—becomes part of the Department of the Environment and Welsh Office programmes. Finally, the cost of 'tax expenditures' on housing is listed entirely separately. The cost of mortgage interest relief is discussed below; for a general discussion of what constitutes tax expenditures, see Chapter 11.

TRENDS IN PUBLIC SPENDING ON HOUSING SINCE 1976

Bearing these limitations in mind, the trends shown in Table 3.1 are clear. Even including spending on Housing Benefit, there has been an almost continuous fall in UK public spending on housing since 1976/7 (which represented the peak year for total spending). By 1989/90 the total was half its initial level in real terms. Whereas in 1976/7 public spending on housing had been equivalent to 4.1 per cent of Gross Domestic Product (GDP) and 9.0 per cent of General Government Expenditure (GGE), by 1989/90 these proportions had been cut to 1.5 and 4.0 per cent respectively. In both the cuts following the International Monetary Fund visit in the mid-1970s and following the change of government in 1979, housing suffered more than virtually any other government programme.

Within this total, the balance between current spending (mostly 'general subsidies'—Rate Fund Contributions and central government payments into HRAs) and Housing Benefit is of particular interest. Throughout the period their combined cost was remarkably constant at or just below £6 billion (on a UK basis at 1988/9 prices). As general subsidies were cut back between 1979/80 and 1982/3, the cost of Housing Benefit rose by an almost equivalent amount. Much of this was cause and effect. As general subsidies fell, real local authority rents rose by half between 1979/80 and 1982/3 (see Chapter 4). This increase in rents both increased the entitlements of those already receiving benefit and brought many more tenants into benefit (see Chapter 10). About half of the higher rents re-emerged immediately as higher Housing Benefit. At the same time, higher unemployment also led to greater numbers of benefit recipients. The fall in the real value of net capital spending was even more dramatic than that of current spending. By 1988/9, real net capital spending (in Great Britain) was only 18 per cent of what it had been in 1976/7. (As is discussed below, what happened to *gross* spending was somewhat different.)

For comparison, Table 3.1 also shows the cost of mortgage interest relief (including Option Mortgage Subsidy until 1983/4). By contrast with the explicit spending programmes, this rose almost continuously. Its real cost was almost twice as high in 1989/90 as in 1976/7, and by 1989/90 was equivalent to 87 per cent of the total of public spending on housing, including Housing Benefit. If one adds the cost of the relief to the other items, the real total in 1989/90 is higher than in 1981/2 and is only 5 per cent lower than in 1978/9, putting a rather different perspective on what has happened to the net public resources going to housing over the last decade from that given by the spending figures alone. On this basis, there has been a switch, not an overall cut.

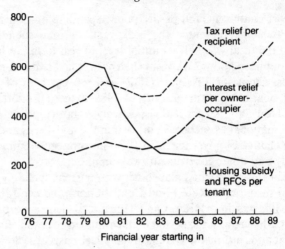

Figure 3.1 Conventional subsidy measures (£ per household at 1988/9 prices)

Note: Subsidy figures are for Great Britain, interest relief figures are for United Kingdom.

Sources: As Table 3.1 and DoE (1989*a*), table 9.3, and equivalents.

Figure 3.1 shows what this has meant for the real value of 'conventional subsidies' per household in the local authority and owner-occupied sectors. As can be seen, the balance has been reversed. The value per tenant of general subsidies to local authority tenants (in Great Britain) fell from around £600 per year in the late 1970s to just over £200 per year in the late 1980s (at 1988/9 prices, as are the figures below). Meanwhile, the value of interest relief (for the UK and including Option Mortgage Subsidy) per owner-occupier rose from around £250 in 1978/9 to £430 in 1989/90. Looking at mortgagers alone, the value of interest tax relief per recipient (in this case the available figures exclude Option Mortgage Subsidy) rose from £440 to £700 over the same period.

The phrase 'conventional subsidies' is used here advisedly: one of the contentions of this book is that, for a series of reasons, such cash flow measures may be misleading as a guide to the true value of the advantages of owners and tenants (see Chapters 5, 11, 13, and 14).

TABLE 3.3 *Local authority Housing Revenue Account, England and Wales* (£bn. at 1988/9 prices)[a]

	Spending				Income			
	Manage-ment & main-tenance	Debt charges	Other	Total[b]	Gross rents[c]	Rate Fund Contri-butions	Housing Subsidy	Other
1976/7	1.9	4.4	0.3	6.6	3.4	0.6	2.3	0.2
1977/8	2.0	4.0	0.4	6.5	3.5	0.6	2.2	0.2
1978/9	2.2	4.3	0.3	6.7	3.4	0.7	2.3	0.3
1979/80	2.3	4.6	0.1	7.0	3.3	0.8	2.5	0.4
1980/1	2.4	4.6	0.2	7.2	3.4	0.9	2.4	0.5
1981/2	2.5	4.3	0.4	7.2	4.5	0.7	1.3	0.7
1982/3	2.6	3.9	0.4	7.0	4.5	0.7	0.8	1.0
1983/4	2.8	3.6	0.3	6.7	4.5	0.7	0.4	1.0
1984/5	2.8	3.6	0.3	6.6	4.5	0.6	0.5	1.1
1985/6	2.8	3.6	0.4	6.8	4.5	0.6	0.6	1.2
1986/7	2.8	3.4	0.4	6.6	4.5	0.5	0.5	1.0
1987/8	2.9	3.2	0.4	6.4	4.5	0.5	0.5	1.0

[a] Adjusted by GDP deflator.

[b] Including change in balances and so equal to total income.

[c] Including rent rebates.

Sources: DoE (1989*a*), table 10.26 and earlier equivalents;
HM Treasury (1990), table 21.2.1.

CURRENT SPENDING

The bulk of current public spending on housing has consisted of central government ('Exchequer') subsidies and Rate Fund Contributions (RFCs) made from the local authorities' general funds to HRAs. As can be seen in Table 3.3, showing the aggregate HRA for local authorities in England and Wales, there was a much faster fall in the real value of Exchequer subsidies—from £2.5 billion in 1979/80 to £0.5 billion in 1987/8 (at 1988/9 prices)—than in RFCs— from £0.8 to £0.5 billion over the same period. What the table also shows is that the dramatic fall in public spending (subsidies) after 1980/1 does not correspond to a similar fall in the total amount spent on the management and maintenance of local authority housing. This *grew* steadily over the period. Real spending per unit

TABLE 3.4 *Indices of real HRA spending and income per unit,[a] England and Wales* (1976/7 = 100)

	Spending				Income			
	Management & maintenance	Debt charges	Other	Total	Gross rents	Rate Fund Contributions	Housing Subsidy	Other
1976/7	100	100	100	100	100	100	100	100
1977/8	102	91	136	96	99	92	92	100
1978/9	110	95	96	100	98	104	98	130
1979/80	116	102	32	103	93	130	105	153
1980/1	123	102	71	107	97	144	100	211
1981/2	127	97	134	107	129	108	56	294
1982/3	137	92	154	108	135	113	35	416
1983/4	151	86	113	106	138	122	20	445
1984/5	153	87	105	107	139	105	22	482
1985/6	157	90	131	111	142	97	27	533
1986/7	161	85	135	109	145	91	25	468
1987/8	167	82	137	109	146	86	25	463

[a] Number of units in December each year.

Sources: As Table 3.3 and DoE (1989a), Table 9.3 and earlier equivalents.

(Table 3.4), increased by two-thirds between 1976/7 and 1987/8, an annual growth rate of 4.8 per cent.

Ideally, it would be useful to relate this to changes in the relative costs of providing management and maintenance to give an indication of the growth in the volume of services. Unfortunately a suitable index is not available, but these costs mainly depend on earnings growth. The growth rate of real spending was more than twice that of average earnings as a whole over the period (and manual earnings grew more slowly), so the volume of management and maintenance spending per unit clearly rose significantly. (Of course, with the emergence of problems on system-built stock of the 1960s and early 1970s, this does not necessarily mean that the service grew in relation to the need to spend.)

Table 3.3 also shows that the real cost of debt servicing was 30 per cent lower in 1987/8 than in 1979/80. What has happened is that local authority housing as a whole has been in the same position as

TABLE 3.5 *Real gross public capital spending on housing, England* (£bn. at 1988/9 prices)

	Local authorities and new towns		Housing associations (to rent)	Other	Total gross spending	Capital receipts	Total net spending
	New-build	Capital repairs					
1976/7	4.7	0.9	1.3	0.9	7.8	0.8	7.0
1977/8	3.7	0.9	1.2	0.6	6.5	0.9	5.5
1978/9	3.0	1.1	1.1	0.8	5.9	1.2	4.8
1979/80	2.5	1.4	1.1	1.0	5.9	0.9	5.0
1980/1	1.9	1.1	1.1	0.7	4.7	1.0	3.7
1981/2	1.2	0.9	0.9	0.7	3.7	1.5	2.2
1982/3	1.0	1.3	1.0	1.1	4.5	2.5	1.9
1983/4	1.0	1.5	0.9	1.8	5.2	2.5	2.7
1984/5	1.0	1.6	0.8	1.5	4.9	2.2	2.7
1985/6	0.8	1.5	0.7	1.1	4.2	2.1	2.1
1986/7	0.7	1.7	0.8	0.9	4.1	2.4	1.7
1987/8	0.7	1.9	0.8	0.9	4.2	2.7	1.5
1988/9	0.7	1.9	0.8	0.8	4.2	3.6	0.6
1989/90	0.6	2.3	0.7	0.8	4.3	3.4	0.9

Sources: As Table 3.1.

an owner-occupier with a mortgage, whose mortgage payments fall in real terms as a result of inflation more quickly than they rise as a result of new borrowing. The effect has been particularly marked since 1979 with the tightening restraints on new local authority borrowing. More than half of the fall in the real value of housing subsidies since 1979/80 could be justified on the grounds that greater subsidy was needed when the real cost of servicing debt was at its highest, but less is needed now (that is, greater subsidy was needed to cope with the 'front-loading' discussed in Chapter 5, but this has now receded).

As the income side of the tables make clear, however, this is only part of the story. While aggregate debt charges fell by £1.4 billion (at 1988/9 prices) between 1979/80 and 1987/8, the total of Rate Fund Contributions and Exchequer subsidies fell by £2.3 billion, with the fall in the latter being particularly rapid. As a result, rents had to rise, with gross rents collected per unit being 57 per cent

higher in real terms in 1986/7 than in 1979/80 (see Table 3.4).
Meanwhile, there was also a substantial rise in 'other' income,
mainly interest credited to HRAs in respect of accumulated capital
receipts from Right to Buy sales, only part of which authorities have
been allowed to spend.

The fall in 'current public spending' on housing thus represents a
switch from general subsidies towards a mixture of rent payments
and Housing Benefit, while gross spending on recurrent services has
actually *increased* in real terms per unit. The fall in the cost of debt
servicing has allowed a substantial rise in real spending on services
to tenants despite a static level of total income.

CAPITAL SPENDING

One also has to make a distinction between what has happened to
gross capital spending and in the way it has been financed. It is also
important to note the switch which has occurred between new building and renovation of the existing public-sector stock. Table 3.5
shows that while net capital spending has collapsed—by 1988/9 it
had fallen to less than a tenth of its 1976/7 real level (although it
recovered a little in 1989/90)—the fall in the gross total is not
nearly so dramatic, although the 44 per cent real drop would be
striking in most other contexts. The difference in the behaviour of the
two totals after 1980/1 is particularly interesting: the net total continues to fall, but the gross total has been higher since 1982/3 than it
was in 1981/2. The explanation lies, of course, with capital receipts,
which quadrupled in real terms between 1979/80 and 1988/9 as
properties were sold under the Right to Buy.

Within the gross total, particular components have fared very
differently. Real spending on new local authority and new town
construction fell continuously, the 1989/90 total being 87 per cent
lower than in 1976/7. Real spending on housing association rental
provision (either through new construction—'new build'—or rehabilitation of existing buildings, and financed either through the
Housing Corporation or local authorities) also fell, but the smaller
proportionate fall meant that by 1986/7 spending on housing association rented housing exceeded that on new council housing. However,
the position looks very different if one takes account of spending on
the renovation of existing council houses. This more than doubled,
so that total gross capital spending on local authority and new

TABLE 3.6 *Indices of volume of capital spending on housing, England* (*Adjusted by public housing output price index.*) (1976/7 = 100)

	Local authorities and new towns		Housing associa-tions (to rent)	Other	Total gross spending
	New-build	Capital repairs			
1976/7	100	100	100	100	100
1977/8	85	104	103	72	89
1978/9	70	123	96	99	84
1979/80	57	156	92	119	82
1980/1	41	117	86	78	62
1981/2	28	101	73	78	50
1982/3	25	159	91	141	65
1983/4	24	183	77	243	76
1984/5	25	196	72	197	73
1985/6	21	193	67	144	63
1986/7	18	216	73	123	63
1987/8	17	237	72	128	65
1988/9	17	236	71	108	63
1989/90	14	270	63	103	63

Sources: As Table 3.5 and DoE (1989a), Table A and equivalents for other years.

town housing has actually grown in recent years—by 38 per cent since the low point of 1981/2. The other items—support for the private sector or home ownership schemes (some organised through housing associations)—have had a much more variable history. The bulk of this spending is on improvement grants. This increased rapidly during the grants 'boom' between 1981/2 and 1983/4 but has subsequently fallen back, taking the total of 'other' spending by 1988/9 below its 1976/7 level.

Table 3.6 gives indices for the *volume* of capital spending adjusted by the output price index for new public-sector housing. Construction costs for new public-sector housing rose less rapidly over the period than prices in general, so capital spending in volume terms fell less rapidly than real spending. Using this index (which does not allow for the changes in land costs and may not be entirely accurate for renovation activity), the volume of gross capital spending fell by only 37 per cent, compared to the 44 per cent fall in real terms. That on new council housing fell by 86 per cent (compared to 88 per cent in real terms), that on renovation of existing council

TABLE 3.7 *Public housing completions and renovations, GB ('000)*

	New completions		Renovations		
	Local authority and new town	Housing associations	Local authority and new town[a]	Housing associations	Grants to private owners
1976	145	16	75	14	83
1977	136	25	94	20	71
1978	107	23	106	15	70
1979	85	18	111	20	80
1980	85	21	100	18	95
1981	65	19	79	14	94
1982	37	13	109	22	139
1983	35	16	127	18	293
1984	34	17	123	21	320
1985	27	13	157	13	200
1986	22	12	208	15	163
1987	19	12	241	13	159
1988	19	11	243	13	157
1989[b]	15	11	n.a.	n.a.	n.a.

[a] 1977 to 1983 figures omit Wales.

[b] First three quarters at annual rate.

Sources: DoE (1989*a*), tables 6.1 and 7.4 and earlier equivalents;
 DoE (1990*a*), table 1.2.

dwellings rose by 170 per cent (against 139 per cent in real terms), while the fall in housing association rental provision was 37 per cent (against 44 per cent in real terms).

Table 3.7 shows the main results of this spending. In line with the spending figures, local authority and new town completions in Great Britain collapsed from 145,000 in 1976 to 15,000 by 1989. Housing association completions of new dwellings reached a maximum of over 25,000 in 1977, but then fell back to 11,000 in 1989. Their renovations mainly represent additions to the sector, so their total new units, although well down on the peak year of 1977, have exceeded local authority completions since 1986.

As stressed above, new building represents only a part of the picture: there was a significant switch towards renovation and rehabilitation to improve the standards of existing dwellings. Local authority and new town renovations grew rapidly from 1976, reaching nearly a quarter of a million local authority dwellings in 1988.

The pattern of grants for the renovation of privately owned property (including grants to tenants) was much more erratic. The number of grants remained below 100,000 until 1981 (it had previously reached nearly 250,000 in 1974) but jumped rapidly to reach a peak of over 300,000 in 1984, before falling back again, at the end of the grants boom.

SUMMARY

■ Net public spending on housing halved between 1976/7 and 1989/90, while the cost of relief for mortgage interest nearly doubled.

■ Throughout the period, falls in net current spending (mainly general subsidies to local authority housing) were largely offset by increases in the cost of Housing Benefit.

■ At 1988/9 prices, annual general subsidies per tenant fell from about £600 in the late 1970s to £200 in the late 1980s, while interest relief per owner-occupier rose from just above £200 to over £400.

■ Despite the cuts in subsidies, real management and maintenance spending per unit rose by nearly 5 per cent per year throughout the period. This was possible because rents rose substantially and the real burden of debt servicing fell.

■ While real net capital spending in 1989/90 in England was only one-eighth of that in 1976/7, gross capital spending only fell by 44 per cent, the difference being due to capital receipts.

■ While new local authority building fell substantially, there was a large increase in spending on renovation of existing local authority housing. Including this, total real gross capital spending on local authority and new town housing (adjusted by an index of general inflation) was 38 per cent higher in 1989/90 than in the trough of 1981/2.

4

Trends in Housing Costs

This chapter provides further background to the rest of the book by examining trends in the rents for local authority and housing association tenants which have resulted from their subsidy systems, and in house prices and interest rates. A final section examines net cash outgoings on housing in all tenures in relation to disposable incomes.

LOCAL AUTHORITY AND HOUSING ASSOCIATION RENTS

Although the two organisations house similar people, local authorities and housing associations set rents according to different principles. Local authorities have been free to set individual rents as they themselves chose, although 'ring fencing' from April 1990 means that they will have rather less freedom to choose overall rent levels—as opposed to relativities—in future. In the past housing associations were not allowed to charge more than a 'fair rent' set by the local rent officer (in practice, they almost invariably charged fair rents). This continues for their existing (pre-1989) tenants, but associations themselves now set rents for new 'assured' tenants.

LOCAL AUTHORITY RENTS

Local authority rents are the outcome of two decisions: the aggregate rent to be collected from the authority's stock; and the relativities set between different properties. The first of these depends on the total costs carried on its Housing Revenue Account (for current items like management and maintenance and capital items like interest on debt), and on the level of subsidy to the HRA from central government. Until April 1990, it also depended on whether the authority made Rate Fund Contributions into the HRA from its general resources (or, in some cases, transferred a surplus out of the HRA). Overall rent levels have thus been the outcome of a mixture of local and central political preferences, the structure of the subsidy system, and historical accident in terms of the date at which property was built and hence the level of debt still being carried. One aim of the new subsidy system described in Chapter Seven is greatly to reduce the influence of historic debt charges and to produce rents which vary between local authorities in proportion to their capital values. This reverses the effect of the subsidy system in the 1980s, which encouraged all authorities to increase their rents by equal cash amounts, tending to reduce the variations between different parts of the country.

Relativities within an authority's stock have been determined by a variety of methods: 'about half of [English] authorities based rents on Gross Annual Values or Rateable Values. The remainder used some other property comparability scheme and these could be sub-divided into "implicit" schemes where rents varied by broad categories of property or "explicit" schemes where a formal, de-tailed points system was adopted' (Maclennan 1986, p. 52). In general, rents have varied rather little between different property types and dwellings of different quality in the same authority. While the Government has exhorted authorities to set relativities which 'reflect the value or popularity of different dwellings' (DoE 1988*b*, para. 18), the new subsidy system does not remove authorities' dis-cretion over relativities within their stock.

HOUSING ASSOCIATION RENTS

Under the 1965 Rent Act, 'fair rents' are supposed to reflect the characteristics of the dwelling (not of its tenant), but on the assump-tion that the demand for rented dwellings of the kind in question 'is not substantially greater than the number of such dwelling houses in the locality which are available for letting on such terms' (Section 70). Given that a price is usually determined by the interac-tion of supply and demand, this definition is almost meaningless in economic terms. In practice fair rents have been fixed by reference to similar properties in the area and to the level of rents set in the recent past, in essence through an exercise which holds itself up by its own bootstraps. Doling and Davies reported from a study in the West Midlands that the rules followed by rent officers within their own areas, 'are followed with varying degrees of consistency, but overall they bear limited similarity to the rules and performances in other areas ... rent officers from different areas would make very different

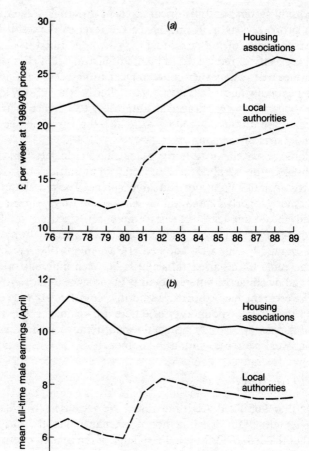

Figure 4.1 Average rents, 1976–1989 (GB):
(*a*) Average rents at 1989/90 prices
(*b*) Rents as percentage of average earnings
Note: Local authority rents at April each year (September in Scotland);
housing association rents for calendar year (first half of 1989).

Sources: DoE (1989*a*), tables 11.1 and 11.5; DoE (1990*a*), table 1.14; DE
(1990), table 5.6; Scottish Development Department (1990), table 15.5.10;
HM Treasury (1990), table 8.11.

determinations for identical dwellings' (1984, p. 104). Results from the Department of the Environment's 'Beacon' exercise (intended to encourage consistency in the setting of fair rents) confirm this impression of inconsistency. In July 1987 the net rent left after deducting estimated management and maintenance costs (based on the allowances given to housing associations for rehabilitiated property) from fair rents varied from less than 1 per cent of a dwelling's capital value in several London boroughs to over 3.5 per cent in Northumberland (Hills 1988*a*, appendix 2). While some variation between regions might be justified by differences in expected house price inflation, even within the same county the net rents for different property types can have completely different relationships with capital values: in West Yorkshire the net rent given for a 1960s purpose-built flat was 1.4 per cent of capital value, while that on an improved late Victorian terraced house was 3.6 per cent of capital value.

Under the 1988 Housing Act, new lettings by associations are no longer covered by fair rents (although they will be retained for existing tenants who stay put or move to another property of the same association). Instead, rents are set at the discretion of the association in the light of the subsidies it receives. The pattern of rents implied by the current system of subsidies to associations is discussed in Chapter 8. While relative capital costs of providing new dwellings will have a strong influence on this pattern, it will also reflect management and maintenance costs which vary rather less across the country. Combined with differences in their overall structures, the new subsidy arrangements will not produce much more consistency between association and authority rent setting than there was in the past, although both will be affected—in different ways— by local market conditions.

TRENDS OVER TIME

Figure 4.1 shows what has happened to average local authority and housing association rents in Great Britain since 1976; (a) shows rent levels in real terms (at 1989/90 prices, adjusted by the Retail Price Index), while (b) shows rents as a percentage of average earnings (the mean GB figure for men in full-time employment). The series for housing association rents is for registrations of rents for new tenants and re-registrations for existing ones. Until 1989 any increase in a

TABLE 4.1 Indices of housing costs and earnings by region (London = 100)

	House prices (1988)	Gross earnings (men, April 1988)		Local authority rents (April 1988)	Housing association rents (1st quarter, 1990)[a]	
		All	Manual		Fair rents	Assured tenancies
Greater London	100	100	100	100	100	100
Rest of South-East	93	81	93	90	99	98
South-West	75	73	85	85	97	87
East Anglia	74	73	90	81	85	84
West Midlands	54	71	87	84	85	76
East Midlands	52	70	87	82	94	80
Wales	44	68	86	90	n.a.	n.a.
North-West	44	72	87	82	75[b]	68[b]
Yorkshire & Humberside	42	70	87	79	82	80
Scotland	41	72	86	75	n.a.	n.a.
North	39	70	88	83	85	74

[a] Data are for National Federation of Housing Associations regions, which differ slightly from standard regions.
[b] Simple average of NFHA 'North West' and 'Merseyside' regions.

Sources: DoE (1989a), table 10.11.
DE (1989a), Part E, tables 108 and 110.
CSO (1989a), table 2.3.
NFHA CORE Quarterly Bulletin, 1st Quarter 1990.

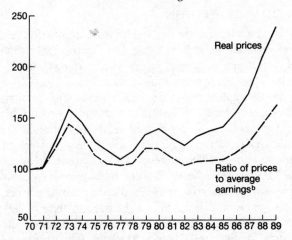

Figure 4.2 UK house prices, 1970–1989[a]
Mix-adjusted index (1970 = 100)
[a] 1989 figures are average of second and third quarters.
[b] Average: adult males in full-time employment (GB).

Sources: DoE (1989*a*), table 10.11; DoE (1990*a*), table 1.13; DE (1990), table 5.6; and equivalents for other years.

fair rent was phased in over two years, so the actual rents paid were somewhat less than those illustrated. It should also be noted that the figures for associations include 'service charges' as well as the rent itself, while those for authorities do not; the differential between them is thus rather smaller than that shown.

Both kinds of rent rose substantially in real terms over the period as a whole, but with a different pattern: the big increase in local authority rents happening between 1980 and 1982, when subsidies were cut (see Chapter 3), while association rents rose fairly steadily after 1981. However, there is no consistent upward trend in relation to earnings; both kinds of rent represented much the same proportion of average earnings (for all full-time men) in 1989 as they did in 1981. Changes in subsidy arrangements for both authorities and associations will lead to a rather different pattern in the 1990s; see Chapters 7 and 8.

VARIATION BY REGION

The way in which local authority and housing association rents have varied by region is shown in Table 4.1, together with figures for regional variations in house prices and earnings. While house prices—the major factor determining the relative costs of providing housing in different areas—vary widely across the country, rents have varied much less. For instance, house prices in the North of England were less than 40 per cent of those in London in 1988, but local authority rents (in April 1988) and housing association fair rents (at the end of 1988) were only 17 per cent below those in London. The fair rents being charged by housing associations (to existing tenants transferring between dwellings) in the first quarter of 1990 also varied much less across the country than house prices. However, those being charged to new 'assured' tenants under the new financial regime (see Chapter 8) varied much more than fair rents.

The table also shows the way in which earnings vary between regions. Average earnings for all men in full-time work also vary more between regions than rents. If these were used as the criterion, a wider dispersion of regional rents could be justified on 'affordability' as well as cost grounds. However, the earnings of manual workers—arguably more relevant in discussing the 'affordability' of rents for social housing—vary much less between regions than overall earnings (indeed, rather less than rents have done). This could be taken as a justification for lack of variation in rent levels; as discussed in Chapter 2, it could also be the *result* of such lack of variation, if wages depend on the cost of living for employees.

HOUSE PRICES AND INTEREST RATES

Both for owner-occupiers and for those involved in producing housing to rent, crucial costs are given by house prices themselves and by the interest rates which have to be paid to finance borrowing. As Figure 4.2 illustrates, house prices are notoriously unstable. The prices shown are the Department of the Environment's 'mix-adjusted' series drawn from its continuous 5 per cent survey of all sales financed by building society mortgages. (The adjustment attempts to remove the effects of variations in the mix of dwellings sold, for instance as a result of changes in the building societies' share of the mortgage market—in some periods, banks and other

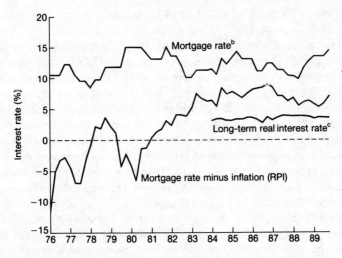

Figure 4.3 Real and nominal interest rates[a]

[a] Rates at end of each quarter.

[b] Building Societies Association recommended rates until last quarter 1983; average rate on building society mortgages from first quarter 1984.

[c] Yield on 2.5% index-linked 2016 stock.

Sources: CSO (1990*a* and *b*); and earlier equivalents.

lenders have increased their share of the top of the market, leading to unadjusted building society prices understating price increases in the market as a whole; in others the reverse has occurred.)

Part of what occurs is the result of a speculative cycle. As a boom gathers momentum, more and more people try to get into the market 'before it's too late', adding to the momentum of the boom. Conversely, once a slow-down is generally perceived, people take their time or even hang back waiting for a more favourable moment to buy, again helping to brake the market even more. Since 1970 there have been three of these cycles, with peaks in real prices in 1973, 1980, and 1989. Whilst there is a general belief that housing is a secure investment, this kind of cycle makes the timing of purchase all-important. Someone buying in 1982 would on average have seen a real increase in the value of his or her house of 90 per cent by 1989, but someone buying in 1973 a 30 per cent real fall in value by 1977. In particular parts of the country, these changes were even more pronounced. With cash prices falling in some regions at the time of writing, it seems likely that there will be a significant real fall from the 1989 peak by 1991.

Given these wide fluctuations, it is hard to establish the underlying trend. However, the figures and data over a much longer period show a historical pattern under which house prices have certainly risen in real terms, but have stayed in a rather more stable relationship with earnings. In Figure 4.2 the second line shows an index of the ratio of prices to average earnings. While this has also fluctuated, the upward trend is much less clear, with the values of the ratio at peaks and troughs relatively close to those at equivalent points in the cycle. The same appears to have been true over a much longer period. In 1970 house prices were twice as high as they had been in relation to the general price level in the late 1930s, but were almost unchanged in relation to average earnings (DoE 1977*b*, table I. 28; see also Holmans 1990). Such long-term stability is not entirely surprising, with factors on both supply and demand sides meaning that prices are affected by income growth. As a result, it seems more plausible to assume that there will continue to be some long-term rise in the real quality-adjusted price of housing in the future, than to assume otherwise. This expected long-run real capital gain has crucial implications for the measurement of subsidies to owners (through the tax system) and to tenants (through rents which give a sub-economic return on capital), which are discussed in Chapter 14.

Short-term interest rates (that is, those which can be varied at short notice, rather than those fixed over a long period) are also highly unstable. For owner-occupiers, the nominal mortgage rate shown in Figure 4.3 has varied between 8.5 per cent and 15 per cent since 1976, and the variable interest rates paid by others will have fluctuated in a similar way. The true cost of borrowing is, however, better measured by looking at *real* interest rates, that is the interest rate paid in excess of inflation. In the short term, as the figure shows, the result of this calculation can be negative, and indeed was negative for much of the 1970s. By contrast, the excess of 5 per cent or more throughout the late 1980s has been unusually high historically: financing housing through short-term borrowing has become a very expensive exercise. If one looks at the financial markets, however, the interest rates on long-term borrowing (which is most relevant for measuring the capital cost of housing) have recently been lower than short-term rates—the markets expect

TABLE 4.2 *Ratio of net housing payments to disposable income by tenure, GB, 1987*

Net payments: % disposable income	% tenure group in range				
	Mortgagers[a]	Tenants			
		Local authority	Housing association	Private unfurnished	Private furnished
Under 5	11	43	24	34	19
5–10	21	23	18	19	16
10–15	24	17	21	16	14
15–20	17	9	11	10	12
20–25	12	4	6	5	8
25 and over	15	3	20	16	32
Payments by tenure group					
Mean % income	14	8	12	10	18

[a] MIRAS recipients only

Source: DoE (1989a), tables 12.9 and 12.10.

TABLE 4.3 *Ratio of net housing payments to disposable income by income, GB, 1987*

Range of disposable household income (£/year)	Mortgagers:[a] net mortgage payments as % of disposable income	Local authority tenants: net rent as % of disposable income
Under 3,000	41	6
3,000–3,999		7
4,000–5,999	31	10
6,000–7,999	19	11
8,000–9,999	17	9
10,000–11,999	15	7
12,000–14,999	13	7
15,000–19,999	11	5
20,000 and over	9	
ALL INCOMES	12	8

[a] MIRAS recipients only.

Source: DoE (1989a), Tables 12.9 and 12.10.

interest rates to fall over the coming years. The best measure of long-run market expectations for interest rates in relation to inflation is given by the yield on long-term government 'indexed' stocks (whose redemption value is linked to the inflation rate). These have only been available for a few years, so a consistent series only stretches back to 1984. The stability of the quarterly data shown in Figure 4.3 is remarkable—in only one of the twenty-four quarters shown was the implied real interest rate outside the range between 3 and 4 per cent, and for most of the time it was close to its average for the period of 3.5 per cent. Again, this measure of the long-term real interest rate has important implications for the value of subsidies to owners and tenants.

None the less, in the short term, what most affects owner-occupiers are the cash flow costs of servicing their mortgages. Here the fluctuations in interest rates and house prices can reinforce one another. In 1982, payments on the mortgages taken out by first-time buyers would have absorbed an average of about 14 per cent of their income (as reported to building societies) at the interest rates applying at the end of the year; by 1989, the equivalent proportion would have been 26 per cent, suggesting a powerful reason why the housing market price bubble burst (own calculations based on DoE 1989a, tables 10.11, 10.16, and 10.25, and equivalents).

CASH FLOW HOUSING COSTS IN RELATION TO INCOME

Tables 4.2 and 4.3 complete this review of the key components of housing costs by presenting figures for the ratio of net housing payments to disposable income (after direct taxes) for tenants and mortgagers in 1987. For tenants, the costs shown are rent net of any assistance with it through Housing Benefit (up to 100 per cent in some cases). For mortgagers, the costs are mortgage payments after allowing for interest relief paid through the 'MIRAS' system (see Chapter 12; they do not therefore allow for the extra relief going to higher-rate taxpayers). As Figures 4.1–4.3 show, 1987 was a fairly average year for the 1980s in terms of rents and house prices in relation to incomes, and for interest rates.

It should immediately be stressed that this does not compare like with like. Unlike tenants, mortgagers can look forward to a substantial period as outright owners, when their costs on this basis would be zero, and they will end up with an asset. On the other hand, owners have to pay their own maintenance and repair costs—taking up on average an additional 2.6 per cent of income (DE 1989*b*, tables 5 and 22). A comparison of equivalent costs and of those over the life cycle is made in Chapter 14.

The clearest conclusion from Table 4.2 is the very poor position of tenants in the private furnished sector, paying an average of 18 per cent of disposable income in rent even after allowing for Housing Benefit, and with nearly a third of them paying out more than 25 per cent of disposable income. By contrast, in the local authority sector, where rents are lower and take-up of Housing Benefit is much higher, two-thirds of tenants pay out less than 10 per cent of disposable income in rent. As Chapter 10 explores, however, the current Housing Benefit system does not prevent the ratio shown becoming very high in some cases. It is striking that even in 1987—when fair rents still applied to all housing association lettings—one-fifth of association tenants were paying out more than 25 per cent of disposable income. With the rents implied by the new grant system, this proportion can be expected to rise substantially (see Chapter 8).

Table 4.3 shows a breakdown by income of the position for mortgagers and local authority tenants (note that mortgagers are concentrated in the higher income ranges shown, tenants in the lower ones). It shows an outcome of the current tax and subsidy systems which recurs in the analysis in later chapters. For mortgagers—and, indeed, for outright owners—the greatest 'affordability' problems measured in this way occur for those with the lowest incomes, with the lowest income mortgagers paying out 40 per cent of disposable income. The lowest-income tenants are much better protected by the Housing Benefit system, with the highest rent to income ratios occurring for those with incomes just too high to qualify for benefit (see Figure 10.5).

SUMMARY

■ Local authority rents rose by more than 60 per cent in real terms during the 1980s and housing association fair rents by 25 per cent. However, these rents were no higher in relation to average earnings in 1989 than they had been in 1981.

■ Rents have varied much less than house prices or average earnings (and hence the costs of provision) across the country.

However, the earnings of manual workers also vary little across the country, giving some justification for lack of rent variation if affordability were the only criterion.

■ Real house prices have fluctuated widely over cycles several years long and have had a rising long-term underlying trend. In relation to earnings, their underlying trend is much more constant.

■ Short-term nominal interest rates have also fluctuated widely. Whereas they were often below the general rate of inflation in the 1970s, they have been well above inflation in the 1980s. Long-run real interest rates have, however, been remarkably stable at around 3.5 per cent since 1984.

■ Private furnished tenants have the highest cash outgoings on housing in relation to their incomes. Nearly a third of them (and 20 per cent of association tenants) paid out more than 25 per cent of disposable income in rent after allowing for benefits in 1987.

■ Whereas it is the lowest-income owner-occupiers who have the highest mortgage payments in relation to income, for council tenants, the highest ratio of rent to income affects those with incomes just too high to qualify for Housing Benefit.

PART II

Subsidy Systems

5

Subsidy Principles and Problems

THE CONCEPT OF 'ECONOMIC' RENTS

Several reviews of British housing finance have concluded that the apparent anarchy of rents in relation to costs described in Chapter 4 should be swept away and replaced with a more rational structure, in particular one in which rents would be set at unsubsidised or 'economic' levels, with assistance given only through income-related allowances. Such proposals—which include those of the Duke of Edinburgh's Inquiry—are discussed in Chapter 16. Whether or not it would be appropriate actually to charge 'economic rents', the concept is a useful starting-point for analysing housing costs and the structure of subsidy systems.

Essentially, the idea of an economic rent is that it would reflect the true long-run cost of providing rented housing. Such costs would allow the landlord to go on providing rented housing indefinitely, with the same return on investment as is available elsewhere in the economy. Some of these costs are straightforward to measure—day-to-day management and maintenance, for instance. Others are not, in particular how to allow for the capital tied up in a dwelling—capital which could have produced an alternative financial or social return if used elsewhere. Difficulties arise because this 'opportunity cost of capital' is usually different from what are conventionally described as 'capital costs' in financial accounts.

ECONOMIC RENTS WITHOUT INFLATION

Imagine, to start with, a world where prices, costs, and earnings are all constant, that is, without inflation or real earnings growth. An economic rent would have to cover three elements. First, there are management and maintenance costs, including provision for regular redecoration and repairs ('cyclical maintenance'). Second, there should be a charge for the opportunity cost of the capital tied up in the dwelling, that is, the return which could be generated on alternative investments; in this case, with no inflation, a measure of this would be given by the market interest rate.

Finally, there should be a provision to reflect that, even with normal repairs and maintenance, houses will not last for ever. There are three ways in which this could be done:

1. a depreciation allowance calculated so that by the time the house fell down, the allowances put aside would have built up into a sum large enough to replace it;
2. a provision for periodic 'major repairs' which were extensive enough to keep the house in good condition indefinitely; or
3. financing arrangements under which the debt would all be paid off by the time the house did fall down, and the process of building a new house with a new loan could start all over again.

Each of these three provisions has an equivalent effect: it makes sure that the landlord's balance sheet does not deteriorate as a result of depreciation. Crucially, only *one* of them has to be made. As Grey, Hepworth, and Odling-Smee put it, 'if a proper charge has been made for modernisation and management then ideally the tenant ought not to bear any element of capital redemption' (1978, p. 68). If the rent charged covered, say, both major repairs and principal repayment (paying off the debt), the landlord would end up with a net increase in assets: the rent would have paid for the *purchase* of the property, even though the tenant did not, at the end of the process, actually own it. In reality, the major repairs actually carried out on a property will not be enough to produce an everlasting house, so that what has to be allowed for in practice is a *combination* of major repairs below the full replacement level and depreciation at a correspondingly lower rate than without major repairs.

Suppose, in this simplified situation, that a unit had a capital value of £50,000, that its management and maintenance costs totalled £600 per year, that the rate of interest used to calculate the opportunity cost of capital was 4 per cent, and that the allowance for depreciation was 1.2 per cent of a £40,000 rebuilding cost (excluding the part of capital value reflecting land, as this does not depreciate; the 1.2 per cent is merely a plausible, not a scientifically assessed, figure). The economic rent would then be £3,080 per year (£600 plus £2,000 plus £480), or about £59 per week, representing 6.2 per cent of the property's capital value. With no changes in costs and values this would stay constant in perpetuity.

THE EFFECTS OF INFLATION

Inflation affects the calculation in two ways. Most obviously, the cash amounts of values and costs will rise from year to year, and with them the cash value of the economic rent. A further effect arises as a result of the way in which the loans which have traditionally financed housing (like most other forms of loan) are expressed in *cash terms*. With inflation, the real value of a debt which is constant in cash terms falls. In compensation for this, interest rates (expressed in 'nominal' or cash terms) tend to be higher.

Suppose that the inflation rate was a steady 6 per cent (with all costs and values increasing at this rate) and that the nominal interest rate was 10 per cent. There are then two equivalent ways of looking at the opportunity cost of capital. One is to look at the situation in cash terms. The cost of borrowing would be measured by the nominal interest rate (10 per cent), but against this should be allowed the rise in the nominal value of the property (6 per cent). The opportunity cost of capital net of this gain would remain at 4 per cent, as in the case without inflation (strictly, the nominal interest rate would have to be 10.24 per cent for this to be exactly true). The alternative is to look at the situation in 'real' (inflation-adjusted) terms. The cost of borrowing is then measured simply in terms of the *real* interest rate of 4 per cent (that is, 10 per cent less the 6 per cent inflation rate to allow for the effect of inflation on the value of outstanding debt). In real terms the capital value of the house is constant (by assumption), so this does not have to be allowed for.

Applying this to the example, the economic rent in the current year would be unaffected, as the real interest rate is still 4 per cent. In subsequent years, all the components of the economic rent would rise by the inflation rate, but in real terms would remain constant.

ALLOWING FOR REAL GROWTH IN COSTS AND VALUES

Even with the inclusion of the effects of inflation, this still makes the important over-simplification that earnings and costs remain constant in real terms. In fact they do not. This introduces two further complications. First, the components of an economic rent may rise in real terms over time. Management and maintenance costs largely consist of wages and salaries. If real earnings rise, so will real management and maintenance costs. Depreciation (or major repair) costs depend on building costs; these also tend to rise more rapidly than general inflation. Finally, if the dwelling is becoming more valuable because real house prices are rising, then the charge for the capital tied up in the dwelling should rise too.

The second complication is that if the asset is becoming more valuable in real terms, allowance has to be made for this *real capital gain* in determining rents. If part of the return on the asset comes in the form of a real capital gain, the *rental* income required to give a particular *total* real return will therefore be lower (to start with, at least).

This last point makes it very important whether it is plausible to expect real increases in house prices to continue in the long term. As discussed in Chapter 4, historically house prices certainly have risen more rapidly than prices in general: with very wide fluctuations, they have kept more in line with earnings than prices.

There are several reasons why one might expect this relationship to carry on (for an alternative view see Duncan 1990). If there has been technical progress in house construction, it has been slow: the attempt to change this in the 1960s through industrialised building methods was a notorious failure. If real earnings in general are rising because of faster productivity growth elsewhere, this will mean a continuing real increase in construction costs. At the same time, land is in fixed supply. Meanwhile, increasing incomes will be increasing the demand for housing: to the extent that it is in fixed supply, this has to be choked off by rising prices. There is nothing particularly strange about a dynamic equilibrium of this kind: many assets are priced in such a way that their return comes partly as an expected trend capital gain, balanced by a lower current return than on assets whose real value is expected to remain constant (stores of wealth like gold being the extreme cases of this).

Part of the observed increase in house prices will of course be a result of quality improvements (partly offset by the move of owner-occupied housing down-market). None the less, the experience of the last fifty years suggests that even after allowing for quality improvements, it is reasonable to expect that real house prices will increase in the long run (in the short run, this will not be true if one is starting from a peak in the cycle). How much they can be expected to increase is both controversial and uncertain. This contributes to the difficulties of assessing precisely what an economic rent would be, and hence of calculating the advantage given by the difference between actual and economic rents. The effects of different assumptions are explored in Chapter 14. For the illustrative examples below it is assumed that expected long-run real growth in capital values is 1 per cent per year, a fairly conservative assumption (Holmans 1990, p. 57, suggests a post-War trend of 1.2 per cent).

ECONOMIC RENTS ALLOWING FOR REAL INCREASES IN CAPITAL VALUES

Allowing for these complications, an economic rent will now be calculated as follows. As before, on the cost side will be management and maintenance costs, an allowance for the real opportunity cost of capital, plus an allowance for depreciation/major repairs (to the extent that such an allowance is needed after normal recurrent repairs). On the return side will be the expected real capital growth in the value of the dwelling plus the rent paid that year.

As with other parts of the calculation, setting a realistic level for the opportunity cost of capital is controversial. However, as shown in Figure 4.3, between February 1984 and December 1989 the yield on long-term indexed government stocks—the best available measure of the long-run real interest rate—averaged 3.5 per cent, so the assumption of 4 per cent is in some ways conservative, incorporating something of a risk premium. Remember that this opportunity cost does not correspond to any particular debt repayment schedule.

Returning to the example, we thus have the following calculation:

	Management and maintenance costs
plus	Opportunity cost of capital (4 per cent of capital value)
plus	Depreciation/major repairs (1.2 per cent of rebuilding cost)
equals	Expected real capital gain (1 per cent of capital value)
plus	Economic rent.

For the house discussed above, the economic rent would be £2,580 per year (£600 management and maintenance, plus £2,000 for the opportunity cost of capital, plus £480 for depreciation, less £500 for the expected real gain) or about £49.50 per week and 5.2 per cent of capital value. It is important to note that this is *lower* than the result of the earlier calculation which ignored future real increase in capital values. However, real capital values are now expected to rise in the long term, contributing to a rise in the economic rent in real terms. The effect of allowing for the real increase in capital values is that rents are lower to start with, but rise more rapidly over time.

It is important to note that the landlord does not have to plan to sell the property and realise the capital gain for it to enter the calculations: the fact that the rental stream will rise in real terms contributes to the required return.

This way of calculating the rent required to give a given real return corresponds (with some differences in the detailed assumptions) to the proposals of Grey *et al* (1978) and of the Inquiry into British Housing (1985*b*). It does *not* necessarily correspond to a 'market' rent, as this would reflect existing shortages and imperfections of the housing market, as well as almost certainly incorporating a very substantial premium to cover a private investor against the possibilities of future rent control and changes in security of tenure legislation (although it does equal the rent which would result in the long run in a theoretical fully adjusted market without any imperfections).

CAPITAL VALUE AND CAPITAL COST

The problems of appropriate valuation for this kind of calculation are explored in the Byatt Report on public-sector inflation accounting (HM Treasury 1987). A particular problem concerns the differences between market *values* and replacement *costs*. If the economy is out of equilibrium (which in the case of housing is probable), the two will not necessarily be the same. If current values exceed the cost of replacement with an equivalent dwelling, it is replacement cost which it is appropriate to use to measure the capital resources being used (as replacement would be the most efficient way of using new resources). On the other hand, if current value is lower than replacement cost, the latter is not relevant (as replacement is a more expensive option than buying an existing unit). If they differ, it is therefore the *lower* of the two which is appropriate to use in calculating the opportunity cost of capital. A particular reason for a difference between capital value and replacement cost could be revealed maintenance and repair problems with a particular design of dwelling. If an *existing* dwelling has an unusually high need for recurrent maintenance, its capital value will be depressed (reflecting this additional liability it brings to its owner).

A related issue is that there may be a choice when constructing new dwellings between those which are cheaper to construct but more expensive to maintain, and those which are the opposite. An economic rent for the latter would incorporate the opportunity cost of its higher capital value, but a lower figure for management and maintenance than the former. A rational investment decision—if it was unbiased by subsidy arrangements—would go for the option which offered the lowest economic rent. For simplicity, in the rest of this book the choices between possible mixes of capital and recurrent costs are generally ignored, except where they result from regional differences in the balance between relative capital and recurrent costs (for instance, because wages and salaries vary less across the country than land and building costs).

HOW HOUSING SUBSIDIES WORK

Suppose, for some of the reasons discussed in Chapter 2, that it is decided that rents should be below the economic cost of provision, with subsidy provided in some way. One solution would be an annual subsidy to the landlord equal to a proportion of total unsubsidised costs, reducing them to the level required. This is not, in general, what has been done in Britain. Governments have been reluctant to pay a proportion of actual spending on items like management and maintenance as they are less easy to monitor and control than, for instance, the costs of new construction. The 'rising costs' element of the 1972 local authority housing subsidy system was an exception but, given the rapid increase in management and maintenance spending which occurred while it was in operation, this experiment has not been repeated (see Holmans 1987, pp. 355–7).

Instead, subsidy has acted by reducing *capital costs* (sometimes including 'capitalised' or major repairs) to a level which can be financed out of the desired rent level. This can be done in two ways. The first includes what Holmans (1987, p. 306) describes as 'the "classic" type of British housing subsidy': local authorities had to borrow to cover the full capital cost of new dwellings, but received annual recurrent subsidies towards their costs. Holmans reports that in 1924, for instance, the subsidy for each new house was £9 per year for forty years; by 1946 the subsidy was £16. 10s. per year for sixty years. An alternative way of achieving much the same result would be an initial capital *grant* sufficient to reduce the cost of the loan required for the balance to the desired level. This is, essentially, how the Housing Association Grant (HAG) system established in 1974 works.

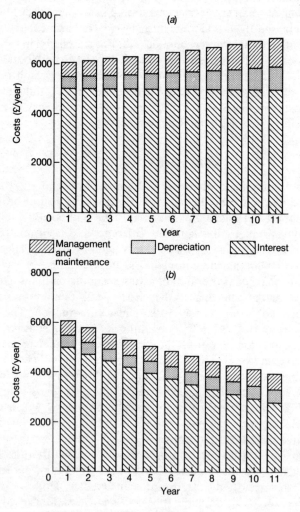

Figure. 5.1 Unsubsidised cash flow costs:
(*a*) 7% growth in costs, nominal terms
(*b*) 7% growth in costs, real terms (6% inflation)

THE EFFECTS OF INFLATION ON HOUSING FINANCE: THE 'FRONT-LOADING PROBLEM'

Inflation causes immense problems for housing finance. At their heart is the way in which the loans traditionally used to finance housing have servicing costs (interest plus principal repayment) calculated so that equal *cash* payments are made each year until the loan is paid off (through what are known as fixed annuity payments). This means that if interest rates do not change, the *real* value of debt servicing falls year by year (as owner-occupiers with old mortgages experience). To offset this, nominal interest rates are, other things being equal, higher at a time of inflation.

Figure 5.1 illustrates the 'front-loading' problem which this causes. It shows a simplified representation of the cash flow costs a landlord would face over the first eleven years with the dwelling described above, if there were no subsidies and if purchase was financed by an indefinite 'interest only' loan (for simplicity avoiding the double counting if debt was repaid while also providing for full depreciation). In Year 1, costs total £6,080 (£5,000 interest at 10 per cent on the £50,000 capital cost, plus £480 provision for depreciation/major repairs and £600 for management and maintenance). After that, it is assumed that inflation runs at a steady 6 per cent, but management, maintenance, rebuilding costs, and capital values rise by a further 1 per cent in real terms each year (although in reality there is no necessary reason why they should all rise at the same rate).

As shown in panel (*a*), showing the position in nominal (cash) terms, by Year 11 these costs would have risen to £7,125. Adjusting for inflation, however, the total of these cash flow costs falls in real terms, as shown in panel (*b*). While management and maintenance and depreciation/major repairs costs (proportional to rebuilding costs) rise gradually, the real cost of the interest payment falls, losing 44 per cent of its real value by Year 11. The real burden of the interest payments can be seen to be 'front-loaded'.

Figure 5.2 illustrates the problems which this causes for subsidy design. Suppose that it was intended that the rent charged should only be 3 per cent of current capital value (below the 5.2 per cent calculated above to give an economic rent), so that it started at £1,500 in Year 1. Allowing £600 for management and maintenance and £480 for depreciation, this would only leave £420 in Year 1 to give a return on capital. With a 4 per cent real opportunity cost of

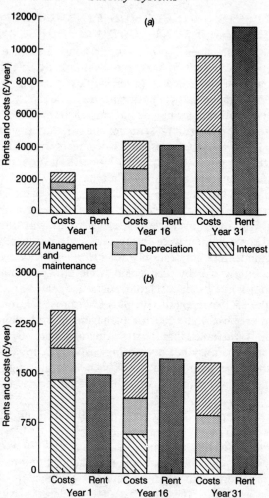

Figure 5.2. Costs and rents (72% capital grant):
(*a*) 7% growth in costs, nominal terms
(*b*) 7% growth in costs, real terms (6% inflation)

capital, but also allowing for a 1 per cent per year expected continuing rise in real rents (in line with costs and the property's value), a discounted cash flow analysis would suggest that the landlord could afford to have up to £14,000 of capital tied up in the dwelling.

As the full capital cost is £50,000, an initial 72 per cent capital grant would be needed to give the landlord an economic return at the given rent level.

Panel (*a*) of Figure 5.2 shows the nominal cash flow costs which would result after allowing for such a grant and with the same management, maintenance, and depreciation costs as before, and with an interest-only loan at 10 per cent on the £14,000 balance of the capital costs after grant. The interest payable is therefore £1,400 in Year 1, and this remains constant in cash terms. The cash costs faced by the landlord thus total £2,480 in Year 1.

The rent starts at only £1,500, however. Despite what theoretically should be an adequate capital grant, the landlord would still be in deficit in the first year. As the figure shows, however, the deficit falls and eventually turns into a surplus (after eighteen years). The reason for this is clear from panel (*b*), showing the fall in the real value of the interest payments. If one carried out a discounted cash flow analysis, the present value of the eventual surpluses would equal that of the initial deficits, confirming that the capital grant was adequate. However, this would not necessarily solve the initial cash flow problems caused by the front-loaded pattern of real interest payments shown in the figure. As Holmans (1987, p. 374) puts it, 'How to close this gap was in reality the problem to which successive [local authority] subsidy regimes were addressed.'

RENT POOLING AS A WAY OF COPING WITH INFLATION

One way of coping with this problem for landlords with a mixture of stock, some financed a long time ago and hence with low 'historic' debt in relation to current values is 'rent pooling'. Essentially what would happen is that the cash loss on new property (on the left-hand side of Figure 5.2) would be offset by the cash surpluses being made on old property (on and beyond its right-hand side). After all, if the property built at different times is of equal value to tenants, there is little reason why rents should differ just because of the vagaries of mortgage financing. When local authorities realised that inflation during and after the War had put them in this position, more and more of them used rent pooling instead of setting rents on the basis of the debt contracted on each individual dwelling; after the mid-1950s, it became the norm (Holmans 1987, p. 326).

There is a limitation to this approach. If all local authorities built houses at a constant rate and if inflation remained unchanged from year to year, rent pooling might give a permanent solution to front-loading. Neither assumption is well founded, however. Some authorities have had large recent building programmes and have debts on which inflation has yet to have much of an effect. They do not have enough old stock from which they can cross-subsidise. Others have built little in recent years but have immediate post-war stock on which the debt has been greatly eroded by inflation. The former group have either had to charge high rents or to make transfers from their general funds to keep rents down. The latter have been able either to charge low rents or (until 1990) to transfer surpluses *into* their general accounts. This leads to the absurdity that unpopular 1960s system-built flats can have higher rents than popular 1940s cottage estate houses owned by other local authorities. Similar effects can occur *within* authorities which carry out only limited pooling.

GENEROUS CAPITAL GRANTS WITH LATER CLAW-BACK OF SURPLUSES

If rent pooling is not an option (as when housing associations were growing rapidly from a small base in the early 1970s), another approach is to give a generous enough initial capital grant to allow cash costs to be covered in Year 1. This is illustrated in Figure 5.3 for the same example as above. To achieve initial break-even, the capital grant would have to be 91.6 per cent (as this reduces the initial debt interest at 10 per cent to £420 as required). This gets rid of the initial deficit, but, as before, in subsequent years the value of the interest falls in real terms. This means that a gap opens up between rents and costs and the landlord benefits from a steadily growing surplus throughout the dwelling's life.

This is essentially what happened to housing associations in the 1970s (or would have happened had rents not been frozen at various points). The Government decided that giving such a large capital grant by itself was over-generous and introduced a device known as 'Grant Redemption Fund' to claw back surpluses of this kind (for further details and recent changes, see Chapter 8). The combined system copes with inflation through the combination of a very generous initial grant coupled with a claw-back as the front-loading problem subsides.

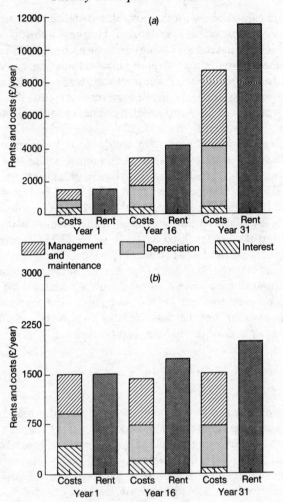

Figure 5.3. Costs and rents (92% capital grant):
(*a*) 7% growth in costs, nominal terms
(*b*) 7% growth in costs, real terms (6% inflation)

RECURRENT SUBSIDY WHICH STARTS AT A HIGH LEVEL BUT THEN FALLS

By contrast, local authorities do not receive capital grants when they construct a new dwelling, but have to cover the loan charges on the entire capital cost with the possible assistance of recurrent subsidies. For instance, the system of Housing Subsidy for local authorities in England and Wales introduced by the 1980 Housing Act worked so that a high level of *initial* subsidy was given when a new house was built, but a lower level was given in subsequent years as rents were assumed to rise but loan servicing costs did not. The system introduced in April 1990 has much the same effect (see Chapter 7 for a further discussion).

The way this kind of system would have to operate for the example being discussed is that the landlord would face the full cash flow costs of £6,080 in Year 1, so that in order to charge a rent of only £1,500, a first year recurrent subsidy of £4,580 would be needed. Later on, the recurrent subsidy required would fall. For instance, by Year 16 the cash rent in the example would reach £4,139, but the unsubsidised costs only £7,980. The recurrent subsidy required falls to £3,841 (worth £1,603 at Year 1 prices). Eventually—after thirty-seven years—recurrent subsidy is no longer needed, and in later years a surplus could be creamed off. (Again, discounted cash flow analysis would confirm that the value of the flow of recurrent subsidies less the later surplus repayments would equal 72 per cent of the £50,000 capital cost.)

INDEXED OR LOW-START FINANCE AS A SOLUTION TO FRONT-LOADING

Another approach is given by the new arrangements which have been introduced for grants to housing associations (see Chapter 8). This is the idea that borrowing should be on 'indexed' or 'low-start' terms. This attacks the front-loading problem directly, without the need either for devices to cream off future surpluses or for initially high recurrent subsidies. The principle of this kind of loan is illustrated in Figure 5.4. Essentially, the payment in the first year is lower than with a conventional loan, but in subsequent years the *cash* amount payable rises. The increase could either be with the rate of inflation in the case of an indexed loan, or according to a predetermined rate of escalation with low-start finance (such as 'deferred interest' or 'stepped interest' loans).

In Figure 5.4, the cash amount payable each year rises with the inflation rate of 6 per cent; the real interest payment shown in panel (*b*) is therefore constant. The example uses the same 72 per cent grant

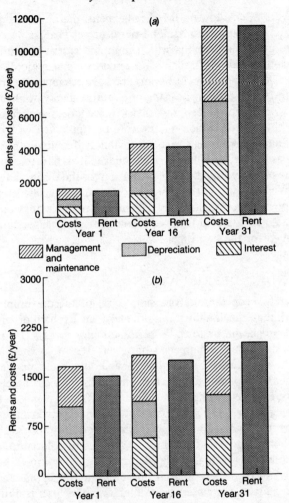

Figure 5.4 Costs and rents (72% grant, indexed loan):
(*a*) 7% growth in costs, nominal terms
(*b*) 7% growth in costs, real terms (6% inflation)

illustrated for conventional borrowing in Figure 5.2. As can be seen, the initial deficit is a fraction of that with conventional finance (a small initial deficit and eventual surplus remain because the interest payments are constant in real terms, while the real income stream from rents after allowing for management, maintenance, and depreciation is assumed to rise at 1 per cent per year).

There are complications which limit the extent to which such loans can be used. First, such arrangements are at present unusual: lending institutions may charge an expensive premium for providing them, and those running housing organisations may not be familiar with how they work. Secondly, they involve a degree of risk—or at least a kind of risk which differs from that involved with conventional finance. What happens, for instance, if rents do not rise as quickly as the rate of inflation (if an indexed loan has to be financed) or as the predetermined rate of escalation (in the case of a low-start loan)? While they might be suitable for organisations which already have a portfolio of outstanding debt and/or reserves, they might not be suitable as the sole form of finance for an organisation being established for the first time.

UNFUNDED DEPRECIATION

In order to keep the analysis simple, all of these examples have assumed that the landlord would make an explicit provision to offset depreciation or towards periodic major repairs. In practice, this has not actually happened until very recently, when housing associations have been told that they should build up funds for future major repairs on their new developments, as these will no longer be eligible for grant (see Chapter 8). This may not, in fact, be a sensible strategy. The return which would be received on funds put aside for future major repairs will almost certainly be less than the cost of borrowing. It is not therefore sensible to hold large funds at the same time as owing substantial debt.

Returning to the example, if no actual provision was made for major repairs, £900 would be available in the first year for debt servicing. This would not be enough to cover the full nominal interest at 10 per cent on an outstanding loan of £14,000, but it would be more than enough to pay interest on an indexed loan (or a low-start loan escalating at a similar rate). This means that a mixture of conventional and indexed/low-start finance could be used. With such a mixture, the value of debt will fall in real terms and in relation to debt over time. This opens up the possibility that when major repairs are carried out, they could be financed by *new* borrowing—remortgaging the property—without pushing the ratio of outstanding debt to the property's value beyond where it was at the start. Provided that the initial capital grant was enough to allow rent to cover the theoretical cost of depreciation and to cover the opportunity cost of the balance of capital, a strategy of building up *unfunded* major repairs liabilities while borrowing in such a way that the real value of outstanding debt falls over time could be best. What is important is the total liability from the combination of debt and outstanding unfunded depreciation, not the precise combination.

SUMMARY

■ An economic rent would cover the costs of managing and maintaining a dwelling, plus a provision for depreciation (or periodic major repairs to prevent it), plus an amount representing the real opportunity cost of the capital tied up in the building, less an adjustment for the long-run real capital gain expected on the property. Over time this would rise with costs and values, which could well be faster than general inflation.

■ Housing subsidy systems do not only have to reduce the costs of landlords to a level where the desired level of rent gives an economic return. They also have to cope with the cash flow effects of the front-loading of conventional debt payments.

■ If there is a mixture of stock of different ages, 'rent pooling' can cope with front-loading by setting the low debt on old property against the high debt on new property.

■ Alternatively, landlords can be given very large initial capital grants, with some kind of system to claw back the surpluses which appear later on as the real value of the residual debt servicing falls.

■ Another approach is to use recurrent subsidies which are high initially, but fall as the front-loading problem subsides.

■ The problem can also be tackled directly through the use of low-start or indexed finance, but this may not be suitable for all organisations.

■ In practice, it may well be more sensible not to build up explicit funds to cope with future major repairs, but instead to borrow on terms which allow debt to fall in relation to rents and property values, leaving room for new borrowing to cover major repairs when they are carried out.

6

Local Authorities: Finance and Control

Britain is unusual in the extent to which local government has been used as the provider of subsidised rental housing. Elsewhere in Europe 'social housing' has been provided by non-profit organisations (the equivalents of British housing associations) or subsidised but controlled private landlords. An effect of the British system has been that the system of subsidies and finance for local authority housing has been tangled up with the rest of local government finance. This interaction became simpler—at least for the time being—with the 'ring fencing' of local authority Housing Revenue Accounts in England and Wales in April 1990. None the less, the workings of overall local authority revenue finance and of central government controls on capital spending remain important in their own right and for an understanding of how the system of housing subsidy to local authority housing has evolved. Readers should skip to Chapter 7 if they are interested in specific housing subsidies only.

A second effect is that the structure of local authority housing follows that of local government. As successive reorganisations of local government have produced larger authorities in many areas, so the typical size of the stock managed as a single unit has increased (see Power 1987a, ch. 4 for discussion of the management consequences of this). As Table 6.1 also shows, a great diversity now exists in the size of organisations running local authority housing. The average stock size for Inner London boroughs and metropolitan districts is above 30,000. Birmingham has a stock of over 100,000; Glasgow of over 150,000. The Northern Ireland Housing Executive, performing a similar role, rented out 173,000 dwellings in 1987 (Department of the Environment (Northern Ireland) 1988). Meanwhile, the average for non-metropolitan districts in England and Wales is below 7,500. A few rural districts run fewer than 1,000 dwellings. This diversity has to be borne in mind in the discussion which follows: 'local authorities' are not a homogeneous group.

TABLE 6.1 *Local authority housing stock 1987/8, GB*

	Number of author- ities	Total stock (*'000*)	Average stock (*'000*)	Range of stock size[c] (number of authorities)		
				Under 10,000	10,000 –39,999	40,000 and over
Inner London boroughs[b]	13	440	33.9	2	5	5
Outer London boroughs	20	341	17.0	3	17	—
Metropolitan districts	36	1,375	38.2	—	26	10
Non-metropolitan districts						
England	297	2,197	7.4	240	44	3
Wales	37	244	6.6	26	7	—
TOTAL England and Wales	403	4,597	11.4	271	99	18
Scotland[c]	56	843	15.1	29	25	2

[a]Estimates for 1987/8 in England and Wales. Information missing for one Inner London borough, ten English and four Welsh non-metropolitan districts.

[b]Includes City of London.

[c]1986/7 estimates.

Sources: CIPFA (1989*a*), Summary Tables; CIPFA (1987*a*); SDD (1987).

CENTRE–LOCAL RELATIONS

Local authorities being the providers also means that this part of housing finance has become embroiled in the overall relationship between central and local government. In the British system, local government can only do what it is allowed to do by central government (the reverse of the situation in Sweden, for instance). Central government has—especially in recent years—used this constitutional power to direct and limit local government activity, and central control over both the revenue side of local authority housing (that is, policy towards rents and subsidies) and towards capital spending (through limits on borrowing and other ways of raising capital finance) has increased.

This is not the place to go into detail on the arguments for and against different models of the relationship between central and local government (see, for instance, Layfield Committee 1976;

Foster, Jackman, and Perlman 1980; Glennerster 1985, chapter 3;
Travers 1986). It is enough to note the tension between the advantages of local decision-making and those of overall macroeconomic
control. Local decision-making allows different communities to
make varying decisons about the use of their own resources, contributing to political pluralism. Decisions can also be made using
local knowledge and thus more efficiently than by a remote
Whitehall department. Accountability is improved if there is close
access to those making the decisions which affect people's lives.

Against these arguments, central government has found it important to control local authorities for macroeconomic reasons, for
instance as a way to influence overall economic demand. Central
government is also concerned to limit the taxes which it has to
charge. While these arguments give some support for control over
local borrowing or the size of central grants, neither implies a need
to control local spending paid for out of local taxation. Intervention, especially since 1979, has, however, attempted to achieve precisely this. The rationale appears not so much to lie in macroeconomics as in the following (see in particular DoE 1986):

- A desire to 'protect local government from itself', preventing the
  US 'flight from the cities' phenomenon—a vicious circle of high
  local tax rates leading to exit of the middle classes, narrowing of
  the local tax base, and even higher tax rates;
- Concern with the 'overall burden' of government, even where
  local communities themselves vote for a larger local government
  role; and
- Concern to protect business ratepayers and those with valuable
  property (argued to be the hostages of non-ratepaying voters).

Whatever the merits of such arguments, they have led to a whole
series of measures which have limited local government's freedom
of action:

1. Total central government grants to local authorities have been
   cut, so that more of their spending has to be paid for from local
   taxation.
2. The pressure through the Block Grant system of central government grants on individual authorities to reduce spending was
   steadily increased (see below).
3. Controls on borrowing and capital spending in general have
   steadily tightened and loopholes have been blocked (see below).

4. From 1982, authorities lost the power to set 'supplementary rates' to finance extra spending plans during a financial year.
5. From 1984, 'rate capping' enabled central government to limit the rate set by certain authorities selected as 'high spenders' (the power being carried over to 'charge cap' in the new system in 1990).
6. In April 1986, the Greater London Council and the six metropolitan county councils, which had been seen as 'high spenders', were abolished.
7. From April 1988 Housing Benefit was changed so that everyone, on no matter how low an income, would have to pay at least 20 per cent of their rates or Poll Tax bill.
8. The Poll Tax (Community Charge) replaced domestic rates from 1989/90 in Scotland and 1990/1 in England and Wales. Non-domestic rates have been taken out of the control of individual authorities and replaced with a centrally fixed 'National Non-Domestic Rate', with its revenue distributed by population. Under the new grant system all spending at the margin falls on the local Poll Tax (see below).

These changes have affected local authority housing in two ways. First, until the 'ring fencing' introduced by the 1989 Local Government and Housing Act, it was possible for authorities to make Rate Fund Contributions (RFCs) from their general funds into their Housing Revenue Accounts in order to reduce rents or to pay for greater spending. Such transfers (which could also go *from* the HRA *to* the general fund) affected the authority's total spending as used to calculate its entitlement to central government 'Block Grant', with extra spending either attracting extra grant or—more commonly in recent years—leading to loss of grant. As a result, the subsidy to council housing depended on the Block Grant system as well as on specific housing subsidies. Secondly, since the introduction of the Housing Investment Programme (HIP) system in 1977 (and earlier for improvement spending), housing has been within the overall capital spending control system.

THE BLOCK GRANT SYSTEM

Table 6.2 shows the substantial change between 1979/80 and 1989/90 in the balance of local revenue sources in England and Wales. While total local authority 'rate- and grant-borne expenditure'

TABLE 6.2. *Local authority income and expenditure 1979/80 and 1989/90, England and Wales* (£bn.)

	1979/80 (current prices)	1979/80 (at 1989/90 prices)[a]	1989/90	% change
Total rate- and grant-borne expenditure	16.0	31.4	36.0	+15
(of which RFCs to HRAs)	(0.37)	(0.72)	(0.35)	(−51)
Financed by:				
Change in balances	0.5	1.0	0.6	−36
Block grant[b]	7.1	13.9	9.8	−30
Specific grants etc.	1.7	3.3	4.7	+41
Domestic rate relief	0.7	1.3	0.7	−44
Domestic rates[c]	2.6	5.2	9.5	+83
Non-domestic rates[c]	3.4	6.7	10.7	+59

[a]Adjusted by GDP deflator (from HM Treasury 1989, table 21.4.1).

[b]Rate Support Grant 'needs' and 'resources' elements in 1979/80.

[c]Apportioned according to aggregate rateable values (after allowing for domestic rate relief).

Sources: CIPFA (1979, 1989*b*).

grew by 15 per cent in real terms (in a period during which national income grew by about a quarter), the amount raised by domestic rates increased by 83 per cent. This was because it had to make up for an 18 per cent fall in the real value of central government grants (Block Grant, specific and other grants, plus 'domestic rate relief'). Non-domestic rates also rose in real terms, but were not affected by the fall in the real value of domestic rate relief.

Much of this change came about through the evolution of the Block Grant, which replaced the 'needs and resources' elements of Rate Support Grant from 1981/2. Like its predecessors, the idea of Block Grant was that of 'equalisation' between authorities in different circumstances. For each authority, central government set a standard level of spending, or 'Grant Related Expenditure' (GRE), derived from a formula which gave weight to factors argued to affect its particular need to spend (such as the local demographic profile). If an authority decided to spend at exactly this level, it would receive enough Block Grant to allow it to balance its books while setting a standard 'rate poundage' (the number of pence charged to each ratepayer per pound of rateable value). Thus, if all authorities decided to spend amounts equal to their GREs, they would—by and large—all end up charging the same rate poundage, despite variations in their needs or resources (size of tax bases). This principle of equalised tax levels for spending at GRE (renamed 'Standard Spending Assessment') is carried forward to the new Revenue Support Grant accompanying the Poll Tax.

If an authority chose to spend a different amount from GRE, grant would be changed so that it had to adjust its rate poundage according to a fixed 'Grant Related Poundage' (GRP) schedule. Figure 6.1 illustrates this as it applied in England (the rules in Wales were slightly different) between 1986/7 and 1989/90, showing the position for Salford Council in 1987/8. Panel (*a*) shows the Grant Related Poundage schedule for that year. If Salford had spent at its GRE (£508 per capita that year), it would have received enough grant to allow it to charge that year's standard rate poundage (197.4p in the pound for metropolitan districts). For every pound per capita by which spending was higher (or lower), the poundage would have had to rise (or fall) by 1.1p. However, if spending exceeded Salford's 'threshold' of £553 per capita, the slope of the schedule increased, with higher spending increasing the rate poundage more rapidly, by 1.5p for each pound per capita of extra spending.

Panel (*b*) shows how grant adjusted to match this schedule. Given Salford's level of rateable value per capita, if spending had equalled GRE, grant of £257 per capita would have been needed. Grant would fall by nearly 40p for each extra pound of spending. The 'marginal grant rate' was *minus* 39.6 per cent. In other words, to spend an extra £1—for instance on a Rate Fund Contribution— Salford would have had to find £1.40 from its ratepayers. Above the 'threshold' the marginal grant rate became minus 90.4 per cent—£1.90 would have had to be raised for every extra £1 of spending. If spending had been high enough—over £817 per capita—Salford would have received no Block Grant at all (and above this level the marginal grant rate would be zero). Conversely, if spending had been low enough—£328 per capita—grant would have covered all spending and the grant related poundage would have been zero. In fact, Salford opted to spend £550 per

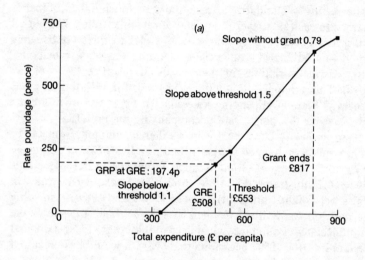

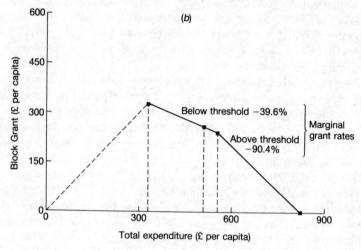

Figure 6.1 Block Grant, 1987/8, Salford:
(*a*) Effect of spending on rate poundage
(*b*) Effect of spending on Block Grant

Sources: CIPFA (1987*b*) and author's calculations.

capita, keeping it just below the 'threshold' and implying a Grant Related Poundage of 244p in the pound (CIPFA 1987*b*).

For authorities with little in the way of resources—low rateable value per capita—the change in Block Grant as spending moved away from GRE was less severe. Conversely, those with high rateable value per capita (perhaps because of substantial non-domestic rateable value) lost grant more quickly as their spending rose. Figure 6.2 shows the extent to which the Block Grant system became progressively more severe after its introduction in 1981/2. Panel (a) shows the original proposal, with the majority of authorities having positive marginal grant rates—extra spending led to extra grant. Only a few lost grant with higher spending. This effective incentive towards *higher* spending was first countered by a complicated system of grant 'penalties' if spending exceeded certain 'targets' (which bore no relation to the principles of GRE) and then by steepening the poundage schedule, ending up with the picture just illustrated for Salford. As a result, as Figure 6.2(b) shows, by 1988/9 the majority of authorities faced negative marginal grant rates. In some cases, they lost more than £1 in grant for every £1 of spending.

RATE FUND CONTRIBUTIONS AND BLOCK GRANT

Rate Fund Contributions came into this in two ways. First, central government calculations allowed for some authorities to be making Rate Fund Contributions. This was through an element of the GRE formula known as 'E7', based on a calculation of a *notional* deficit on the authority's Housing Revenue Account. To complicate matters, the E7 calculation was based on different assumptions from those used to calculate Housing Subsidy described in Chapter 7 (see Gibson 1981, and Hills 1987*a* and *b* for more detailed discussion). Originally, *negative* values of 'E7' were included in calculating GRE—Block Grant was based on the assumption that some authorities were making surpluses on their HRAs which would be transferred to their general funds. This provoked strong opposition from those affected, mainly Conservative-controlled district councils, and was dropped from 1982/3. Second, *actual* Rate Fund Contributions contributed to the total expenditure used to calculate Block Grant, while 'negative RFCs' going into the general fund reduced total expenditure.

The net effect on Block Grant depended on the balance between

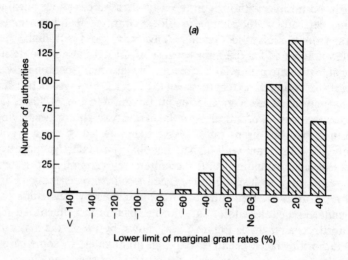

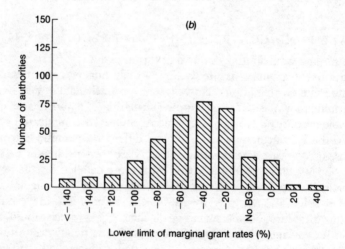

Figure 6.2 Marginal Block Grant rates:
(*a*) English housing authorities 1981/2 (original)
(*b*) English housing authorities 1988/9

Sources: CIPFA (1981, 1988*a*); Society of County Treasurers (1981).

the notional RFC (E7) and the actual transfer. For instance, in 1987/8 Salford's notional RFC was assessed at £7.24 million (Society of County Treasurers 1987). It actually made a discretionary RFC of £7.39 million (CIPFA 1989a). Given its marginal grant rate of minus 40 per cent, the additional transfer of £150,000 would have led to a reduction in Block Grant of £60,000. Note that an authority with a zero E7 (in notional surplus on its HRA) which actually transferred a surplus *from* its HRA to the general fund would reduce total expenditure by the whole transfer; if it faced a negative marginal grant rate, as was likely, this would have increased its Block Grant.

The increasing severity of the Block Grant schedule and the fact that council tenants would themselves have to pick up part of any increase in rates made RFCs increasingly unattractive. Returning to Salford, 20 per cent of its rateable value related to council dwellings in March 1988 (CIPFA 1989c). The transfer in excess of the E7 brought a benefit to council tenants of £150,000, but cost ratepayers £210,000, of which £42,000 would have been borne by council tenants themselves. Had Salford's spending been slightly higher, its marginal grant rate would have been minus 90 per cent, and the total cost of the £150,000 transfer would have been £285,000, with £57,000 coming from council tenants.

Other councils were in an even worse position. For instance, the London Borough of Islington faced a marginal grant rate of minus 197 per cent in 1987/8 and council dwellings accounted for 23 per cent of its rateable value. This meant that every £100 of Rate Fund Contribution had a total cost to ratepayers of £287, of which £66 came from council tenants. A decision to hold council rents down by £1 per week would only have given council tenants a net benefit of 34p, while implying higher rates totalling more than six times this benefit for other ratepayers. In fact, Islington's 1987/8 budget included a discretionary RFC of £33.6 million, lower than its £35.5 million E7 (CIPFA 1987a, and Society of County Treasurers 1987).

The advantage of Rate Fund Contributions to council tenants was further reduced by the April 1988 Housing Benefit changes, which reduced maximum benefit to 80 per cent of rates, while it remained 100 per cent of rents. For tenants on benefit, a decision to hold down rents at the expense of the rates actually made them worse off. Not surprisingly, as Table 6.2 shows, such pressures—combined with the falling real debt charges shown in Table 3.3—contributed to a

halving of the real value of Rate Fund Contributions in England
and Wales between 1979/80 and 1989/90.

Meanwhile in Scotland a rather different approach had been
taken. Rate Fund Contributions had not affected Scottish Rate
Support Grant—a £1 transfer had simply cost the ratepayers £1.
Instead of using the grant system to make RFCs expensive, from
1984 the Secretary of State for Scotland took direct powers to limit
them, reducing RFCs from £139 million in 1984/5 to a planned
level of £3.5 million in 1989/90 (Scottish Development Department
1989). In this way and others, the 'ring fencing' of HRAs and
elimination of RFCs in England and Wales from April 1990 was
following where Scotland had led.

LOCAL GOVERNMENT FINANCE FROM 1990

Despite all the measures it had already taken to rein in local spending, the Government decided on a major reform of local government
finance in England and Wales from April 1990. The best-known
element of this was the replacement of domestic rates by the Poll
Tax (officially known as the Community Charge). This was, however, only one element of a four-part package of reforms. The other
parts included the 80 per cent maximum to rate/Poll Tax rebates,
the National Non-Domestic Rate, and the new Revenue Support
Grant, replacing the previous general grants to local authorities
including Block Grant (see DoE 1986 for the Government's arguments, and Esam and Oppenheim 1989 for a critical commentary).

These changes have distributional effects both between those living in one local authority area and between different local
authorities. Some people 'gain on the swings' of the switch to the
Poll Tax, but 'lose on the roundabouts' of the change in revenue
sources for their local authority. Others may lose on both or gain on
both. Complicated arrangements were made in an attempt to limit
the speed with which some of these gains and losses take effect—with
complex (and limited) 'transitional relief' for some of those losing
substantially from the April 1990 changes, and a system of 'safety
nets' limiting the losses and (for the first year) gains of local
authorities. It will be several years before the ultimate distributional effects of the new system become clear.

There are two important effects on local authority spending decisions. First, Revenue Support Grant is calculated so that if spend-

ing equals its Standard Spending Assessment, the authority receives enough grant to balance its books while charging a standard Poll Tax, after allowing for its population-based share of National Non-Domestic Rate. Grant is fixed, with no adjustment if the authority chooses to spend at a different level. The marginal grant rates under the new system have therefore become zero for all authorities. Given that they were mostly negative before (see Figure 6.2), this might be thought to have weakened the pressures on authorities to reduce spending. However, the second factor, removal of non-domestic rates from the local tax base (so that local decisions no longer affect revenue from non-domestic rates) means that any additional spending has to be financed from a narrower tax base.

Taking the case of Salford again, in March 1988 49 per cent of its rateable value was domestic. Given its marginal grant rate of minus 40 per cent in 1987/8, this meant that a £100 increase in spending cost its domestic ratepayers about £70 (49 per cent of £140). Had it been spending above its 'threshold', with a marginal grant rate of minus 90 per cent, the cost to domestic ratepayers would have been £95. Under the new system, the £100 would be fully borne by the Poll Tax payers. Nationally, roughly half of rateable value was domestic, so the switch implies an increase in the effect of extra local spending on local domestic taxpayers for most of the majority of authorities where marginal grant rates were less severe than minus 100 per cent (but in others the effect has been reduced). The new tax is also more regressive (has more of an effect on those with low incomes) than rates, which makes it less attractive to councils wanting to increase spending on services which would benefit those with low incomes.

Another way of looking at this is through the effect of a percentage increase in local spending on the Poll Tax which the authority has to set. For a typical authority where about a quarter of its revenue comes from the Poll Tax, spending 10 per cent more than its Standard Spending Assessment means that the local Poll Tax has to be *40 per cent* higher than the national standard. This four to one 'gearing' can be compared with the old system shown in Figure 6.1(a). Salford in fact spent 8.3 per cent more than its GRE, resulting in a rate poundage 24 per cent above the national standard, a gearing of just below three to one. The Government's justification for gearing is that much local authority spending is simply a result of statutory responsibilities. Only a small part of spending is really discretionary, so a 10 per cent rise in total spending is equivalent to a much larger rise in discretionary spending, to which the rise in tax rate should be related.

Note that a 10 per cent 'error' in the Government's assessment of an authority's spending needs has precisely the same effect as a decision by that authority to provide a 10 per cent better service than the standard. The increase in gearing makes the political haggle about needs assessment even more important than it was, as was immediately clear when the new system was introduced in England and Wales in 1990. The central assessment of 'spending needs' for 1990/1 was well below local authorities' own assessments. For instance, inflation of only 4 per cent was allowed for at a time when most costs were rising at twice that rate. Gearing meant that this by itself added about 16 per cent to Poll Tax bills, explaining half of the discrepancy between the Government's forecasts and actual levels even before allowing for the costs of administering the new tax and allowing for increased non-payment compared with the rates.

Even though the greater pressure against spending might have been expected to continue the decline of Rate Fund Contributions, 'ring fencing' removes the possibility of making them at all. The consequences of this for the HRA are discussed in Chapter 7. The effect on general funds is, however, worth noting. As RFCs—and, in most circumstances, negative RFCs—are no longer to be allowed, the notional contributions allowed for through the E7 element of GRE disappear. This means a *gain* to the general funds of those which had previously been making RFCs in excess of any E7 allowed for them, but a *loss* to the general funds of those which had been making a lower actual RFC than their E7 level, including all those which were making contributions to the general fund from the HRA. While most of the other aspects of the April 1990 reforms benefited 'low spending' authorities and penalised 'high spenders', this particular part of the change had something of the opposite effect.

CONTROLS ON LOCAL AUTHORITY CAPITAL SPENDING

Once upon a time central government offered local authorities subsidies if they chose to provide new housing, and left them to decide how many units to build. For accounts of how that free and easy world disappeared, see Malpass and Murie (1987, chs. 3–5), Leather

(1983), Leather and Murie (1986), and Malpass (1990*a*). Apart from short periods of constraint, before the 1970s central government set minimum *standards* for local authority housing (such as 'Parker Morris') and limits on its *costs* (such as the 'Housing Cost Yardstick'), but not controls on total spending. Authorities had to make bids for part of a central allocation for spending on capital improvements from 1974, but new building did not come under control until 'Housing Investment Programmes' (HIPs) were introduced from 1977/8. The HIP system allowed central government to set a limit for total local authority housing investment and to distribute that allocation between individual authorities, with the authorities choosing their own mix of spending. (Note that 'allocations' merely constitute permission to spend or borrow, not any kind of grant.) When introduced, the new system was said to be in the interests of local discretion as well as giving central control of aggregate spending. In fact, the system has accompanied an almost continuous fall in net public capital spending on housing (see Chapter 3), and by 1983 it was being said that, 'The local autonomy and planning objectives of the system have been almost fully subservient to central decisions on the distribution of resources, strong encouragement to follow national policy initiatives and a tightly controlled and uncertain financial climate' (Leather, 1983, pp. 223–4).

Originally the plans put in by each authority—the 'bid'—had an important part in the allocation process, but as time went by, an index of the housing needs of each authority—the Generalised Needs Index (GNI)—became more important. This did not mean that allocations followed an objective assessment of need. First, spending power from capital receipts was not controlled by this process (see below). Second, DoE regional offices had substantial discretion, weakening the importance of the needs allocation. While such discretion can clearly be useful to temper a mechanistic formula, Leather and Murie report that 'In practice, at local level discretion has to date been used very selectively in order to match the allocations suggested by GNI scores more closely to commitments and to past spending patterns' (1986, p. 48). They also go on to suggest that 'The annual changes in regional GNI scores suggest strongly that it is not an independent or "objective" measure, but one which has been subject to constant amendment as a result of political pressures' (1986, p. 49).

The capital receipts problem resulted from changes made from 1981/2 under the 1980 Local Government Planning and Land Act, which extended the kind of control provided by HIPs to cover all local authority capital spending. Whereas before 1981/2 capital receipts did not increase an authority's permitted spending, from 1981/2 they were allowed to add a specified proportion of receipts, for instance from Right to Buy sales, to this total. The change was made to encourage Right to Buy sales but had two further results. First, the aggregate capital allocation took receipts into account, but the distribution between individual authorities did not. As those with the most capital receipts were not necessarily those with the biggest problems, capital spending was not directed towards the areas of greatest need.

Perhaps of greater concern to the Government, the system did not give the year-to-year control over total spending it wanted. Much of the rationale for the whole system was to set a limit on local authority net borrowing, as this contributed to the Public Sector Borrowing Requirement, reduction of which was seen as a key macroeconomic policy aim, but the treatment of capital receipts did not allow this. Originally, authorities were permitted to spend half of housing capital receipts in the year in which they arose. The balance would be accumulated, with half of it permitted to be spent the next year (plus half of any new receipts), and so on. The initial receipt thus generated a 'cascade' of permitted spending in subsequent years. But authorities did not have to spend up to their limits—they could carry unspent amounts forward. In 1981/2 and 1982/3, total net spending in England was less than the Government had planned. But in the next three years, authorities used more of the receipts which they had now accumulated and 'overspent' the Government's plans—by more than 50 per cent (£1 billion) in England in 1985/6, for instance (DoE 1988*a*, p. 8).

The Government's first response was to cut the proportion of housing capital receipts which could be spent each year to 40 per cent in 1984/5 and 20 per cent from 1985/6. Then in the 1986 Green Paper (DoE 1986), the Government indicated that the system of control was to change again. An added reason was that some authorities had found ways to evade the control—for instance, by leasing deals which gave them use of new assets, but paid for out of future revenue, not out of capital spending.

CREDIT APPROVALS—THE 1990 SYSTEM

The system which came into force in England and Wales in April 1990 was first outlined in a 1988 consultation paper (DoE 1988*a*) and introduced by the 1989 Local Government and Housing Act. It has five main features:

1. Central government sets 'credit approvals' covering local authority capital spending resulting from both borrowing and leasing deals. These are divided into 'basic credit approvals', issued by the DoE for the following financial year, and 'supplementary credit approvals', issued by any department for specific spending (not necessarily restricted to use in one year).
2. The size of individual credit approvals takes some account of the DoE's assessment of the authority's likely level of capital receipts.
3. New (and already accumulated) capital receipts are divided into two parts—the 'reserved part' (75 per cent of housing receipts and half of other receipts) and the 'usable part' (25 per cent for housing; half of other receipts).
4. The 'reserved' part must either be used to redeem debt, or put aside to meet future liabilities. Authorities will be free to use the 'usable part' for capital spending as and when they choose (except for the proceeds of large-scale transfers of local authority housing, where there are special restrictions on the rate at which they can be spent).
5. For some kinds of spending, initial capital grants are replacing the previous system of recurrent subsidies to help with loan charges.

The new system, illustrated in Figure 6.3, gives the government better control over net capital spending in two ways. In contrast to the old system, where 20 per cent of housing capital receipts could be spent in the first year with the remaining 80 per cent carried over for spending in later years (via the 'cascade'), under the new system 25 per cent of housing receipts (and 50 per cent of others) can be spent immediately (or later), but the rest will never increase capital spending power. This substantially reduces the DoE's difficulty in guessing what amount of accumulated capital receipts will be used each year, and hence in forecasting net capital spending. Second, the inclusion of leasing (which had grown to account for 5 per cent of

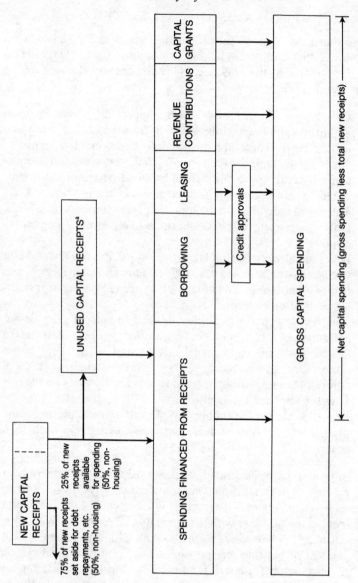

Figure 6.3 Local authority capital controls from 1990/1
[a] 75% of housing receipts accumulated before 1990/1 set aside for debt repayment (50% for non-housing receipts).

gross capital spending by 1985/6) removes a loophole in the old system.

The fact that credit approvals can take account of individual receipts could lead to what has been called 'a quite sensational redistribution of resources towards inner city areas which find it hard to generate receipts' (Warburton 1989). Whatever else the effects of the new system, this has the potential to generate a more rational distribution of capital spending. Whether it is, in fact, used to do so remains to be seen.

The new system of capital controls—together with the new fixed Revenue Support Grant—should also be seen in the context of the new 'planning total' for government spending which excludes 'self-financed' local authority spending, that is, spending financed by the Poll Tax or from capital receipts (see Chapter 3). By limiting its objectives to planning the parts of spending which it can, in fact, control, the Government is more likely to meet its own targets. However, its implementation of 'charge capping' in April 1990 suggests that it actually retains a wider set of objectives than the new planning system ostensibly suggests.

SUMMARY

■ The overall system of local government finance has impinged on local authority housing through the revenue effects of Rate Fund Contributions to the Housing Revenue Account (and of 'negative RFCs') and through capital spending controls.

■ Throughout the 1980s pressures on local authority spending increased. In particular, the rules of the Block Grant system evolved so that extra spending (including RFCs) meant lost grant, increasing the impact on ratepayers (including council tenants themselves).

■ This culminated in the replacement of domestic rates by the Poll Tax, with non-domestic rates taken out of local control. Although central grant no longer falls with extra spending, all additional spending from the general fund falls on the narrow and regressive tax base provided by the Poll Tax. This means that the proportionate effect on the Poll Tax is much greater than the increase in spending (or shortfall in needs assessment) which caused it—a phenomenon known as 'gearing'.

■ 'Ring fencing' of HRAs ends most transfers between general funds and HRAs, separating council housing from general local authority finance.

■ The new revenue finance system is accompanied by new controls on capital spending. The new 'credit approvals' cover spending financed from both borrowing and leasing deals. Individual approvals take capital receipts into account. Only a proportion of capital receipts is available to increase capital spending; the rest can no longer be carried forward to future years.

■ The new system increases central government's control over aggregate net capital spending. It also has the potential for capital spending to relate better to the needs of different areas.

7

Local Authority Housing Subsidies

HOUSING REVENUE ACCOUNTS

Local authorities have to keep a special Housing Revenue Account (HRA) recording accruals of income from and spending on their own housing stock. Other housing services—Housing Benefit administration or paying for temporary accommodation for homeless families—are recorded within their general funds. The distinction is not always clear, however. For instance, some authorities charge street lighting or maintenance of open spaces on their own estates to the HRA, even though such services are provided to other local residents through the general fund, paid for from the Poll Tax (rates in the past); in such cases, tenants are not receiving an equal benefit to other residents from the general fund. Partly because of this—but mainly to prevent effective transfers which would evade its 'ring fence' round the HRA—the Government has said that it wishes HRAs to be 'more tightly defined': 'The Government's view is that the HRA should include income and expenditure in respect of an authority's own housing stock, and other transactions arising from the authority's enabling role should fall outside the HRA' (DoE 1988c, para. 14). There are some legitimate grey areas, however. Being a 'good landlord' may involve housing managers in what might otherwise be regarded as personal social services. It would be unfortunate if a rigid interpretation of landlord functions ruled out this kind of activity (but paid for from the general fund where this would be done for equivalent services to other residents).

Under the 1989 Local Government and Housing Act (Schedule 4), the main HRA income items are:

- Gross income from rents, etc.;
- Charges for services (heating, etc.);
- Central government subsidy; and
- Amounts equivalent to interest received (on the 'reserved' part of capital receipts not yet used to redeem debt).

The main expenditure items are:

- Repairs, maintenance and management;
- Revenue contributions to capital outlay (RCCO);
- Rents, rates, etc. to be paid by the authority;
- Rent rebates to the authority's tenants (but not their administration); and
- Amounts covering 'loan charges' on borrowing for building or renovating the authority's dwellings.

The HRA also includes items for bad debts, transfers to or from a Housing Repairs Account (if kept to smooth out the cost of irregular repairs), and the balances on the account at the start and end of each year. The 'ring fencing' described below has virtually removed the possibility of transfers between the HRA and the general fund. The treatment of rebates has also changed as a result of the 1989 Act, before which authorities counted *net* rents after rebates as an income item.

Most of the items are straightforward. However, the 'loan charges' do not directly relate to specific housing debts. Instead, authorities 'pool' the loans taken out for all their activities, and the HRA can be thought of as borrowing from this pool. The interest rate charged to the HRA therefore equals an average or 'pool' rate of interest on the authority's total debt—some at low interest rates, some at high ones—not the rate paid on the loans which were actually used to finance housing.

THE EVOLUTION OF SUBSIDIES TO LOCAL AUTHORITY HOUSING

Detailed accounts of the evolution of local authority housing subsidies up to 1979 can be found in Holmans (1987, ch. 7) and in Malpass (1990*a*, chs. 4–6). Housing subsidy systems in Britain have succeeded one another at roughly five-yearly intervals for the last seventy years. However, as Malpass stresses, for much of this time their basic rules did not change much and, even when they did, the transition to new arrangements generally incorporated more in the way of continuity than dramatic change. Apart from the 1919 'Addison Act' subsidies, which provided an open-ended deficit grant (so that the Treasury picked up the whole cost of any deficit, provoking inevitable concerns about cost control), subsidies between

1923 and 1967 followed Holmans's 'classic British housing subsidy' pattern: x pounds per year per house for y years, with 'x' (and sometimes 'y') changing in each Housing Act (and with differences at various times in the amounts provided for different kinds of construction and—after 1961—authorities in different circumstances). The 1967 system partially broke with this pattern by basing the annual subsidy for new dwellings on the difference between the costs of loan charges at an interest rate of 4 per cent and at the actual rate at which it was carried out (or, at least, a 'representative' rate for the year).

The Conservative Government's 1972 Housing Finance Act introduced several significant breaks with this kind of system. The intention was to accompany a move to 'fair rents' on local authority housing, as already set by rent officers for the private rented sector. Importantly, this was backed by legal compulsion, provoking confrontation with those who resisted, most notably the councillors of Clay Cross in Derbyshire. The move towards fair rents also broke with the past (in another way which has not been repeated since 1974) in removing local authority discretion over the rents of individual dwellings. The rate at which rents increased was, however, limited. Subsidy was the sum of various elements, with the overall intention that subsidies granted under previous legislation would be phased out (another innovation) as rents rose faster than costs. In the event, inflation turned out to be much faster and interest rates higher than the Government had anticipated and it was the costs which rose fastest, so that the total cost of housing subsidy actually grew rapidly between 1972/3 and 1974/5. As Malpass points out, the Act failed in its own objectives on two grounds: politically, legal compulsion was inept; technically, the subsidy system left central government exposed to the effects of inflation (by the same token, protecting authorities from it).

The incoming Labour Government in 1974 first froze council rents and then limited increases as part of its anti-inflation policies. It repealed the Housing Finance Act, replacing it with new subsidy arrangements under the 1975 Housing Rents and Subsidies Act. These included removal of the idea of fair rents for local authority housing, restoration of the 'no-profit rule' (which outlawed transfers *from* the HRA to the general fund), and subsidy calculations including 66 per cent of the loan charges on new investment and extra subsidy for authorities in 'high cost' areas. The new system was to be temporary, pending the results of what started as the Housing Finance Review (eventually producing the 1977 Green Paper). In the event, the 1979 election intervened, and it was the Conservative 1980 Housing Act which changed the system.

THE 1980 SUBSIDY SYSTEM

The Housing Subsidy system in England and Wales between 1981/2 and 1989/90 worked on the basis of *notional* calculations of the *change* in income and expenditure on authorities' HRAs each year. In contrast to 1972, there was no compulsion to raise rents, but the withdrawal of subsidy on the *assumption* that they were increased by certain amounts gave a powerful push to authorities to follow the Government's wishes.

Under the 1980 system, a starting-point was taken each year as the result of the subsidy calculation made the previous year (for 1981/2, the first year of the system, the starting-point was the total of subsidies payable under previous legislation in 1980/1). To this 'base amount' was added central government's assessment of what was to be allowed for spending (the change in 'reckonable expenditure'), while assumed increases in income (the change in 'reckonable income') were deducted. Put simply, if the DoE's assessment of the need for spending to rise exceeded the proceeds from the assumed rent increase, subsidy would increase accordingly; conversely—and by far the more common case—subsidy fell where rent income was assumed to rise faster than spending.

The change in reckonable expenditure included a percentage increase (set nationally each year) in management and maintenance costs per dwelling from the previous year's reckonable costs. For the first year of the system, the allowance for reckonable management and maintenance spending was taken as the average of its actual spending per dwelling over the three years 1978/9 to 1980/1 (at 1980/1 prices). Thus by 1989/90, the final year of the 1980 system, each authority had its subsidy calculation based on an increase in cash spending on management and maintenance by 77 per cent from that base, this being the cumulative effect of the annual percentage allowances. The change in reckonable spending also included 75 per cent of the loan charges on new capital spending (or a notional equivalent if it was not, in fact, financed from borrowing).

The main change in reckonable income was a deemed increase in the rent on each dwelling in an authority's stock (based on the number of dwellings in the previous year). These annual rent guidelines were set as flat-rate amounts per dwelling across England and Wales. For instance, the guideline for 1989/90 was £1.95 per week per dwelling, while the guidelines between 1981/2 and 1989/90 totalled £12.50.

If the result of the annual calculation was negative, no subsidy was payable, nor did the authority have to pay out 'negative' subsidy (but the 'base amount' for the following year was the negative result of the previous year's calculations, not zero). In 1981/2 95 per cent of English housing authorities received subsidy; by 1986/7, three-quarters of them were 'below the subsidy floor'.

EFFECTS OF THE 1980 SYSTEM

The most important results of the 1980 system have been seen in Chapters 3 and 4. It allowed a massive cut in central government spending on housing subsidy to local authorities, the main effect being a substantial rise in real rents. It also had the following features:

1. It did leave authorities with some discretion over rents and spending. Rent relativities between dwellings within each authority's stock were at its discretion (as remains the case after 1990), while variations in management and maintenance spending could be paid for by an equal change in rents (thus there was 'zero subsidy at the margin' on current spending—which is also carried over to the new system).
2. In addition, higher spending or lower rents could be paid for through Rate Fund Contributions (with the consequences for Block Grant outlined in Chapter 6). 'Ring fencing' has now ruled this out.
3. The annual flat-rate rent guidelines had the effect of encouraging equal cash increases in rents in parts of the country where housing is in very short supply and in those where rents were already high enough to leave property unlet. For instance, between 1980/1 and 1988/9 rents in England and Wales as a whole rose by £11.17 from £7.71 to £18.88 (DoE 1989*a*, table 11.1; this compares with the accumulated guidelines of £10.55 over the same period). Within this overall average, rents in London rose by £12.27 to £21.69, only a little more in cash than the

national increase, so that the differential between London rents and those elsewhere fell in real terms. While there was variation between different authorities in their rent increases, that variation was around a pattern dominated by a flat-rate increase, rather than one of a percentage increase from original rent levels (Mullings 1989).[1]

4. What was allowed for management and maintenance did not depend on the particular characteristics of each authority's stock (as is the case with allowances to housing associations), but on what it was spending ten years ago. The 77 per cent increase allowed for between 1980/1 and 1989/90 compared with one of 70 per cent in the Retail Price Index and 116 per cent in average male earnings. None the less, actual management and maintenance spending per unit rose significantly in real terms over the period (see Table 3.4).

5. It coped with the 'front-loading' of loan charges by giving substantial help with new borrowing (when this was allowed), but with subsidy withdrawn later as rents were assumed to rise faster than costs.

6. As more and more authorities dropped out of subsidy, the annual rent guidelines ceased to have any direct effect on them. In the event, authorities which were out of subsidy still tended to follow the DoE's guideline (but this might not have been the case if the government had attempted to raise rents even faster).

7. While Block Grant penalties for higher spending on the general fund did give an incentive for Rate Fund Contributions to be cut (or greater transfers *from* the HRA to be made), the removal of assumed HRA surpluses from the calculation of 'Grant Related Expenditure' from 1982/3 limited the pressure on relatively low-debt authorities to increase their rents (see Chapter 6).

8. Authorities could receive subsidy for their HRAs both through Housing Subsidy (going directly to the HRA) and the Block Grant system (through the allowance for notional Rate Fund Contributions). These were based on two *different*—and in some ways inconsistent—notional calculations for each authority (see Hills 1987*b*). Some authorities were deemed not to need Housing Subsidy by one part of the DoE's calculations, but to need extra Block Grant for an assumed Rate Fund Contribution by the other. For others, the reverse was the case.

THE NEW SUBSIDY SYSTEM IN ENGLAND AND WALES FROM 1990

Partly because of some of these features of the 1980 system, the Government announced in its 1987 White Paper (DoE 1987*a*) that it was going to introduce a new subsidy system. Under the 1989 Local Government and Housing Act, this came into effect from the 1990/1 financial year. Its rules are laid out in the *Housing Subsidy and Accounting Manual 1990* (DoE 1990*b*).

AIMS OF THE NEW SYSTEM

The aims of the new system given in a July 1988 Consultation Paper were that the new system should be 'simpler, fairer and more effective' (DoE 1988*b*). The new system will, indeed, be simpler in some ways, notably through the end of the interaction between subsidy to the HRA and subsidy to the general fund. The second aim was expanded as:

It should be fairer towards tenants and [community] charge payers alike, and fairer between tenants in different areas. Rents generally should not exceed levels within the reach of people in low paid employment, and in practice they will frequently be below market levels. They should, however, be set by reference to these two parameters: what people can pay, and what the property is worth, rather than by reference to historic cost accounting figures. (DoE 1988*b*, para. 11)

Effectiveness would mean 'directing the available subsidy to those areas where it is needed, and providing an incentive for good management rather than a cover for bad practice and inefficiency'.

Key elements of the change are illustrated by the main flows into the HRA before and after the changes shown in Figure 7.1. First, HRAs have been 'ring fenced', so that authorities can no longer choose to make RFCs into them (or 'negative RFCs' out of them, except in initially rare circumstances). Secondly, what was Housing Subsidy has been amalgamated with the central government subsidy which used to pay for rent rebates to authority tenants, producing a new 'Housing Revenue Account Subsidy'. As discussed above, the HRA is also supposed to be 'more tightly defined'.

Underlying this there appear to be two key objectives. The first is greatly to reduce local authority discretion over the relationship between rents and management and maintenance spending. Within the new system, once one is fixed, the other follows automatically

(a)

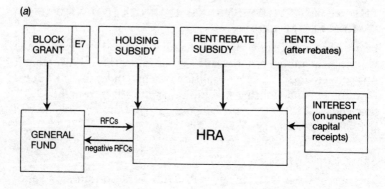

(b)

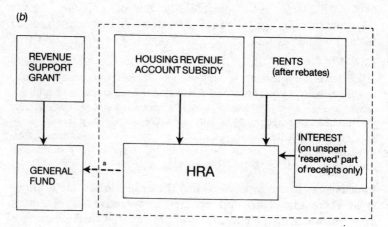

Figure 7.1 Sources of HRA income before and after ring fencing:
(*a*) Before ring fencing (up to 1989/90)
(*b*) Ring fencing (from 1990/1)
[a] Transfers out of HRA only allowed in restrictive circumstances.

(barring the effects of changes in balances and of certain capital
spending items), with no possibility of a transfer from outside the
HRA to blur the relationship: 'Tenants will thus be given clear
signals about the performance of their council's housing operation'
(DoE 1988*b*, para. 14).

The second is to regain a lever over the three-quarters of
authorities which had dropped out of Housing Subsidy. Under the
new system, all but a very few authorities will be 'in subsidy', thanks

to the amalgamation with rent rebate subsidy, and all will be under equal pressure to go along with the government's guidelines.

Coping with inflation

A reason given for the change is the front-loading problem discussed in Chapter 5:

> Because local authorities borrow on a historic cost basis, the cost of their borrowing is effectively eroded by inflation, even at its current level. As a result there is a growing trend towards more and bigger surpluses in HRAs. In the past this was generally offset as new capital projects at current prices entered the account.... It follows that HRAs in general will increasingly generate surpluses.... It is essential that those surpluses should not be available to be used as a cushion for bad practices and inefficiency. (DoE 1988*b*, para. 10)

In the past, one of the ways in which local authority housing finance has coped with front-loading was 'pooling' of costs between old (low-debt) and new (high-debt) stock. As there is not much new stock around any more—a situation which the Government intends to continue—the potential surplus on the old stock is not being pooled away. In the absence of any changes to the system, this could have allowed authorities to set rents which fell behind inflation, to boost management and maintenance spending, or to make transfers out of the HRA.

A main objective of the new subsidy calculation is to cream off such potential surpluses before they arise. This is not entirely un-reasonable, given that the relative debts carried by different authorities are only in small part related to need or their past record of good management, but owe much to historical accident. Why should an authority which has refused to provide any new housing for the last twenty years be placed in a far more favourable position than one which has been trying as hard as it can to meet local housing needs, but therefore carries a much higher—and more re-cent—level of debt?

One way of tackling this—calculation of Block Grant allowing for transfers to the general funds of authorities assumed to be in surplus on the HRA—had already been tried and abandoned. A second would have been an explicit 'negative Housing Subsidy', which authorities deemed to be in surplus would have to remit to central government (as housing associations have to do through Rent Surplus Funds; see Chapter 8). With the proceeds redistributed to those assumed to be in deficit, this would provide a mechanism for the 'national rent pooling' which has been called for in some proposals for reform of housing finance (see Chapter 16).

What the Government has chosen to do is rather different. Instead of keeping rent rebate subsidy—really part of the social security system—separate from general housing subsidy calculations, it has amalgamated the two. However, it is rather easier to understand the new HRA Subsidy if it is regarded as having two parts, one equal to what would have been the old rent rebate subsidy in full, the other roughly equivalent to the old Housing Subsidy, but with the latter now allowed to become negative.

Looked at in this way, the new system can be seen as a device for introducing negative Housing Subsidy while avoiding explicit remittances of notional HRA surpluses to central government. Instead, they are netted off the amount the authority needs to cover rent rebates. The hope would seem to have been that this would defuse the opposition which had defeated the earlier attempt to achieve a similar result through Block Grant. However, the change has still proved politically difficult. Its effect is that some authorities receive HRA Subsidy which falls short of the cost of their rent rebates. The rest of the cost has to come from making a surplus on the rest of their HRA. Inevitably this is seen as meaning that the Housing Benefit of the poorest tenants is being paid for from the rents of the slightly less poor tenants. Although this is not true in the sense that the rent paid by one tenant is not, in fact, affected by the rebates given to any other tenant, it is true in a highly visible—if narrow—accounting sense. This may be perceived as far more unjust than would explicit rent pooling payments whose purpose would at least be clear. Rent Surplus Fund payments may not be popular with housing association committees, but they are not open to this kind of interpretation by tenants.

A 'smooth transition'

In moving to the new system, the Government said that it wanted a 'smooth transition' so that 'the introduction of the new system should not *of itself* introduce any sharp change in the level of rents or management and maintenance spending in any individual authority' (DoE 1988*b*, para. 15; emphasis added). This did not, however, mean that nothing else changed at the same time—the smooth transition was along an upward slope for rents. It did mean that the new system incorporates initial protection through extra subsidy—as a result of 'damping' arrangements—for authorities starting with rents well below the levels implied by the guidelines in the new system, perhaps because they used to make sizeable RFCs or because they have little HRA debt.

It may be unduly cynical to suggest that the point of the smooth transition was to avoid rocking the boat too much in advance of a general election, but it is certainly clear that the DoE's primary aim was to make sure that all authorities were hitched up to the engine of the new subsidy system first, before pulling the levers which will take rents off in the—undisclosed—direction which it wants.

The ring fence

As Figure 7.1 shows, under the old system as well as rents (net of rebates), rent rebate subsidy, Housing Subsidy and interest on accumulated capital receipts, the HRA could receive Rate Fund Contributions from the authority's general fund. These could in turn be backed by the part of Block Grant which depended on the notional HRA deficit given by the E7 element of Grant Related Expenditure (although the actual RFC could have been entirely different). Alternatively, negative RFCs could have been made *out of* the HRA into the general rate fund.

Under the new system, a single payment of HRA Subsidy replaces the old Housing Subsidy payments (if any), rent rebate subsidy, and existing RFCs. The E7 element of GREs disappears, and the new Revenue Support Grant introduced alongside the Poll Tax is unaffected by the state of an authority's HRA. Negative RFCs are only to be allowed if an authority's HRA Subsidy falls below zero, whereupon there will be a compulsory minimum transfer out of the HRA—a sort of 'negative HRA Subsidy'—to which authorities will be allowed to *add* at their own discretion. (These arrangements are designed to avoid the previous possibility that authorities receiving subsidy could still make transfers out of the HRA.)

Interest receipts

Around 15 per cent of HRA receipts in England and Wales in 1987/8 came from 'other income'—mainly interest on accumulated capital receipts from Right to Buy sales (DoE 1989*a*, table 10.26). Under the new capital control rules described in Chapter 6, the size of interest receipts may fall, as 75 per cent of new and accumulated receipts (the 'reserved' part) must be either used to repay existing debt (which will, in turn, affect the interest being paid *out of* HRAs on such debts) or set aside to cover what would otherwise be new borrowing in the future. The HRA is now only credited with the interest on the 75 per cent part of receipts (until used to redeem debt). Interest on the rest —which authorities can choose what they do with—goes to the general fund.

Balances

In order to stop authorities building up reserves within their HRAs in advance of the new system which could have been used to delay its impact, the Local Government and Housing Act set a limit to the working balances which could be carried on the HRA at the *start* of the new system in April 1990 (£150 per dwelling up to a maximum of £5 million for any authority). Any negative balance on the HRA at the end of 1989/90 (or any credit in excess of the limit) had to be transferred to the general fund. There is, however, no limit on working balances in subsequent years, but authorities must budget to avoid a deficit on the HRA.

Arrears

As mentioned above, the HRA records accruals of income and spending rather than actual cash flows. This might be thought to remove the housing department's incentive to collect rents and reduce arrears (as rents will be credited as they accrue on occupied property, regardless of the date of payment). However, normal accounting conventions will require a proportion of old arrears to be written off each year, which will directly affect the HRA. Second, the net interest credited to or debited from the HRA will include an 'appropriate proportion' of interest received on an authority's cash balances (or paid on an overdraft), which will reflect the contribution from arrears—or lack of them—on the HRA. Together these put housing departments in much the same positions as, say, a housing association in terms of the advantages of keeping arrears low.[2]

THE NEW SUBSIDY CALCULATION

The pre-1990 Housing Subsidy system was based on *differences* between entitlement to subsidy in one year and the next. By contrast, the new system is effectively being based on a fresh calculation each year—working on a 'fundamental' rather than an 'incremental' basis, as the DoE puts it. As a result, the new system in England and

Wales has much in common with the system of Housing Support Grant in Scotland, discussed below, which was already based on 'fundamental' principles.

In many ways this will make the workings of the new system much clearer than those of the old one, where subsidy entitlements depended on amounts paid in previous years under long-forgotten rules. In essence, the new system provides each local authority with the amount needed to balance its Housing Revenue Account at a guideline level of rent for that authority after allowing for a notional allowance for its management and maintenance spending, for actual loan charges net of receipts, and for the cost of rent rebates. That is, so that:

	HRA Subsidy
plus	Guideline rents (gross)
equals	Rent rebates
plus	Management and maintenance allowance
plus	Net interest payments.

For instance, as a very simplified example, suppose that two authorities are identical in that each has 10,000 dwellings, a guideline rent of £1,000 per dwelling per year, is expected to have rebates costing 50 per cent of its gross rent roll, and has a management and maintenance allowance of £600 per dwelling (in practice, guideline rents and management and maintenance allowances vary from authority to authority). However, for historical reasons one has net (admissable) interest payments of £5.5 million and the other of £2.5 million. Then HRA Subsidy is:

Authority A

	Management and maintenance allowance	£6.0 million
plus	Net interest payments	£5.5 million
plus	Rent rebates	£5.0 million
less	Gross rent guideline	£10.0 million
Equals		£6.5 million

Authority B

	Management and maintenance allowance	£6.0 million
plus	Net interest payments	£2.5 million
plus	Rent rebates	£5.0 million
less	Gross rent guideline	£10.0 million
Equals		£3.5 million.

Each authority can therefore balance its HRA if it charges the guideline rent of £1,000 per dwelling and spends the £600 per dwelling on management and maintenance implied by their allowance, despite the difference in interest payments (which become pretty well immaterial under the new system). If management and maintenance spending differs from the allowance built into the subsidy formula, actual rents have to vary from the subsidy guideline by a corresponding amount. For instance, management and maintenance spending of £700 per dwelling would mean that rents would have to be £1,100 per dwelling.

In setting subsidy initially, the DoE uses an estimate of what rebates will cost, but if this turns out to be incorrect, subsidy is adjusted retrospectively, so that subsidy effectively depends on *actual* rent rebate costs (at the rent level the authority actually sets). This adjustment is important. It means that it is *not* the case that, if half the tenants receive rebates and there is a rent guideline increase of £2 per week, the other tenants will end up paying an extra £4 per week. Nor does an increase in the number of rebate recipients change the gross rents which have to be charged for the HRA to break even.

In effect, the new subsidy has two elements, one covering the full cost of rent rebates (£5 million in each case), and the other set to balance the rest of the HRA. This second element would be £1.5 million for Authority A, but *minus* £1.5 million for Authority B. For Authority A, this result could have been achieved under the old system. It could have received Housing Subsidy of £1.5 million plus rent rebate subsidy of £5.0 million, giving the same £6.5 million total. The difference arises for Authority B. Under the old system, it would have received *at least* the £5.0 million of rent rebate subsidy. It could well have received zero Housing Subsidy, but not a negative payment. Its combined subsidy would have been £5.0 million, not the £3.5 million calculated above.

RENT GUIDELINES IN THE NEW SYSTEM

As far as rents are concerned, the DoE originally said that under the new system,

assumptions about rent increases ... will be somewhat better targeted than the recent practice of assuming a single across-the-board increase for all authorities. This may be done, for instance, by differentiating between authorities on the basis of their current rents and perhaps also by making different assumptions for different groups of authorities (perhaps, but not necessarily, on a geographical basis). (DoE 1988*b*, para. 8)

In the event, rent guidelines for individual authorities depend on the relativities between average Right to Buy valuations. As the then Secretary of State, Nicholas Ridley, put it as the Local Government and Housing Bill passed through Parliament,

The starting point would be a decision each year . . . on the average increase to be assumed. That would produce a new national total of the income from rents . . . . The new national total can be shared between housing authorities according to the number of dwellings that they have and an assessment of their local circumstances . . . . We want rents to vary geographically, not as they do now in a way which is unfair, discriminatory, haphazard and often based on historical or political bias, but in a way which takes more account of the geographical spread of housing, its type and the demand for it . . . . A good measure of the variations in the value of property can be found in the right-to-buy prices of council sales. (Official Report, 14 June 1989, col. 961)

A more detailed idea of how the system works was given in various 'determinations' published in 1989 (DoE 1989*b* and *c*). Under these, the Department of the Environment makes an annual decision about the national average rent increase it would like. Given the starting level of rents, this implies a national guideline rent per dwelling. In turn, this implies an 'underlying guideline rent' for each authority (implicit in the system rather than described as such by the DoE, which lays out its calculations in a more roundabout way) depending on its relative Right to Buy valuations (adjusted for the mix of flats and houses in the total stock and in sales). The change in rent built into the subsidy calculation for each authority for the coming year is then calculated to move towards this under- lying guideline from existing rents.

For instance, in the determination (DoE 1989*c*) for HRA Subsidy in England in 1990/91 (the determination for Wales follows similar principles), the national average rent guideline works out at £22.80 per week (£21.76 at 1989/90 prices plus £1.04 per week added for inflation between 1989/90 and 1990/91). The valuation of the Lon- don Borough of Islington's stock (based on Right to Buy valuations over the four years up to 1988/89), works out at 190 per cent of the national average for each dwelling, while that in Blackburn is only 49 per cent of it. Applied directly to the national rent guideline, these would generate 'underlying guideline rents' of £42.42 per week in Islington and £11.78 per week for Blackburn (the precise numbers following from the slightly odd procedure of working out relativities at 1989/90 prices and then adding a *constant* £1.04 across all authorities for inflation). Given their starting 1989/90 rents, this would—left to itself—have meant a £16.46 per week guideline rent increase in Islington, but a *fall* of £10.22 per week in Blackburn.

However, the Government recoiled from the implications of immediate moves towards rents directly proportional to capital values. To prevent too great a movement in rents from year to year there are 'damping' arrangements built into the subsidy formula. These limit the speed at which it is assumed that rents will reach the implicit guidelines. For 1990/91, they are based on a change in rents making up 35.2 per cent of the difference between actual 1989/90 rents and the 'underlying rent guideline' (at 1989/90 prices, with £1.04 then added for inflation to 1990/91). They also incorporate a maximum assumed rent increase of £4.50 and a minimum assumed increase of 95p. The first of these applied to Islington, the latter to Blackburn.

Table 7.1 illustrates the situation for these two authorities and others at the top and bottom of the valuation range. Note that, apart from Kensington and Chelsea, there was little difference between actual rents in 1989/90 in the high- and low-value authorities. However, the 'underlying guidelines' imply rents more than doubling where values are high, but nearly halving where they are low. In the short term the relative movements in rent assumptions are restrained by the 'damping' mechanisms, which is the way in which the 'smooth transition' to the new system is achieved. The underlying system may imply that Islington rents ought to rise by roughly two-thirds while those in Blackburn halve, but this will only happen gradually. Indeed, it may never get there given that the DoE has said that, 'damping is not seen as a transitional arrangement only but as a continual feature of the system' (DoE 1989*b*). This statement implies that the intended end result may not be to have relative rents in direct proportion to capital values, but leaves us none the wiser as to what the eventual structure is intended to look like. Each year the DoE will take a decision on the shape of the damping formula and for the foreseeable future this will almost certainly be more important for most authorities than the rest of the system. This makes the new system much less transparent than it would otherwise

TABLE 7.1 *Housing Revenue Account Subsidy: guidelines for 1990/1, England; selected authorities*

	Stock valuation as % of national average[a]	1989/90 actual average rent[b] (£/week)	'Under-lying rent guide-line' for 1990/91[c] (£/week)	1990/91 rent guide-line with 'damping'[d] (£/week)	1990/91 manage-ment and mainten-ance guideline[e] (£/week)
England	100	20.73	22.80	22.80	n.a.
High value authorities					
Kensington & Chelsea	226	38.74	50.22	43.24	28.19
South Buckinghamshire	195	25.01	43.57	29.51	17.17
Windsor & Maidenhead	190	21.64	42.48	26.14	15.37
Islington	190	25.96	42.42	30.46	18.56
Mole Valley	185	17.74	41.20	22.24	17.97
Low value authorities					
Wolverhampton	59	22.13	13.78	23.08	14.80
Bolton	51	18.90	12.23	19.85	11.06
Rossendale	49	21.52	11.79	22.47	14.19
Blackburn	49	22.00	11.78	22.95	11.58
Burnley	46	19.50	10.94	20.45	10.95

[a] Based on Right to Buy valuations 1985/6 to 1988/9 adjusted for house/flat composition of sales and stock.

[b] With allowance for voids.

[c] £21.76 national guideline at 1989/90 prices adjusted by relative stock valuation plus £1.04 for inflation to 1990/1 (see text).

[d] Maximum increase of £4.50 or minimum increase of £0.95.

[e] Based on average spending 1986/7 to 1988/9, except Islington which is based on 1988/9 'reckonable' spending for old Housing Subsidy (i.e. average spending 1978/9 to 1980/1 uprated).

Source: DoE (1989c) and associated documents.

be. It also gives the DoE almost complete freedom of action—through choice of a suitably baroque damping formula—in what happens to individual authorities each year.

The Government has been at pains to stress that it is not proposing 'market rents' but rather moves towards a 'market-like pattern of rent differentials', in the words of the housing minister Lord Caithness (at the US–UK Conference on Affordable Housing in London in July 1989). However, whether that is what the current proposals will achieve is perhaps open to question. The four to one differentials shown in Table 7.1 are almost certainly *greater* than those which one might expect to see in a market which had reached some kind of long-term balance (although not necessarily in one where short-term distortions were still paramount). To be sure, some of the variation in market rents across the country would be in direct proportion to the capital tied up in a property, but some would also relate to management and maintenance costs (see Chapter 5). As these vary much less across the country than capital values, the total of the two—and hence long-run 'market' rents— would vary less than capital values. In other words, the new system may end up driving towards (albeit kept in check by the *ad hoc* damping formulae) a structure of rent relativities which varies more across the country than would an undistorted market—which is more 'market-like' than the market!

Of course, as with the old system, actual rents do not have to be set at the notional levels implied by the subsidy formula, for instance if management and maintenance spending does not equal the allowance built into it, or if the authority is carrying 'inadmissible' loan charges on the HRA. Actual rent increases in 1990 followed the guidelines in some cases, but not in others. In the cases listed in Table 7.1, Islington, Mole Valley, and Windsor and Maidenhead followed their £4.50 guideline, Kensington and Chelsea increased rents by less, and South Buckinghamshire by far more. The others raised rents by more than their 95p guideline (information supplied by CIPFA; no data for Bolton).

This all concerns rent relativities. For the overall level of rents likely to result once the 'smooth transition' is over, there is at the time of writing little to go on other than the statement that 'rents generally should not exceed levels within the reach of people in low paid employment, and in practice they will frequently be below market levels' (DoE, 1988*b*, para. 11). Indeed, a housing minister has stated; 'We have no preconception about the level to which rents should eventually rise' (David Trippier, reported in *Inside Housing*, 21 April 1989). It will not therefore be clear where the annual rent guidelines are taking us until we get there, which may not be for several years. However, an almost identical form of words has been used to describe the 'affordable rents' which result from the new system of housing association finance (see Chapter 8). If this is what the Government has in mind, it would mean that average local authority rents could more than double. Note that changes in local authority rents apply to all their tenants, whereas the new housing association rents only apply to new tenants, while existing tenants retain the right to a fair rent.

MANAGEMENT AND MAINTENANCE IN THE NEW SYSTEM

Under the old Housing Subsidy, a part of the change in subsidy each year resulted from a uniform percentage applied to a base figure for each authority which ultimately depended on how much the authority was spending on managing and maintaining each of its dwellings in the three years 1978/79 to 1980/81. This has not necessarily reflected the relative needs of authorities particularly well. A further paper (DoE 1989*d*) suggested that ultimately HRA Subsidy should depend on an allowance for spending by each authority derived from a national total of management and maintenance spending which the DoE is prepared to allow for and on a 'score' for each authority, reflecting the type, date of construction, and sizes of its stock. If, for instance, research suggested that a particular authority's stock cost 20 per cent more than the average to manage and maintain (giving it a 'score' of 120), while the national total of management and maintenance allowed for that year implied an average of £12 per week per dwelling, then that authority would have £14.40 per week per dwelling built into its subsidy calculation.

These 'spending allowances' could well be very different from actual current spending levels (or those built into the old subsidy formula). Again, in order to achieve the 'smooth transition' to the new system, the DoE proposed special 'damping' arrangements to ensure that the jolts in moving to the new system are not too large, perhaps with limits (up and down) put on the proportions by which it would be expected that spending would change in real terms from year to year.

Basing subsidy on explicit allowances for the amounts needed to manage and maintain different kinds of stock could be a great improvement in terms of directing resources to where they are needed, but it is not clear when this will actually happen. As well as the prospect of 'damping', the actual allowances for 1990/1 were set on the basis of past spending, not taking account of any assessment of relative spending needs. The 'score' system is now unlikely before 1992.

The allowances for 1990/1 are calculated from the *higher* of: 'reckonable spending' under the old system in 1988/9; actual spending over the three years 1986/7 to 1988/9 (at 1988/9 prices; in both these cases uprated by 19.63 per cent, intended to incorporate a real increase in spending over 1988/9 levels); and a regional minimum figure set by the DoE. Given that most authorities were in fact spending well over the 'reckonable' levels allowed in the old subsidy system, in all but a few cases it will be the average of spending in the three years up to 1988/9 which will count. The others are authorities with unusually low recent management and maintenance spending on their HRAs, in several cases because they had 'capitalised' repairs spending to take advantage of the rules of the old subsidy system (or to evade rate capping). This kind of spending can now only be capitalised if there is 'enhancement' of the properties, so some of these authorities now face problems, as the allowance in the subsidy formula does not take account of previous repairs financed in this way (except to the extent that they are protected by the minimum allowances given regionally or by their previous 'reckonable' spending).

As Table 7.1 shows, Islington's 1990/1 allowance works out at £18.56 per week per dwelling (one of the few based on spending between 1978/79 and 1980/1), while Blackburn's is £11.58. These allowances compare with the 'underlying rent guidelines' of £42.42 and £11.78 respectively. The formulae chosen by the Government imply that rents in Islington could (if damping ever unwinds) end up more than twice as great as management and maintenance costs, while rents in Blackburn barely covered them. In Wolverhampton and Rossendale the underlying rent guidelines are actually *lower* than the 1990/1 management and maintenance allowances.

LOAN CHARGES

Under the new system, HRA Subsidy allows each authority to balance its books if its rents and management and maintenance spending equal its guidelines, almost *regardless* of the net loan charges on the HRA. This will (once the 'damping' arrangements unwind) iron out the differences between authorities which used to result from their historic debt levels. In calculating subsidy, the DoE allows completely for any changes in loan charges resulting from reduction in debt (for instance, as a result of capital receipts) or from movements in the 'pool' rate of interest on existing debt. As far as new borrowing—for instance for new building or for renovation—is concerned, the resultant loan charges are also allowed for pound for pound in the subsidy calculation and so have no effect on the level of rents the authority has to charge (except where they result from borrowing in excess of a guideline set by the DoE for total HRA-related capital spending set as part of the credit approval system). From 1990/1, the 'admissible cost' limits, which previously limited the amount of spending on any particular project which could attract subsidy also disappeared (except on leasing deals). At the margin, therefore, there is a subsidy rate of 100 per cent on capital spending within the overall annual limit, above which the marginal subsidy rate drops to zero.

This is a major change of principle from previous subsidy systems. For instance, in the 1980 system authorities were affected by at least 25 per cent of any variation in capital costs (and by 100 per cent for the majority which were out of Housing Subsidy). Under the new system this part of the incentive for cost control has disappeared—and this applies to virtually all authorities. Of course, authorities will still retain an interest in the value for money they achieve, as this will determine the number of units built or renovated which they can deliver from within the credit approvals set by the DoE.

The implications of this switch—from a system where 100 per cent marginal subsidy rates were avoided to one which incorporates them (up to the overall annual HRA capital spending guideline)—is discussed further in Chapter 15. It looks a little strange beside the changes which the same department made for housing associations in 1988, described in Chapter 8, one of the main aims of which was to remove the possibility of 100 per cent subsidy to capital projects at the margin. On the other hand, it brings local authorities in England and Wales in line with the Scottish system described below.

As far as tenants are concerned, new borrowing—unless outside the HRA capital spending guideline—has no effect on rents (until it begins to affect Right to Buy valuations). A renovation programme will thus have no effect on the total rent income which has to be collected, while any new dwellings will be assumed for subsidy purposes to have rents equal to the average for the existing stock, regardless of their type or cost. This does nothing to re-inforce DoE exhortations that 'more should be done to encourage authorities to reflect the value or popularity of different dwellings in establishing rent differentials between properties in the same area' (DoE 1988b; however, the document did go on to stress that this was a matter of 'local authority practice rather than the subsidy regime'). It contrasts with the old system, where the break-even rent on a new dwelling for an authority receiving Housing Subsidy equalled 25 per cent of the resultant loan charges (see Hills 1988a, p. 165).

Under the new system, the limits set by the capital control system are more important than before. This is because there is an important difference between the consequences of capital spending for housing and for other purposes: loan charges resulting from the former are completely covered by increased HRA Subsidy, but other loan charges have no effect on Revenue Support Grant. In the past, authorities were able to allocate their capital spending between different areas within the *total* of the annual guidelines set for different purposes. The limit referred to above on the extent to which capital spending can affect HRA Subsidy has been introduced to stop authorities concentrating capital spending on housing, thereby taking advantage of the asymmetry in subsidy treatment. While authorities can theoretically spend more on HRA capital than the guideline, they cannot transfer resources into the HRA to cover the loan charges, making this very expensive for tenants. The division between HRA and non-HRA capital spending guidelines has become more rigid and the freedom of local authorities to choose their mix of capital spending has been further restricted.

HOUSING SUPPORT GRANT IN SCOTLAND

As mentioned at various points in this and the previous chapters, arrangements in Scotland have differed significantly from those in England and Wales, but the 1990 changes have the effect of bringing the English and Welsh systems much closer to the Scottish system.

First, during the 1980s Rate Fund Contributions were not 'reckonable' for Rate Support Grant in Scotland: the complications of including an element for RFCs in Grant Related Expenditure assessments or of RFCs affecting grant entitlement at the margin (as described in Chapter 6) were therefore avoided. Second, the Scottish Office has limited RFCs (now 'General Fund Contributions') since 1984. From 1989/90 the only GFCs allowed were those needed as a 'safety net' to prevent rents rising too rapidly (for instance, the limit on rent increases was £2 per week in 1989/90).

The other major difference was that the Scottish Housing Support Grant (HSG) has, since the early 1980s, been based on 'fundamental' principles like the new HRA Subsidy in England and Wales, not 'incremental' ones. HSG is calculated to allow authorities to balance HRAs assuming:

1. A fixed level of management and maintenance spending per dwelling across Scotland (£330 per year in 1989/90) with additions for authorities with small stocks or high-rise dwellings;
2. 100 per cent of actual loan charges (but based on a 'pool' rate of interest for the whole of Scotland); and
3. A standard rent figure for the whole of Scotland (modified by GFCs if this would imply too large an increase in rent).

Like the new system in England and Wales this gives a 100 per cent marginal subsidy rate to new capital spending (except in so far as the authority's interest costs differ from the Scottish 'pool rate'). Since the early 1980s the only constraints on capital spending have been the overall capital allocations to each authority (kept completely separate from other capital allocations), with no system of 'project control' analagous to the old admissible cost limits in England and Wales.

Where Housing Support Grant differs most from HRA Subsidy is that rent rebate subsidy remains separate (and there is no proposal to change this). Roughly half of Scottish authorities are 'out of HSG', which leaves them to set their own rents and spending without subsidy influence (subject to the limits on GFCs). Scottish authorities thus divide into two groups: those receiving HSG where the relationship between rents and management and maintenance spending is fixed by a guideline across Scotland; and those out of HSG where the relationship is determined by historic debt.

SUMMARY

■ The 'ring fence' round Housing Revenue Accounts is intended to stop the relationship between rent levels and spending on management and maintenance being 'blurred' by Rate Fund Contributions, but for the immediate future, changes in rent levels will have much more to do with changes in the subsidy than with management effectiveness.

■ The new HRA Subsidy in England and Wales restores a lever to central government over rents and spending for nearly all authorities. It is equivalent to a combination of the old rent rebate subsidy in full and the old Housing Subsidy (but with the latter now *negative* in some cases).

■ HRA Subsidy is calculated so that each authority can balance its HRA if rents and management and maintenance spending equal guideline levels set by the DoE. Any variation in spending from the guideline requires an equivalent change in rents.

■ Ultimately subsidy will be based on rents for different authorities with relativities in proportion to the capital values of their stocks (based on Right to Buy valuations). This implies large shifts in relative rents, and the variation could end up *greater* than would result from 'market' rents. The speed at which this occurs is limited by 'damping' adjustments, intended to ensure a 'smooth transition' to the new system.

■ The Government has said it has 'no preconception' about the overall level of rents, but the words used to describe this level are almost identical to those used for rents under the new housing association subsidy system, which could imply average local authority rents more than doubling from their levels of the late 1980s.

■ Subsidy should eventually incorporate allowances for the relative costs of looking after each authority's stock. This would be a better way of distributing subsidy than the use of past spending, but in the short term subsidy will be based on actual spending in the late 1980s.

■ The new system embodies a marginal subsidy rate of 100 per cent on net HRA loan charges (unless total capital spending exceeds a certain limit). Net loan charges will have no effect on rents, removing differences between authorities resulting from historic debts (although these affect the rents from which the 'smooth transition' to the new system starts) and making the front-loading of debt charges virtually irrelevant.

■ The new system greatly increases central control over local authority housing. A corollary is the potential for a more rational distribution of subsidy between authorities, but, in the short term at least, the intricacies of the 'damping' formula chosen each year will be more important than the underlying subsidy structure, giving further power to the DoE over the out-turn for individual authorities.

■ The 1990 changes in England and Wales bring that system much closer to Scottish Housing Support Grant than before. However, rent rebate subsidy remains separate in Scotland and about half of Scottish authorities are out of Housing Support Grant.

NOTES

1. Note that this is not contradicted by Malpass's finding (1990*a*, pp. 148–9) that authorities with high rents in 1988 had large rent increases between 1980 and 1988, while those with low 1988 rents had small increases. This in itself is hardly surprising—more than half of 1988 rent *levels* resulted from of the increases since 1980—and is perfectly compatible with the overall dispersion of rents in 1988 being less than that in 1980. However, the wide variation between high and low rent authorities in 1988 (the average for the top ten was nearly twice that for the bottom ten) shows that it would be a mistake to think that a great deal of variations in rents did not survive.

2. At the point of transition to the new system in April 1990 the DoE laid down complicated regulations (see DoE 1990*b*) with the general effect that pre-1990/1 arrears come outside the new ring-fenced HRA, but with authorities given a choice as to how much of old arrears were written off on the 1989/90 HRA, written off on the 1989/90 general fund, or carried forward on to the 1990/1 general fund.

8

Housing Association Subsidies

Housing associations are non-profit organisations whose main activity is providing housing to let at below market rents. Their status hovers between public and private sectors. On the one hand, their capital finance has come overwhelmingly from central government grants and loans, making their development programme very much part of public policy. On the other, they are controlled by voluntary management committees, independent of central or local government control, putting them into the private sector for some purposes (although under the supervision of the Government-appointed Housing Corporation or its equivalents in Wales and Scotland).

This ambiguity has brought associations distinct political advantages in the last fifteen years. In the mid-1970s, they shared in the growth of publicly funded building programmes, but they suffered less severely than local authorities from the cuts in public spending on housing during the 1980s, and the Government now intends more rapid growth for them in the early 1990s, while restraint for local authorities continues.

The housing association movement includes a great diversity of organisations, ranging from charitable trusts established to run a handful of almshouses anything up to eight hundred years ago to organisations with large professional staffs managing more than ten thousand dwellings, as large as the average local authority housing department. Their origins vary from Victorian philanthropic trusts, through radical groups established in an attempt to mitigate the housing problems of the 1960s, to those which started life as central government agencies or—in a few recent cases—local authority housing departments (see Baker 1976, for an account of the origins of the movement).

As well as providing 'general needs' housing at below-market rents (the main focus of this chapter), associations are involved in running hostels and other housing for those with special needs of one kind or another, and in various initiatives to promote 'low-cost' owner-occupation. Their legal status varies. To receive grants from central government they have to be registered with the Housing Corporation (Tai Cymru in Wales or Scottish Homes in Scotland). Most registered associations are charities, but they can also take other forms—such as friendly societies—provided that they do not distribute profits to their members.

Their stock—605,000 units in the UK at the end of 1988 (DoE 1989*a*, table 9.3)—is only 2.6 per cent of all dwellings and just over a tenth of the size of local authority housing, but it represents more than a quarter of non-local authority rented housing. They have also grown very rapidly—doubling in size since the early 1970s—and their relative share of new publicly funded provision is much greater than their existing stock. Between 1982 and 1988 associations completed 94,000 new dwellings compared with 193,000 for local authorities and new towns (ibid., table 6.1; GB figures), while associations also completed renovations on about 91,000 dwellings in England alone, most of which were additions to the sector through rehabilitation of former privately owned stock (ibid., table 7.1). The effect of the Right to Buy has been less dramatic than for local authorities because it has not applied to tenants of charitable associations. The 16,000 Right to Buy sales between 1982 and 1988 represented only 3.5 per cent of their initial stock, a quarter of the comparable proportion for local authorities (ibid., tables 9.3 and 9.7; GB figures).

This relative expansion is likely to continue. In its spending plans for the early 1990s, the Government has said that 'the number of new homes provided by housing associations in 1992–93 is likely to be over twice that in 1988–89' (DoE 1989*e*), while new capital spending by local authorities remains tightly constrained. Provisions in the 1988 Housing Act for 'Change of Landlord' on local authority estates are intended to increase the share of rented housing managed by associations as 'voluntary transfers' are already doing.

As Table 8.1 shows, their size varies greatly. The forty-six largest of the 2,256 associations registered with the Housing Corporation owned more than half of the total rented stock in England and Wales in 1989. This concentration of ownership—which has increased in recent years—is somewhat at odds with the popular image of associations as small-scale local organisations, although it does not preclude them from having adopted a less centralised approach to management than local authorities (see Centre for Housing

TABLE 8.1 *Registered housing associations by size*[a],
England and Wales, March 1989

Size range (units)	No. associations in range	No. units owned ('000s)	% associations	% stock
over 10,000	7	111	0.3	20.4
2,501–10,000	39	177	1.7	32.7
1,001–2,500	78	112	3.5	20.6
101–1,000	302	113	13.4	20.8
0–100	1,830	30	81.1	5.5
Total	2,256	543	100	100

[a] Associations owning fair-rent housing.

Source: Housing Corporation (1990).

Research 1989, for a detailed examination of management performance by associations and local authorities).

Two-thirds of the association stock consists of flats (a fifth of them
converted rather than purpose-built), one-third of houses. This is a
significant difference from local authorities, where only 36 per cent
of the stock is made up of flats, nearly all purpose-built (GB figures
for 1987 from OPCS 1989, table 3.29). The stock is not evenly spread
across the country: in December 1988 associations owned 5.4 per
cent of the Greater London stock, and 3.6 per cent in the North of
England, but less than 2 per cent in the East Midlands and Wales
(DoE 1989*a*, table 9.4).

In general, association and local authority tenants have much in
common. Just over half of both groups of household heads were
economically inactive in 1987: 56 per cent for association tenants; 55
per cent for authority tenants (OPCS 1989, table 3.21). As Table 1.3
shows, the two groups of tenants have similar incomes: in 1987 the
mean household income of association tenants was £6,900; for local
authority tenants it was £7,000 (DoE 1989*a*, table 12.1). A slightly
greater proportion of association than authority household
heads—45 per cent compared to 39 per cent—were aged 65 or over in
1987 (OPCS 1989, table 3.21), reflecting the work of associations
which have specialised in sheltered and other housing for the
elderly. Like local authority tenants, a high proportion of association tenants receive Housing Benefit: between October 1988 and

March 1989 57 per cent of new association tenants were receiving it (*Housing Associations Weekly*, 27 October 1989).

Given that many of those housed by associations come from the same waiting lists as local authority tenants and that they have similar incomes, it is not at all clear why—apart from historical accident—the financial arrangements for the two organisations should be structured to result in different levels of rent or effective subsidy for similar properties. Ways of adapting the two subsidy systems to produce equivalent results are discussed in Chapter 17. The rest of this chapter describes how subsidies to associations have evolved and how they now work.

THE EVOLUTION OF HOUSING ASSOCIATION SUBSIDIES

One of the historical differences between housing policy in Britain and in much of the rest of Western Europe was the way in which subsidies for rented housing were channelled to local authorities rather than non-profit organisations. This began to change with the 1967 Housing Subsidies Act, which allowed subsidy to be passed on by authorities to associations on the same terms as for their own new building—subsidy would cut the net cost of new borrowing to the equivalent of a loan at a 4 per cent interest rate.

This was amended by the 1972 Housing Finance Act. As for local authorities, the intention was that association rents should rise to 'fair rent' levels (and in this case the fair rent regime survived the 1974 election). Earlier subsidies on existing dwellings were phased out by an annual 'withdrawal factor', on the assumption that less subsidy would be needed as rents rose. For new developments, a 'new building subsidy' was introduced. This consisted of a recurrent grant which in the first year of a new dwelling's life would bridge the gap between the fair rent and costs, including management and maintenance and unsubsidised loan charges. Grant would be paid at the same cash level for two further years, then phased out at a predetermined rate in subsequent years.

The idea of this system was that grant would start off at a high level but then fall, precisely in order to cope with the front-loading problem discussed in Chapter 5. However, there was no guarantee that the predetermined subsidy withdrawal would match the actual way in which the gap between fair rents and costs would narrow.

Technically, the system did not work. One of the consequences of this is that there are some associations which still need 'Revenue Deficit Grant' to break even because of the losses they would otherwise make on their pre-1974 stock.

HOUSING ASSOCIATION GRANT

This technical problem was remedied by the 1974 Housing Act, which switched the system of housing association finance away from annual subsidies to large initial capital grants—Housing Association Grant (HAG). Fair rents were retained, but a large enough payment of HAG was now made available to reduce the 'residual loan' (from either the Housing Corporation or a local authority) covering the balance of capital costs to the amount which could be financed from the difference between standard allowances for management and maintenance costs and whatever fair rent was set by the rent officer *in the first year of the project's life*. That is:

HAG = Capital cost − Residual loan

where the residual loan is calculated so that:

Loan servicing = Fair rent − Management and maintenance allowance

(with the loan servicing covering interest and repayment over sixty years for 'new-build' projects or thirty years for 'rehabilitation' projects, and rents allowing for a standard 4 per cent level of empty property, or 'voids').

Thus, to take an example (roughly corresponding to the situation in 1988, the last year of this system), suppose that a newly built unit in the North of England had a capital cost of £34,000 (including any interest paid and 'rolled up' during the development period), that the fair rent set for it yielded £950 per year (after voids), and that the appropriate management and maintenance allowances totalled £396 (as they would have done in 1988/9 for a large association). The amount available to service the residual loan would then be £554, which could cover a loan of £5,522 (if the interest rate was 10 per cent, with repayment on a standard annuity basis—that is, by constant cash amounts—over sixty years). Housing Association Grant would then cover the remaining £28,478 (84 per cent) of the capital cost.

As a second example, a rehabilitated unit in London could have had a capital cost of £90,000, rent (after voids) of £1,200 per year, and management and maintenance allowances of £742 (higher because rehabilitated dwellings are more expensive to maintain and, to a lesser extent, because costs are higher in London). In this case, only £458 is left to service a residual loan, which could then only be £4,318 (with an interest rate of 10 per cent but repayment over thirty years). HAG would have to be £85,682, or 95 per cent of capital cost.

There are several things to note about this system:

1. The grant was the true residual: rents were established first, and then grant was adjusted to allow the association to break even while charging them.
2. If capital costs were £1 higher, HAG would be £1 higher, provided that the Housing Corporation accepted that costs did not depart too far from the 'Total Indicative Cost' (TIC) guidelines which it set for that kind of project and area (and that none of them were judged to be 'non-qualifying' or a result of preventable over runs).
3. Given that the residual loans generated payments which stayed the same in cash over their life, and that associations broke even in the first year, the potential for a surplus to accrue in later years as rents rose was built into the system (see Figure 5.3 above). Running into deficit would be unlikely unless management and maintenance costs started above the allowance level or rose very rapidly later on (or rents rose only very slowly).
4. No allowance was made for future major repairs—the assumption was that further grant—'major repairs HAG'—would be available for them when they were required.

GRANT REDEMPTION FUND

Originally HAG was the grant its name suggested (although it was repayable if the buildings it financed were sold off for some other purpose). Kilroy speculates that the system, 'was supported in Whitehall on the premise that so far as a public financial liability was concerned there was no difference between a grant and a loan: both had to be raised from somewhere at the outset of expenditure' (1975, p. 97). While this is all too plausible, the possibilities of emerging surpluses led the Public Accounts Committee of the

House of Commons (1978, p. x) to criticise the system as bestowing 'an uncovenanted financial benefit' and the 'possibility of windfall benefits' on associations, which they argued should be recouped by the Exchequer.

In response, in February 1979 the then Labour Government proposed that a new system of 'Grant Redemption Funds' (GRFs) be established in which these surpluses would accumulate, and then be either used to offset other grants to which the association was entitled or remitted to the Department of the Environment (DoE 1979). At the same time, associations were to be allowed to set rents at their own discretion, the GRF contributions being based on *deemed* rather than actual rent increases (much along the lines of the 1980 local authority Housing Subsidy).

In the event, the Conservative's 1980 Housing Act did introduce Grant Redemption Funds, but retained fair rents for associations. GRF was calculated on the basis of the surplus of *actual* (fair) rents over the total of actual loan charges and management and maintenance allowances. The calculation was made for each scheme which had been financed by HAG (with pro-rating arrangements if part of the finance had come from elsewhere) and, if the total was positive, the association had to make a payment (in most cases remitted centrally).

The introduction of GRF changed the nature of Housing Association Grant. Receipt of it opened up the probability of future GRF payments—it became only in part a grant, gaining some characteristics of a loan. The calculation described above meant that the total of residual loan servicing and GRF would always equal the difference between management and maintenance allowances and fair rents. If the latter two were both to increase over time at the rate of inflation, so would the total of GRF and loan servicing. In real terms, the total would be constant, but the faster the rate of inflation, the more important the GRF element would become. Although this could not be expected to happen exactly, it meant that the combination of a (conventional) residual loan and GRF was rather like an *indexed* loan—where loan-servicing costs rise in cash from year to year with prices (in this case, with the difference between allowances and rents).

Once an association was liable to GRF, any increase in rents on its HAG-funded stock would accrue to GRF, with no effect on the association's net finances—GRF acted as a '100 per cent tax' at the margin. As a result, although in theory fair rents are supposed to represent an arbitration between landlord and tenant, an association liable to GRF would have no reason to press for any change in rents (although it had every incentive to collect rents once they were set, as the calculations involved fixed voids allowances).

While fixed allowances for general management and maintenance rather than actual costs were taken into account (leaving associations an incentive to keep recurrent costs under control at least), associations could deduct the whole of any deficit they made on their 'service' account. This could occur legitimately if the service charge which a rent officer was prepared to allow in addition to the fair rent did not cover the full cost of providing the service. However, this also offered a way of avoiding GRF; the greater the proportion of spending which could be classified as 'service costs', the lower GRF would be.

Grant Redemption Fund took effect for association accounting years starting after September 1982. By 1987/8 its yield had risen to £14.7 million (Duckworth 1989*a*). While this was not very large by comparison with other association costs or the annual development programme allocated by the Housing Corporation, it was set to grow rapidly. The rate at which this would have occurred depended on future inflation, interest rates, and the size of the new development programme. On a range of assumptions in an earlier analysis based on a simulation model of housing association finances, I calculated that by 2003/4 its annual yield could have reached between £50 million and £300 million (at 1984/5 prices), with the most plausible estimates in the middle of this range (Hills 1987*c*, pp. 48–59). In fact, the system has now been substantially modified, as is explained below.

REVENUE DEFICIT GRANT

The 1974 Act also introduced a recurrent grant, Revenue Deficit Grant (RDG), for associations which would otherwise make a loss while charging fair rents (but spending no more than the amount given by the management and maintenance allowances for their stock). Given the HAG and GRF arrangements described above, this is rather unlikely for post-1974 developments, but it can happen to associations with stock financed under the earlier subsidy systems.

RDG is calculated for an association's rented stock as a whole (excluding hostels and any dwellings financed under the 'New HAG' system described below). An association can be in surplus on its HAG-funded stock—and so liable to GRF,—while being in deficit overall—and so liable to RDG. In this rather complicated case, any GRF liability would count towards costs in calculating RDG, but then the association would retain its GRF payment, setting this against its RDG entitlement (see Hills 1987*c*, pp. 103–8, for full details of the possible interactions).

Unlike calculations of HAG or GRF, entitlement to Revenue Deficit Grant depends on *actual* management and maintenance spending (up to the allowances). This means that subsidy is given pound for pound for spending up to allowance level—the system implies a 100 per cent marginal subsidy rate on recurrent spending—so that there is no financial reason for associations receiving RDG to spend any less than their allowances.

As the cost of pre-1974 loans has gradually been eroded by inflation, so the overall cost of RDG has fallen—from £38.3 million in 1982/3 to £12.2 million in 1987/8 (England and Wales figures; Duckworth 1989*b*). Not only can this process be expected to continue, but the Government has also proposed to refinance the pre-1974 stock of certain associations, so as to 'buy them out of RDG'. Given that RDG is not available on schemes financed under the new system described below, RDG may disappear altogether within the next few years.

Associations also provide hostel accommodation—44,000 bedspaces in England and Wales in 1989 (Housing Corporation 1990). An equivalent to RDG—Hostel Deficit Grant (HDG)—was also introduced in 1974 to meet deficits on the costs of running hostels. In this case, the deficits have arisen mainly as a result of the high recurrent expenses of providing this kind of housing rather than because of high capital costs. Under the proposals for reforming the funding of 'special needs housing' discussed below, HDG would disappear.

HIGHER MANAGEMENT ALLOWANCE

As well as the normal allowances for management and maintenance costs (which depend on a fixed matrix of unit types and location), some associations receive an additional Higher Management

Allowance (HMA), which gives credit for extra costs relating to work in 'stress areas', with particularly socially disadvantaged tenants, or with scattered properties. The size of this allowance is negotiated with the Housing Corporation, and the amount which can be claimed depends on actual spending by the association.

EFFECTS OF THE 1974 SYSTEM

The system as it had evolved by 1987 therefore had the following main features (for more details see Hills 1987*c*):

1. It had given associations almost complete financial security, underpinning their great expansion after 1974.
2. It incorporated a number of features reducing financial incentives for associations to control costs, notably the 100 per cent marginal subsidy rates on capital costs through the HAG system and on recurrent costs (up to allowance level) for those receiving RDG.
3. GRF acted as a 100 per cent tax on additional rental income, removing liable associations' interest in the fair rents set for their tenants.
4. Allowing for GRF, the true level of grant implied by the system was less than the percentage of capital costs covered by HAG.
5. Despite this, the whole of any capital spending counted towards public spending (and came within controls on it), including both HAG and the 'residual loans'.
6. The combination of loan servicing and GRF liabilities acted in many ways as a kind of 'indexed loan'.
7. While associations appear to have used management and maintenance allowances as a 'norm' for spending, they did not have to take into account future needs for major repairs in setting building standards.

THE 'BRAVE NEW WORLD' AFTER 1988

Partly in response to some of these features, the Department of the Environment issued a consultative paper in September 1987 proposing various changes to the system which were then introduced by the 1988 Housing Act, the majority taking effect from April 1989. The paper set out two aims: 'First, they will increase the volume of rented housing the associations can produce for any given level of public expenditure. Second, they will create new incentives to associations to deliver their services in the most cost-effective manner' (DoE 1987*b*, para. 2).

A LARGER PROGRAMME

The first objective is to be met by using 'private finance' (borrowing from the private sector) for costs not covered by Housing Association Grant. Thus, for example, if only 75 per cent of the cost of a scheme comes from public grant, a total of £133 of development can be carried out for every £100 of public spending. However, for residual loans no longer to count as 'public spending' under Treasury accounting conventions, they cannot be 'guaranteed' by government through the possibility of Revenue Deficit Grant if things go wrong. Developments under the new regime are therefore excluded from the possibility of RDG or major repairs grant.

Two further changes were made in order to boost the scope for private finance. First, private finance is assumed be on a 'low-start' basis, so that a larger loan can be supported from a given level of rent at the start of a project, reducing the need for capital grant. With loan costs escalating in cash terms, potential for future surpluses is smaller, so these schemes are not liable to the new equivalent of GRF ('Rent Surplus Fund'). Second, from January 1989 new tenants have 'assured tenancies' and no longer have the right to fair rents (see below for what their rents are likely to be). Higher rents also reduce the grant element, further increasing the scope for private finance.

However, two other changes have *increased* the grant required by associations at any given rent level (or increased the rents for a given grant). First, borrowing from the private sector—particularly without the kind of security which used to be available from RDG— incorporates a 'risk premium' and so is more expensive than money which is borrowed by government and then on-lent to associations. It reduces the size of loan which can be serviced from a given rental income. This has been exacerbated by the form of finance which many associations have been using under the new arrangements— 'deferred interest' loans at *variable* interest rates. These incorporate *short-term* interest rates into the calculation of initial loan servicing. At the time of writing these are well above long-term fixed-interest borrowing rates—the financial markets expect short-term interest rates to be lower in the future, and with them the cost of servicing variable rate loans (a phenomenon known as an 'inverse yield curve', as it is the reverse of the premium which one might normally expect to be paid on long-term loans). In effect, variable interest loans currently involve an additional 'front-loading' element, undoing part of the purpose of 'low-start' finance. The repayment periods for private finance are also shorter than the thirty or sixty years of public-sector residual loans in the past.

The second aspect increasing initial costs is the new requirement that associations put provisions aside for 'Major Repairs Funds', intended to build up to amounts which will cover the cost of future major repairs, for which HAG will no longer be available on schemes financed under the new arrangements. The effects of this at first sight minor change, mentioned only in passing in the original Consultative Document, are substantial. On the basis of the small amount of empirical evidence existing to date, the Housing Corporation and the National Federation of Housing Associations (NFHA) have suggested that associations should make annual provisions equal to 0.8 per cent of the rebuilding cost of new-build schemes, and 1 per cent for rehabilitation schemes (increasing over time with building costs). For a new-build project with a rebuilding cost of £50,000, this adds about £7.70 per week to initial costs—equivalent by itself to an addition of 30 per cent to what had been fair rent levels in 1988/9. Alternatively, if the provision was met by higher initial capital grant to allow reduced loan servicing (assuming a deferred interest loan at a fixed interest rate of 10.5 per cent, with payments escalating at 5 per cent per year over thirty years), grant would have to be about £5,700 higher.

A MORE COST-EFFECTIVE PROGRAMME

The new system is designed to give incentives to associations to be more cost-effective and raise their incomes in several ways:

1. Capital grants no longer cover changes in costs pound for pound as before. For 'tariff' associations (see below), the capital grant for particular kinds of unit and area is a fixed cash sum, unaffected by actual costs. For others, grant is given at a predetermined percentage of estimated scheme costs, with additional grant at this percentage available for only limited overruns.

2. Neither Revenue Deficit Grant nor Rent Surplus Fund apply to new schemes. Where they do apply on existing schemes, associations can now retain part of any rent increases.
3. Rents for new tenants are now fixed by the housing association, not by a rent officer.
4. The withdrawal of major repairs grant increases the interest of associations in building standards which minimise the need for future major repairs.

The intention is that, 'the injection of market disciplines will itself lead to greater efficiency and make associations more independent and more responsible for the quality and effectiveness of their investment decisions and the competence of their management' (DoE 1987*b*, para. 6).

THE NEW HOUSING ASSOCIATION GRANT SYSTEM

The fundamental change from the pre-1988 system is that the order in which grant and rent are determined is reversed. In the new system, grant is fixed first and associations adjust rents to cover the remaining costs. This is the reverse of the old procedure under which rents determined grants.

Fixed-percentage grant rates and guideline capital costs—'Total Cost Indicators' (TCIs)—are now set for different kinds of project and region. For grant purposes, associations fall into three groups:

1. 'Tariff' associations, which agree what was originally intended to be a three-year programme with the Housing Corporation for development of a certain number of units of a particular kind (although the Corporation's 1990 cash crisis meant that this intended stability failed to emerge). Grant is paid at the fixed-percentage rate multiplied by the appropriate TCI. The association benefits fully if costs end up below TCI but bears the full effect of any higher costs.
2. 'Non-tariff' associations, which receive grant at the appropriate percentage on estimated scheme costs (provided that these do not exceed 130 per cent of TCI). Cost overruns up to 10 per cent above the estimate (if out-turn costs are still within 130 per cent of TCI) and any cost savings result in grant being adjusted by the appropriate percentage applied to forecast out-turn costs, so the association carries only part of the risk.

3. Associations receiving public funding which—because of their small size or lack of reserves or property equity—do not have access to private finance can receive residual loans from the Housing Corporation or local authorities. Because these residual loans are cheaper than those from the private sector (but still on 'low-start' terms), grant rates are lower than those applying to schemes using private finance. Small new associations (with fewer than 250 units) may also be entitled to a 'start-up grant' if they run into a deficit on their development work within five years of their first acquisition.

The crucial factors in the new arrangements are the tables each year published by the Housing Corporation for TCIs and grant rates. The first of these consists of a table showing 'basic costs' for dwellings of different sizes in different areas, on the assumption that the project is a normal 'acquisition and works' new-build project. These are adjusted by 'multipliers' for factors which affect costs (for instance, TCI is lower if a project only involves building works, not acquisition, but is higher in most parts of the country for rehabilitation projects). Note that TCI is set when a scheme is approved, so it relates to out-turn costs at some point in the future. Another difference from the old system is that TCIs include an 'on-cost'. This covers fees and the 'acquisition and development' ('A and D') allowances paid to associations for their own costs during development of a project, together with a *fixed*-percentage allowance for interest charges during the development period, whereas actual interest used to be 'rolled up' in the capital costs on which HAG was calculated. The new system therefore gives a much stronger incentive to associations to speed up development.

The published grant rates also vary by area and by project category (such as new-build, rehabilitation, purpose-built for the elderly, or purpose-built for the frail elderly). Grant rates are also adjusted (for non-tariff associations only) to allow for particularly high- or low-cost locations within particular areas.

An example

The workings of the new system can be seen from the following example for a new-build dwelling in TCI area 'C' (the outer South-East) intended for 3–4 people approved in the first half of 1989/90. TCI would be £75,900 and the grant rate 75 per cent (the overall target for England as a whole at the time). Housing Association Grant would then be £56,925 if estimated costs equalled TCI (and this would be the 'tariff' for associations using that system), so £18,975 of private finance would be needed. If this could be raised on terms which involved initial payments equal to 7 per cent of the loan, loan servicing in the first year would cost £1,328 (this would be possible with, for instance, a deferred-interest loan at an interest rate of 10.5 per cent and 5 per cent annual escalation over thirty years, or a 5.6 per cent index-linked loan over thirty years; if interest rates were higher or if borrowing involved less of a 'low start', the cost would be higher).

For a dwelling in this area, rebuilding costs might be about 80 per cent of total cost, that is, £60,720. The recommended annual major repairs provision for new-build projects is 0.8 per cent, or £486. Finally, if the project was completed in 1990/1, management and maintenance costs would be £477 (if they were in line with the allowances set by the Housing Corporation for 1990/1). This gives total costs in 1990/1 of £2,291, so a weekly rent of £45.80 would have to be charged for the association to break even (with the standard 4 per cent allowance for 'voids' or empty properties). Note that for this fairly typical project, the rent implied for 1990/1 is almost twice as high in cash as typical fair rents had been two years before.

All of this assumes that costs turn out to equal TCI. If they do not, the association's finances will be affected, in contrast to the pre-1988 system. In this case, if costs were 10 per cent higher than TCI, for a tariff association the residual loan would have to be £7,590 higher, adding £10.62 to the weekly rent required; for a non-tariff association, grant would cover 75 per cent of an addition of this size, so the loan would only be £1,898 higher, adding £2.66 to the required weekly rent. If costs were 10 per cent lower, required rents would fall by the same amounts. These effects reflect the intentions of the new system—the rents which associations have to charge are sensitive to the capital costs of project, especially so in the case of tariff associations. It is clearly the Housing Corporation's intention that as many associations as possible should be 'on tariff', with the maximum incentive for cost control.

The range of costs and grant rates

Table 8.2 gives an idea of the range of costs and grant rates applying in England in the first year of the new system, 1989/90. The four

TABLE 8.2 *Costs to housing associations with 1989/90 grant rates*

TCI area[a]	A		G	
Type of scheme	New-build	Rehab.	New-build	Rehab.
Size of unit (persons)	1	6–7	1	6–7
Total Cost Indicator[b] (£)	59,000	157,665	24,600	54,340
Grant rate (%)[c]	81	87	63	78
HAG if cost equals TCI (£)	47,790	137,169	15,498	42,385
Residual loan at TCI (£)	11,210	20,496	9,102	11,955
First year loan servicing (£)[d]	785	1,435	637	837
Estimated rebuilding cost (£)[e]	44,250	118,249	20,910	46,155
First-year major repairs provision (£)[f]	354	1,182	167	462
Management & maintenance (£)[g]	552	829	477	736
Total first-year costs (£)	1,691	3,446	1,281	2,035
Initial break-even rent (£/week)[h]	33.80	68.90	25.60	40.70
Estimated 'Indicator Rent'[i]	28.30	51.45	21.50	37.60
Effect on break-even rents if capital costs 10% higher (£/week)				
'Tariff' association	+8.26	+22.08	+3.44	+7.60
'Non-tariff' association	+1.57	+2.87	+1.27	+1.67

[a]TCI area A covers Inner London and part of Outer London; TCI area G includes parts of Northern England.

[b]For projects approved in first half of 1989/90 (from Housing Corporation circular HC 11/89).

[c]For 1989/90 (from circular HC 25/89).

[d]If first-year servicing costs are 7% of loan (for instance, a 30 year fixed interest loan at 10.5% on deferred interest terms with payments rising at 5%, or a 30 year index-linked loan with a real interest rate of 5.6%).

[e]75% of TCI in TCI area A, 85% in area G.

[f]At 0.8% for new build projects, 1.0% for rehab.

[g]1990/91 allowances levels for large associations.

[h]Allowing for 4% voids.

[i]National Federation of Housing Associations 'Indicator Rents' for 1990/91 (from *Housing Associations Weekly*, 2 February 1990; 1989/90 levels increased by 8.1% to give estimate for 1990/1).

examples cover the highest and lowest cost areas (TCI areas 'A' and 'G' respectively), each showing a low-cost unit (a one-person new-build unit) and a high-cost one (a 6–7 person rehabilitated unit). The variation in TCI between the cheapest and the most expensive of these examples is 6 to 1, but the variation in the fixed grant rates reduces the variation in residual loans to just over 2 to 1. However, the variation in suggested major repairs provisions is, at 7 to 1, even greater than that of TCI (because of the greater provision for 'rehab' than new-build projects). Allowing for management and maintenance costs on the assumption that they are in line with the allowances set by the Housing Corporation (but which are not an integral part of the new system), the rents required to break even in 1990/1 (assuming that this is when completion would be) vary by a factor of 2.7 to 1.

The sensitivity of required rents to variations in capital cost can be seen from the bottom of the table. A tariff association rehabilitating a large unit in central London could, theoretically, reduce the rent required by nearly a third if capital costs came in 10 per cent below TCI. By the same token, a project of this kind would carry a risk that rents would have to rise correspondingly if costs overran (for instance, if unexpected problems such as dry rot were found in the building being rehabilitated). Given the inherent risks of rehabilitation and that many associations cannot afford to carry this kind of 'downside' risk, it has been argued that the new system makes rehabilitation much less attractive than it was before (even on non-tariff terms), and indeed much less rehabilitation work was started in 1989/90 than in earlier years.

RENTS AND 'AFFORDABILITY'

Associations are not, however, expected simply to charge rents which cover costs. In setting out the principles which associations should use to set rents under the new regime, the Housing Corporation has laid down that 'Registered housing associations are subject to the *overriding requirement* of the Tenants Guarantee that rents must be set and maintained within the reach of people in low paid employment' (Housing Corporation 1989a, para. 2.1; emphasis added); and that 'On certain new schemes it may be necessary to set rents below the level where they cover costs, in order to ensure that they remain affordable' (ibid., para. 4.2). The problem with this is that no guidance whatsoever has been given as to the meanings of phrases like 'within the reach of', 'low paid' or 'affordable'. As the same document rather unhelpfully puts it, 'Affordability is for associations to determine' (ibid., para. 4.1).

Rents payable without driving people below minimum incomes

The most hardline interpretation of 'affordability' would be to say that rents were affordable if people could pay them without reducing their remaining resources below, say, the minimum provided by Income Support. However, given the current structure of Housing Benefit (see Chapter 10), remaining resources will stay at or above this minimum with *any* rent which is accepted not to be above 'market' levels. This interpretation would mean only that associations should not set rents above market levels—indeed, given their secondary obligation to 'maximise rental income' (ibid., para. 2.2), rents would have to be set *at* market levels.

Rents 'affordable' to those above the Housing Benefit threshold

During discussion of the original proposals one Minister said that the rents which the Government had in mind were to be, 'reasonably affordable by those individuals or households whose income is just above the Housing Benefit threshold' (speech by Mr Ian Grist to the Welsh Housing Associations Council Annual Symposium, September 1987). This recognises that, under the current Housing Benefit system, the maximum ratio of net rent (after benefit) to net income occurs just at the point where entitlement to Housing Benefit runs out. The implication of the statement would be that rents should be set to keep this ratio below some maximum. However, Housing Benefit is not structured in a way which is much help for this aim—this kind of 'affordability ratio' can easily reach very high levels. For instance, the 'break-even rent' of £33.80 shown in the first column of Table 8.2 would, under the 1990/1 social security system, leave single people aged 25 or over paying up to 38 per cent of net income in rent; for those aged less than 25, the ratio would be higher. For families, ratios are lower: the £68.90 rent in the second column could absorb up to 29 per cent of the net income of a married couple with four children.

Given the structure of Housing Benefit, setting a maximum to such ratios would give a clear limit to rents. For instance, a limit of 20 per cent of net income would mean rents no higher in 1990/1 than £10.60 per week for single people aged over 25, or £36.50 for a family of six. If the limit was 33 per cent, the limits would be £25.10 and £86.30. Even with this higher ratio, break-even rents for single people in the *lowest* cost region shown in Table 8.2 still violate this concept of 'affordability'.

Parity with owner-occupiers

Another early Ministerial suggestion was that, 'the best test of what people should pay seems to be to look at what proportion of income people choose to spend on housing when the choice is theirs' (speech by Mr William Waldegrave to the National Federation of Housing Associations, September 1987). By implication, this means looking at housing costs of owner-occupiers (as looking at private tenants would simply get back to 'market' rents). However, it would clearly be inappropriate to use the spending of those with *new* mortgages as a benchmark—unlike tenants, they can look forward to future falls in the real value of their housing costs. If one looks at owner-occupiers as a whole, the 1986 *Family Expenditure Survey* shows that they spent about 16 per cent of their disposable incomes on interest payments, repairs, maintenance, and decorations (DE 1987, tables 5 and 22).

One interpretation of 'affordable rents' is thus that tenants (by implication those not receiving Housing Benefit) should pay a similar proportion of net income in rent. New housing association tenant households with at least one person in paid work had average net incomes of £127 per week in the period October 1988 to March 1989 (*Housing Asssociations Weekly*, 27 October 1989). Even if this was to rise to £150 per week in 1990/1, a 16 per cent ratio would yield a national average rent of £24 per week—in line with *fair* rents, but well below the 'break-even rents' in Table 8.2.

Following this kind of approach, the National Federation of Housing Associations has issued tables of what it calls 'indicator rents', intended to average the somewhat higher figure of 20 per cent of net incomes, with some variation across the country. Table 8.2 shows estimates of 'indicator rents' for 1990/1. As can be seen, the 'break-even' rents are between 8 and 34 per cent higher than these 'indicator' levels. This leaves associations with an as yet unsolved dilemma: if they follow the 'overriding requirement' of 'affordability' on this apparently reasonable basis, their rents will not cover their initial costs; if they cover their costs, they violate affordability.

It should be noted that this approach of looking at cash housing payments by owner-occupiers in fact *overstates* the true cost of housing to them as it incorporates the cost of purchasing an asset (which rents do not). To obtain true 'tenure neutrality' in housing costs would require a different approach based on the cost of capital to owners after allowing for this. How to calculate this is explored in Chapter 12 and proposals for achieving something close to it in Chapter 17.

RENT RELATIVITIES

While confusion still surrounds the overall level of rents which is supposed to result from 'affordability', it is clear from Table 8.2 that the new system is intended to result in rents which vary rather more than fair rents used to (see Chapter 4). Between the highest and lowest cost units, the variation in 'break-even' rents is about 2.7 to 1. For units of the same kind, the variation between high- and low-cost regions is between 1.3 and 1.7 to 1. However, this level of regional variation is considerably less than can be expected to result from the new local authority subsidy system, where the rents on which subsidy is based may end up in direct proportion to capital values (see Chapter 7). The reason for this difference in outcome in the new housing association finance system lies in its concentration of subsidy on *capital* costs alone (which are the component which varies most across the country), and the higher grant rates given to high-cost regions.

EXISTING STOCK UNDER THE NEW ARRANGEMENTS

The discussion of the 'New HAG' system above relates to new developments, mostly approved since April 1989, although there were some pilot '30 per cent HAG' and 'challenge-funding' schemes with similar, if less generous, financial arrangements before then (see Kleinman 1987). For associations' existing stock financial arrangements continue to have some of the same features as before, but with various modifications.

A key difference relates not to the existing *stock* as such, but rather to existing tenants compared with new ones. The former retain a right to a 'fair rent' (and carry this right with them if they move within a single association's stock, including to units funded under the new system). However, since January 1989, if existing units are re-let to new tenants, they come under 'assured-tenancy' rules, and associations are expected to set rents in line with the 'affordable' rents being set for their new stock. The new rules for Revenue Deficit

Grant and Rent Surplus Fund reflect this expectation. At the same time, the new arrangements are intended to allow contributions towards 'Major Repairs Funds' for part of existing stocks as more rents move on to assured tenancy rents.

Rent Surplus Funds

From April 1989, Grant Redemption Funds have been replaced with new 'Rent Surplus Funds'. These have broadly the same intention as GRF—the removal of surpluses resulting from the effects of inflation on conventional debt—but are structured to give associations more of an incentive to maximise rents. For stock liable to RSF, the surplus is calculated in much the same way as before:

	Surplus
equals	Actual rents
minus	Actual loan charges
minus	Management and maintenance allowances.

There are four key differences from GRF:

1. Stock funded under the new system and let on assured tenancy terms is not liable to RSF. However, if existing tenants with the right to a fair rent occupy 'New HAG'-funded stock, the association can deduct the difference between their fair rents and what 'affordable' rents would have been in calculating the surplus for RSF purposes.
2. Some of the rents of 'Old HAG'-funded stock will be at 'affordable' rather than fair rent levels.
3. Arrangements have been simplified for stock funded under pre-1974 arrangements—'Pre-HAG' stock. Where there has been no HAG input into such property, or only HAG for major repairs, the property will be excluded from RSF. Where schemes are 'joint funded'—say, because HAG was used for development on privately funded land (or there was some other privately funded component) or because a Pre-HAG scheme has benefited from HAG-funded 'reimprovement'—a percentage of the surplus counts towards the RSF calculation.
4. Once the aggregate surplus has been calculated, 70 per cent is deducted to go towards building up Major Repair Funds for existing stock. The remaining 30 per cent—which constitutes RSF—is split, with half going to the Housing Corporation, and half retained by the association.

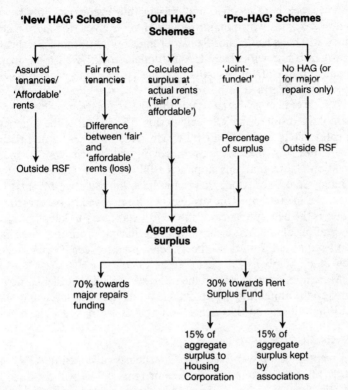

Figure 8.1 Rent Surplus Fund arrangements
Source: Duckworth (1989*a*; adapted).

These arrangements are summarised in Figure 8.1 (adapted from Duckworth 1989*a*, which contains a fuller account of the RSF system).

The bulk of the calculated surplus is therefore intended to build up Major Repair Funds on associations' existing stock. The idea is that the stock will be split into two parts: 'Block A', with funds covering the suggested requirement (calculated at the standard percentages of current rebuilding cost for the number of years—up to thirty—since original completion); and 'Block B', with no major repairs funding, which will remain eligible for HAG on major repairs. As contributions from RSF allow, stock will be reclassified from Block B to Block A, with the general assumption that the most recent stock is reclassified first. It will thus eventually only be the oldest stock for which major repairs HAG is given; the more recent stock will have had Major Repairs Funds built up from RSF, bringing it into line with 'New HAG'-funded stock. Even then, major repairs grant will not be available if the association's other financial reserves are deemed to be adequate.

A further change from GRF is that the association is able to keep half of the result of the RSF calculation, 15 per cent of the aggregate surplus. Thus, for every £1 by which rents increase on its existing properties, 15p goes towards improving the association's financial position. Note that this applies to fair rents as well as assured-tenancy rents, so associations now have an incentive to press for increases in fair rents. One strategy being employed by some associations as the new system came into effect was to try to keep fair rents and 'affordable rents' in line, with the income from increased fair rents requested from rent officers being used to keep down rents on new stock below its full cost (Pollitt 1989).

More minor changes from the GRF system are that there is now a limit on the amount by which deficits on service accounts can reduce RSF liabilities, and that deficits on hostels are now excluded.

Revenue Deficit Grant

As mentioned above, 'New HAG' schemes fall outside RDG entitlement. For existing units let at fair rents, RDG will continue to be calculated as before. If, however, existing units are let on assured tenancies, what counts towards RDG is a notional rent half-way between the average fair rent on the rest of the association's stock and the average actual rent. This means that half of any increase in rent on re-letting is retained by the association and gives it a net benefit. However, any increase in fair rents results in lower RDG. This removes any net benefit from associations in RDG from pressing for higher fair rents; indeed, they have an interest in *lower* fair rents, as these increase the amount which can be retained from rents on assured-tenancy re-lets. (Any RSF liability both contributes to RDG entitlement, and is used to meet part of the RDG requirement before anything is set aside for major repairs or split between the association and Housing Corporation.)

In order to hasten the disappearance of RDG, the Housing Corporation has offered to refinance old schemes with HAG payments which would reduce costs to those which could be met from current fair rents. Being 'bought out' of the need for RDG might have benefits for associations in terms of making them better-looking prospects for private finance, and in terms of allowing them to keep a greater proportion of any surpluses which they make. However, the cost of such an arrangement would be that 75 per cent of surpluses on the refinanced properties would now come within the scope of RSF. For an association which was likely to move out of RDG entitlement in the near future, the loss of potential surpluses from properties which would otherwise come outside the RSF system could well more than offset the advantages of an RDG 'buy-out'.

SPECIAL-NEEDS FUNDING

People with 'special needs' for housing fall into a wide range of categories, including: people with physical disabilities; people with mental health problems; those leaving institutions (including prisons); refugees; people with AIDS/ARC or who are HIV positive; women at risk from domestic violence; and the frail elderly. In some cases, the housing itself needs physical adaptation; in others, the main need is for intensive management and/or provision of care. Many of those living in special needs accommodation are wholly dependent on Income Support.

In the past, funding came from four sources (see Berthoud and Casey 1988 for a detailed discussion of hostel finances):

– Housing Association Grant calculated on the old 'residual' basis (often resulting in 100 per cent capital grants);
– charges to residents, in many cases backed by Supplementary Benefit/ Income Support 'board and lodging' payments (covering items including food) or by Housing Benefit for residents not entitled to Income Support;
– 'topping-up' funding from elsewhere (such as local authority social services departments) to cover the cost of particular kinds of care; and
– Hostel Deficit Grant, making up the income of associations from charges to cover non-care recurrent costs.

This system is changing in three ways. First, the Income Support system has changed to restrict the 'board and lodging' payments. From October 1989 hostel residents have been moved on to the normal system of Housing Benefit, with 'market rent' limits on eligibility, and items like food assumed to come out of the normal Income Support rates. Second, the 'New HAG' system will be extended to special needs housing. Third, Hostel Deficit Grant is to disappear.

In a Consultation Paper issued in October 1989, the Housing Corporation (1989*b*) proposed that capital funding should be brought into line with the rest of the 'New HAG' system, with fixed percentage grant rates, and Total Cost Indicators adjusted to allow for some additional costs of special-needs housing. Associations would then have to make charges which covered the same costs as their other housing—loan repayment, major repairs provision, 'normal' management and maintenance, and an allowance for voids at 4 per cent. At the same time HDG would be replaced by flat-rate annual allowances (£3,600 per year per bedspace was suggested) to cover the additional *management* costs of special needs housing (including a higher level of voids). The cost of *care* provision should come from 'topping-up' funding from other sources.

The intention of these proposals is to integrate the 'housing' aspects of special-needs provision within either the same arrangements as apply to other housing, or within a flat-rate allowance for additional management costs (as opposed to the old deficit grant given by HDG), with care costs in excess of the additional management allowance assumed to come from other sources. At the time of writing, it is not clear when such changes will happen.

SUMMARY

■ At the centre of housing association finance is an initial capital grant, Housing Association Grant (HAG). Between 1974 and 1989 the size of grant was set so that an association would break even in the first year of a new project's life, given the fair rents set by the rent officer, standard allowances for management and maintenance, and servicing of the residual loan.

■ From 1980, associations became liable to make Grant Redemption Fund (GRF) payments, creaming off surpluses which would otherwise arise as rents rose but loan-servicing costs did not.

■ Revenue Deficit Grant was introduced in 1974, primarily to cover the deficits which would otherwise arise on properties funded with less generous pre-1974 subsidies.

■ From 1989 the system has been changed with two main aims: to encourage the use of private finance to supplement public grants, and to give greater incentives to associations to control their costs.

- In the new system, HAG is predetermined, either as a fixed cash sum for 'tariff' associations or as a percentage of estimated scheme costs for others. Rents now have to be adjusted by associations so that they can cover loan charges (assumed to be on a 'low-start' basis) on the balance of capital costs, management and maintenance, and a provision for future major repairs (as HAG for these is no longer available for new developments). The resulting rents are significantly higher than fair rents used to be.
- For existing developments GRF has been replaced by Rent Surplus Funds (RSF). An aggregate surplus is calculated for the association, 70 per cent of which goes towards building up funds for major repairs on existing stock, and the rest to RSF, which in turn is split equally between the association and the Housing Corporation.
- RSF is not applied to new developments, nor are losses on them eligible for RDG.
- Existing tenants retain the right to a fair rent (even if they move within an association's stock).
- The Government expects the need for RDG to disappear over the next few years. In the meantime, associations receiving RDG will retain part of the proceeds of higher rents.
- It has been proposed that Hostel Deficit Grant (HDG) be replaced by a combination of measures, including a flat-rate allowance for additional management costs for special-needs projects.

9

Other Housing Subsidies

ARRANGEMENTS FOR ESTATE TRANSFERS

The Government has been promoting arrangements under which local authority estates can be transferred to new landlords. These include: 'voluntary transfers' under the 1985 Housing Act, where authorities can try to transfer all or part of their stock to a new landlord (a new housing association set up for the purpose in most of the cases which have arisen); transfers under the 'Change of Landlord' provisions of the 1988 Housing Act (under which an alternative landlord or tenants can initiate the process of transfer); and 'Housing Action Trusts' (HATs), the idea of which is that a body set up by central government should take over the running of estates while extensive repairs and improvements are made (an idea which has made no progress at all at the time of writing). There have also been a number of large-scale transfers resulting from the winding up of new towns or the abolition of metropolitan authorities like the Greater London Council.

Such transfers have major significance for housing policy, going well beyond the scope of this book, and the terms on which they will happen (including, in particular, the arrangements for tenants to vote on whether they should) have caused major controversy. Even if very few transfers ever actually took place, the potential given to tenants to 'exit' could still have important effects on how local authority housing is run. The transfers also raise important subsidy issues. Although they consist of estates which already exist, the financial terms set for transfer have much in common with a system of capital grants being given to a new housing project. Once the deal is struck, the new landlord is intended by the Government to be on its own—paralleling the new capital funding system for housing associations. Both sides of the arrangements have to be considered—the situation of the new landlord, and hence of the tenants who transfer, and that of the old landlord, and hence of the tenants who remain.

THE SITUATION OF THE NEW LANDLORD

In making one of the original proposals for estate transfers Henney (1985) suggested that transfer terms should be based on market value after taking account of four factors:

1. rental income net of management and maintenance costs allowing for inflation (starting from rents 'similar to current levels');
2. the present value of the expected level of proceeds from sales under the Right to Buy;
3. the present value of expected sales with vacant possession; and
4. the cost of major repairs (*net* of the higher rents possible after renovation).

The 1988 Housing Act lays down that the price paid for a transferred estate under Change of Landlord should be the price which it would realise if 'sold on the open market by a willing vendor ... subject to any tenancies subsisting on that date but otherwise with vacant possession' (Section 99(2)). It also suggests that the price should take account of the cost of repairs required to put the buildings into 'the state of repair required by the landlord's repairing obligations'. The Department of the Environment expects substantially the same approach to be adopted for valuations for 'voluntary transfers'.

This kind of formulation—effectively tenanted market value, taking account of outstanding major repairs—has three important implications. First, note that the answer can be a negative number— a 'dowry' may have to be given to the new landlord to allow necessary repairs to be carried out without requiring borrowing beyond that which could be financed from rents and receipts from Right to Buy sales. The worse the state of repair and the lower the rents or prospects of sales, the more likely the need for a dowry.

Second, the *current* level of rents is of great importance. The higher they are, the greater the probable value of any future rental stream and hence the higher the value of the estate to a new landlord. As the changes in subsidy described in Chapter 7 are intended to produce major changes in relative rents across the country (and possibly generally higher rents in the future), the precise date of transfer could be very important. Two otherwise identical estates could end up with different rents built into their finances for some years to come, simply because the transferring authority had raised its rents between the dates of transfer.

However, it has not been made clear how rents will be set after transfer. In Henney's formulation they would simply have risen with inflation. As it is, the DoE has laid down only that Change of Landlord and voluntary transfers come under the 'Tenants Guarantee' (Housing Corporation 1988) and hence that rents should be 'within the reach of those in low paid employment', the vagueness of which was discussed in the previous chapter. For new tenants, rents will be constrained by whatever this is interpreted to mean. Where transfers have taken place, existing tenants have—as part of the negotiations preceding votes on transfer—extracted some guarantees about their own rent levels for the next few years. Without more explicit guidance, such guarantees and rents themselves will probably end up varying greatly from transfer to transfer.

A further factor in considering terms of transfer is the possibility of the same front-loading problems with estate transfers as have been discussed in earlier chapters with respect to subsidies on new dwellings. If it was assumed that the capital required to finance a transfer (assuming that the price was positive) was borrowed on conventional terms, the price could be low enough to allow the new landlord to break even initially—in which case a surplus would emerge in later years as debt-servicing costs did not rise with inflation. Alternatively, a higher price could be set which was fair in net present-value terms, but left the new landlord with an initial cash flow problem. Once again, indexed or low-start finance could help lessen the problem— and, indeed, has in the first transfers to take place—but this brings the problems of cost, availability, and unfamiliarity discussed in the previous chapter. It seems possible, given that the Government is keen to encourage transfers, that the terms will be relatively generous, allowing break-even with relatively little escalation of debt repayments. If so, in a few years time we may see a very similar debate to that which preceded the introduction of Grant Redemption Fund for housing associations in 1980.

The position of the new landlord will be similar to that of housing associations for stock financed under the new regime (see Chapter 8), including all its risks. In this case, however, the exposure to risk will be more serious, as the new landlords will have *all* of their stock financed under the new arrangements, rather than just that built since 1989. There will be no other stock available to spread the risk—and the risks are large (with transfer prices depending on 30 year forecasts of cash flows).

THE SITUATION OF THE OLD LANDLORD

Once again, the structure of the new HRA Subsidy in England and Wales greatly simplifies the effects of a transfer on its former landlord. Under the previous subsidy system, the balance on the HRA would have been very sensitive to the terms of any transfer. Depending on these, and on the average level of debt per dwelling carried by on the HRA, a transfer could have left an authority needing to raise rents on its remaining stock or to increase Rate Fund Contributions, or to do the reverse. In the event of a transfer of the whole of its stock, the authority could have been left facing residual HRA debt charges—or receiving interest on residual financial assets—but no dwellings.

While the 1989 Act was still going through Parliament, the DoE published complicated proposals for a new 'Residual Debt Subsidy' to cope with some of these effects. Following responses to these proposals, and following the change in principle to a 'fundamental' basis for calculating subsidy, the situation is much simpler. Residual Debt Subsidy was only needed in certain rather obscure circumstances in 1989/90, the last year of the old Housing Subsidy system (when it protected the HRA from a rise in debt per dwelling following a transfer).

In the new system, the 'reserved part' of the positive proceeds of a transfer (75 per cent, or more if outstanding housing debt is relatively high) has either to be used to pay off HRA debt or retained to generate interest which will be credited to the HRA. In either case this reduces the *net* loan charges carried on the HRA, but leads to a matching reduction in HRA Subsidy (for the reasons discussed in Chapter 7). At the same time, the fall in the number of dwellings reduces the *aggregate* guidelines for rents and management and maintenance spending built into its subsidy calculation, but does not affect the amounts allowed *per dwelling* (unless the transfer results in a change in stock composition affecting either the average management and maintenance allowance or the future levels of Right to Buy valuations).

If the transferred dwellings have an average rent which differs from the authority's subsidy guideline, the rents on the remaining dwellings will have to adjust (except to the extent that the authority has a margin of error built into its rent setting). If, for instance, the transferred dwellings have an actual average rent above the guideline, more rent will have to be found from those left behind to

restore average rent levels (or less spent on their management and
maintenance). Also, management and maintenance costs may not
actually fall in proportion to the change in the size of the stock (or
rather of its aggregate allowance)—for instance, there may have
been economies of scale (or, alternatively, there may turn out to be
the reverse). It will, however, be immaterial to the remaining tenants what price or dowry is set for a transfer (unless the size of a
dowry eats up part of an authority's credit approvals).

The full adjustment of HRA Subsidy for the effect of a transfer on
net loan charges carried on the HRA removes some of the local
authority's financial interest in the terms of a deal. Its incentive for
negotiating reasonable terms lies not in the net effects on its HRA—
these are removed by the 100 per cent marginal subsidy—but in the
'usable' part (up to 25 per cent) of the capital receipts, which will be
credited to its non-housing funds. In the case of transfers under the
Right to Buy or Change of Landlord, the price is in any case set by
the District Valuer. Transfers have to be approved by the Secretary
of State in any case.

THE RIGHT TO BUY

The encouragement of large-scale transfers of local authority
estates to new landlords follows the dramatic effects on British
housing of the introduction of the Right to Buy in the 1980 Housing
Act. Between October 1980 (when it came into force) and 1988, just
over 1 million sales were completed of public-sector dwellings to
their tenants under the Right to Buy in Great Britain (DoE 1989*a*,
table 9.7; note that pre-1989 tenants of non-charitable housing
associations have the Right to Buy, as well as those of local
authorities and new towns). Including other sales, local authorities
and new towns in Great Britain sold 1.3 million dwellings between
1979 and 1988, one-fifth of the stock they had started with (DoE
1989*a*, tables 9.3 and 9.6). Overwhelmingly it has been the better
part of the stock which has been sold, with most sales being houses
rather than flats. Forrest and Murie's survey of Right to Buy sales
found that 'The typical sold dwelling is three-bedroomed and semi-
detached' (1984, p. 27) and that, 'there is nothing in the evidence to
justify modifying the view that it is better quality family dwellings
that are sold' (ibid., p. 31).

While this finding is relatively uncontroversial, there is much more dispute about the effect of this on the subsequent supply of new lettings. Appraising possible effects of the policy, the Department of the Environment argued that experience from earlier sales suggested 'nearly all sitting tenant purchasers would otherwise have remained tenants until their death, when the widow would take over the tenancy. Not until *she* ceases to live as a tenant is there any effect on the number of new tenants that can be accommodated' (DoE 1980, p. 40). By contrast, the House of Commons Environment Committee forecast (1981, p. xx) that the policy would mean a significant loss of re-lets, estimated to start at 2.6 per cent each year of the stock which had previously been sold.

The concern here, however, is not with the social advantages or disadvantages of the policy. It is rather to examine what subsidy is implicit in the current arrangements, with sales at a discount to the market valuation of the property. Both sales and discounts had existed before the 1980 Act. Its innovations were to end local authorities' ability to block sales to tenants of more than three years' standing (later reduced to two) and to introduce a much more generous scale of discounts than had been allowed before. For those who had been tenants for less than four years, the discount was set at 33 per cent of the property's value, and this was increased by 1 per cent for each year of tenancy, up to a maximum of 50 per cent for those who had been tenants for twenty years or more. This was extended in 1984 to allow ten more years of accumulation to give a maximum of 60 per cent. For flats, this was further increased to 70 per cent in January 1987, with a faster rate of accrual, so that this maximum is reached with fifteen years' tenancy. Discounts are restricted by the 'cost floor'—the net sales price cannot be reduced to less than the total of cash amounts spent on the dwelling in the previous eight years or so—and by a maximum discount, originally £25,000 (increased to £50,000 from 1989).

At first sight, it might be thought that selling at a discount automatically bestows a benefit on the purchaser (and loss to the seller) equal to the size of the discount. This is not necessarily so, however, if the comparison is with a situation in which there was no sale, with the potential purchaser remaining as a tenant, paying a sub-economic rent. Forrest and Murie suggest that in setting discounts, 'it could be argued that it is the marginal difference between market value and a rental linked value which the tenant should pay. Such a formula would have just as great a logic as current arrangements if not more' (1984, p. 50). Without advocating that discounts should be set in this way, this formulation provides a point of departure for measuring the extra benefit which current arrangements confer on tenants (and hence the effective cost to central and local government).

Figure 9.1 gives an example of what this kind of formula would imply, depending on the number of years of tenancy which the purchaser would otherwise have enjoyed. It shows the percentage discount required to leave the purchaser in an unchanged position, discounting future costs and benefits at a real interest rate of 3.5 per cent. At the 'fair' discount, the net cost of purchase equals the discounted value of the dwelling (assuming that this increases at 1 per cent per year in real terms) at the end of the period for which it would have been occupied, plus the value of saving the stream of rents which would otherwise have been paid in excess of the management, maintenance, and depreciation costs which the purchaser now faces rather than the landlord. The calculation assumes that the purchase would be fully financed by a mortgage at 10.745 per cent (that is, assuming 7 per cent inflation), over twenty-five years (or the remaining tenancy period, if shorter) and allows for the benefits of mortgage interest relief at the current 25 per cent basic tax rate.[1] (See

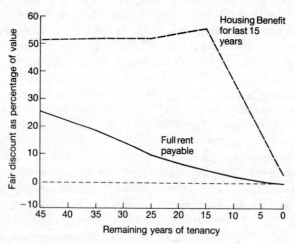

Figure 9.1 'Fair' discount percentage
Net rent 1%, gross rent 3.56%

Chapters 4, 5, and 14 for discussion of the plausibility of these assumptions and of those used below.)

The straightforward case is shown by the lower line, giving the result if rent would have been payable in full throughout the remaining years and would each year have equalled 1 per cent of current capital value in excess of management and depreciation costs. This would correspond, in 1989/90 terms, to a typical local authority house worth £30,000 with a rent of about £20.50 per week, allowing for management, maintenance, and depreciation totalling £14.77 per week. The 'fair' discount falls from about 25 per cent if forty-five years of tenancy would have been expected, to a small *negative* discount (essentially offsetting the value of mortgage relief) if only one or two years remained. The main reason for this pattern is that the shorter the period of tenancy would have been, the less the value of the forgone benefits from paying sub-economic rents.

The second line in the figure shows the 'fair' discount if the tenant could have looked forward to receiving Housing Benefit covering all of rent for the last fifteen years of the tenancy, say in retirement. Here the pattern is very different. By exercising the Right to Buy, someone would sacrifice the help they would have received through Housing Benefit in retirement, as owners receive no help with their repair, maintenance, or depreciation costs even if their incomes are low (except, perhaps an improvement grant if the standard of the property becomes poor enough—see below). The extra discount required to offset this loss takes the fair discount for someone with forty-five years of tenancy ahead to over 50 per cent. In this case, the discount rises slightly as the prospective length of tenancy falls, until the prospective number of 'rent-free' years itself falls.

Innumerable sets of assumptions could, of course, be made, leading to some variation in the pattern shown in the figure (see DoE 1980 for a related sensitivity exercise of this kind). What this analysis makes clear, however, is the importance of whether those exercising the Right to Buy would have ended up receiving Housing Benefit later in their tenancies. If they would not have done, the current discounts—ranging from 32 per cent up to 60 or even 70 per cent— much more than compensate for the loss of sub-economic rents at current rent levels, except for those with very long periods as tenants to look forward to (a result which is robust to relatively large variations in the key assumption made about rents). Notably, the fair discount falls for shorter prospective tenancies, in contrast to the rise in actual discounts with years of completed tenancy, so that the *net* benefit of current arrangements rises even more steeply than the gross discount.[2] By contrast, if rent would have been covered by benefit for the last fifteen years of a tenancy, the actual discounts are not enough to compensate for the loss of this advantage except, perhaps, for those qualifying for discounts of approaching 60 per cent.

Unsurprisingly, this analysis reinforces the finding that the advantage of exercising the Right to Buy depends on the tenant's economic circumstances—it is of greater value to those who can look forward to higher incomes in the future. The main cause of this lies, however, in the asymmetry of benefit rules for low-income owners and tenants, a topic returned to later in the book.

Two further points should be made. First, the kinds of calculation given above understate the value of exercising the Right to Buy, in that once someone has purchased they have greater freedom in what they choose to do in the future. Subsidies to local authority and housing association tenants come 'tied' to a particular property with a particular standard of service, with only restricted chances to vary either. Even if exercising the Right to Buy had a zero effect in net present-value terms, it could well still be to the tenant's advantage.

Secondly, there is an effect on the remaining tenants from consequential changes in the balance of the Housing Revenue Account following a sale to be considered. Under the pre-1990 Housing Subsidy system the result would have been complicated, depending on the balance between the fall in actual costs and the reduction in subsidy (resulting from the stock being one dwelling smaller together with a reduction corresponding—for some reason—to 65 per cent of 'notional loan charges' relating to the property sold). Under the 1990 HRA Subsidy system described in Chapter 7, the result is simplicity itself for the reasons discussed above in connection with large-scale transfers. Virtually all that matters in the new system are the guidelines for rent and for management and maintenance for each authority, and the loss of a dwelling has no effect on the rents and spending implied for those remaining, regardless of the sales price or discount (unless the rent of the dwelling or the spending on it vary from the authority's average, in which case there may be the same kind of effects as with large-scale transfers). To the extent that the Right to Buy does imply a net benefit to those exercising it, it is central government which faces the corresponding loss.

IMPROVEMENT GRANTS

Grants for repair, improvement, or the provision of missing 'standard amenities' are the most important form of direct help (as opposed to the indirect help going through the tax system) given by the government to owner-occupiers and private landlords. As the public spending figures discussed in Chapter 3 showed, commitment to this area of policy has varied greatly. From a peak of 244,000 grants in Great Britain in 1974, the number was cut to below 100,000 between 1976 and 1981 (see Table 3.7). There was then a boom in the number of grants—and more generous rates of grant—with about 300,000 approved in each of 1983 and 1984. Since then the number has fallen to about half this level.

As with much of the rest of housing finance, the system of improvement grants has been revised by legislation in the late 1980s. In this case the new system is planned to be introduced in mid-1990. In many ways the changes represent a major simplification of the incoherent and disjointed structure which had evolved by then (for details of that system, see Bucknall 1984, and for a discussion of it see Walentowicz 1988). Under the old system (following the 1980 Housing Act) there were four different kinds of grant:

1. *Improvement grants* for conversion, improvements, or adaptation for people with disabilities;
2. *Intermediate grants* for missing standard amenities;[3]
3. *Repairs grants* for substantial repairs to pre-1919 dwellings;
4. *Special grants* for 'houses in multiple occupation' (HMOs) for standard amenities and providing fire escapes.

The rules for these grants varied. Some were 'mandatory', that is, the local authority had to provide them, including all intermediate grants and some special and repair grants where the local authority had served a notice that work had to be carried out. Others, including all improvement grants, were provided at the authority's discretion. The conditions for receipt in some cases included a minimum age of dwelling (for instance, pre-1961 for improvement and intermediate grants but pre-1919 for repairs grant), or a maximum rateable value (for improvement and repairs grants). Some conditions were less onerous for properties in 'General Improvement Areas' (GIAs) or 'Housing Action Areas' (HAAs). Maximum grant rates (which the authority had to give in mandatory cases) also varied from 50 per cent up to 90 per cent depending on the kind of grant, the date of application, the kind of property, whether located in a GIA or HAA, and whether the applicant was a 'hardship' case. Different maximum amounts of 'eligible expenses' applied to the different grants and varied across the country. Apart, however, from the proxy effects of the rateable value limits and of poor housing conditions creating the need for work to be carried out in the first place, the grants were not means-tested. Their aim was the improvement of stock in poor condition, rather than directly to help those with low incomes.

Given the complexity of the old system, it is hard to argue with the rationale given for the new grant system:

> There is overlap between the scope of different grants and in some cases there are inappropriate restrictions on the amount of repair and improvement that can be grant-aided. The rules are now difficult for applicants to understand and for local authorities to administer. The Government believes that the structure of the system should be greatly simplified and proposes to introduce a single form of grant for people who lack the resources to do all or part of the work themselves. It will cover both repair and improvement up to clearly defined standards. (DoE 1987c, para. 4)

The controversial element lies in the means-testing which will be applied to the new grants.

Under the new system there will be a single kind of grant replacing the previous four. Rateable value limits will be removed, as will age limits (except for properties built within the last ten years and thus covered by housebuilders' guarantees). Grants will be mandatory if they bring properties up to a revised standard of 'fitness' (including lack of 'serious' disrepair, freedom from damp, natural light and ventilation, and with the old standard amenities). Discretionary grants will then be available to bring property up to—but not beyond—a higher 'revised target standard' (including being in 'reasonable repair', and covering wiring, lighting, heating, and insulation). GIAs and HAAs are replaced by the single category of 'Renewal Areas', in which authorities are expected to focus their work, have wider enforcement powers, and where they may be eligible for greater central government support (limited to 75 per cent of the cost of grants in most other cases).

Under this system the various flat rates of grant are replaced by grants of *up to* 100 per cent of the costs, but with the amount payable dependent on the claimant's resources. The way this will work was explained in a further consultation paper (DoE 1989*f*) and is based on the system of Housing Benefit introduced from April 1988. As such it suffers from similar problems to that system (see Chapter 10).

Under the new system 100 per cent of costs will be met for owners with incomes at or below a 'threshold' of resources, based on the appropriate Income Support rate plus a margin (£20 in 1990/1). Above this level grant will be reduced by an amount depending on the size of loan (at a 'standard national rate of interest'—15.4 per cent in May 1990—and repaid over ten years) which could be serviced by 20 per cent of the excess of annual income over the threshold.

There are two problems with this kind of system. First, the means test effectively applies a rule designed on the basis of income over a ten-year period to income assessed over a single year or less. The example given in the 1989 consultation paper makes the problem plain. At 1988/89 benefit levels, a family of four would have been entitled to a full grant of, say, £10,000 if their net annual income was £5,673. The effect of the means test would be that they would receive no help at all if their income exceeded £14,708. In other words, a £9,035 increase in net income in the year of assessment leads to a loss of entitlement to grant of £10,000! With the higher interest rates applying in mid-1990, the tax rate would be a little lower—almost exactly 100 per cent of annual income. Quite apart from any labour market effects of this kind of tax rate, it means that people will pick the date at which to be assessed very carefully—the year immediately after retirement may become a popular one for grant applications.

Second, the grant is based on 100 per cent of eligible costs, less an amount depending only on income. Even for those only receiving a partial grant, costs £100 higher will mean grant £100 higher. This both greatly weakens the incentive for grant recipients to control costs and opens up the scope for collusion between them and a friendly builder doing the work. To prevent abuse and keep the system under control, local authorities will have to exercise much tighter supervision of cost estimates than used to be the case. The simplicity of the system's structure in one sense will necessitate more administration of a different kind (this is an example of the general problem of 'up-marketing' discussed in the next chapter).

SUMMARY

- The price set for large-scale transfers of local authority stock to a new landlord is supposed to reflect its tenanted market value, allowing for outstanding repairs. This may imply a negative price—a 'dowry'.

- This price may well be very sensitive to the rents previously charged, and so future rents may depend on the date of transfer (although constrained by the vague protection of the 'Tenants Guarantee').

- To cope with the cash flow problems arising from the front-loading problem and to encourage transfers to take place, new landlords may be given what turns out to be a good deal in the long run, although the financial arrangements expose the new landlords to a high degree of risk.

- The new HRA Subsidy largely protects the remaining tenants from being affected by the terms of transfer of other parts of the stock.

- Discounts under the Right to Buy currently rise with length of tenancy from 32 per cent to 60 per cent (or even 70 per cent), with a maximum of £50,000.

- The actual discount does not value the *net* benefit to tenants exercising the Right to Buy, as by doing so they forgo the opportunity to pay sub-economic rents in future, possibly with help from Housing Benefit.

- At current gross rents, actual discounts significantly exceed the 'fair' discount which would just balance these effects. Such 'fair' discounts generally fall with shorter prospective tenancies, in contrast to the actual rise with length of completed tenancy.

- Allowing for the possibility of future Housing Benefit receipt, however, the 'fair' discount could be much higher, possibly higher than those actually available.

- The new improvement grant system greatly simplifies the previous four types of grant with varying qualification conditions. However, the means test now used to calculate entitlement involves a 'tax rate' of around 100 per cent on current income, and the system removes any incentive for the recipient to control costs, creating the need for tighter monitoring.

NOTES

1. If the real interest rate is π, the real annual increase in house prices h, management and maintenance costs are a constant proportion m of current value, depreciation a proportion d of current value, total rent a proportion $(n + m + d)$ of current value (n being the net rent after deduction of management, maintenance, and depreciation), the period of occupancy T years of which rent is paid for the first T' (the later years being covered by Housing Benefit), the length of the mortgage L, then the fair price (FP) for a unit value dwelling is given by:

$$FP = \frac{[(1 + h)^T (1 + \pi)^{-T} + (n + m + d)\, CF(T') - (m + d)\, CF(T)]}{(1 - VMIR)}$$

where $CF(x)$ is the cumulative value of a stream of payments made at the end of each of x years rising annually at the rate h (after the first year) discounted at π, and $VMIR$ is the present value of mortgage interest relief on a unit of borrowing (see Hills 1987c, p. 102). Note that discounting at the real interest rate is equivalent to assuming that alternative investments for owners and tenants would be effectively tax-free. For discussion of the importance of this assumption and of the effects of alternative benchmarks see Chapters 11 and 12.

The 'fair' discount percentage, D, is then given by

$$D = (1 - FP).$$

2. The dominant idea behind the actual rising schedule of discounts with length of *completed* tenancy appears to be that a greater discount is needed to 'catch up' on the position which someone could have reached as an owner-occupier since the beginning. Strictly, this will only be so if the rents paid so far during the tenancy embodied a *smaller* subsidy in economic terms than the value of tax advantages to owners, which does not appear to be the case (see Chapter 14). If it was, there would not be a positive 'fair' discount in compensation for future losses of the kind shown in the figure (except in respect of lost Housing Benefit).

3. The 'standard amenities' were: a bath or shower; a wash basin; a kitchen sink; a hot and cold water supply serving each of these; and exclusive use of an inside WC.

PART III

Housing Benefits

10

Housing Benefit: Principles and Problems

Unlike the general 'bricks and mortar' subsidies described in Chapters 7 and 8, Housing Benefit is an income-related benefit, administered by local authorities, with the size of individual entitlements depending on a household's rent, income, and composition.[1] Its scale has become increasingly important: since 1982/3 the cost of means-tested assistance with rent has exceeded that of general subsidies to tenants (see Table 3.1). In 1989/90 the total cost of Housing Benefit paid in respect of rent (as opposed to rates or the Poll Tax) was £4.1 billion (HM Treasury 1990, tables 14.1 and 14.2; GB figure). Over 4.1 million households were receiving rent rebates or allowances—worth roughly £1,000 each per year on average—including nearly 60 per cent of local authority tenants (ibid. and DoE 1989a, table 9.3). The Housing Benefit system is now more important in determining the amounts which most tenants pay for their housing than the systems of subsidy to local authorities and housing associations described in earlier chapters.

The general issues in the policy choice between general subsidies to keep housing costs down for all and means-tested benefits have been outlined in Chapter 2. The clear advantage of means-tested benefits is their 'targeting' on those who—according to the means test—need them most. The cost of getting a certain amount of assistance to this group will be less than that of general subsidies, some of which would go to others. There are, however, problems.

TAKE-UP AND THE 'COSTS OF CLAIMING'

In 1985, 22 per cent of those eligible for Housing Benefit for rent or rates—1.8 million households—failed to claim the benefit (HM Treasury 1990, table 14.16; GB figure). Those entitled to larger amounts were more likely to claim, so the amount unclaimed was 10 per cent of the total available. None the less, a drawback of the switch from general subsidies to Housing Benefit since 1980 has been that some low-income households have not been protected from rent increases because of their failure—for whatever reason—to claim Housing Benefit. Those reasons include: ignorance; the cost in time, fares, and hassle of claiming; and the stigma attached to claiming means-tested benefits (see Bradshaw and Deacon 1983). If entitlement is high enough, more people find it worth while to claim, but they still face these costs of claiming, which, in aggregate, could be substantial. Fry and Stark (1987) found that a short-term unemployed family would only be more likely to claim Supplementary Benefit (SB) than not if entitlement exceeded £9 per week in 1984/5, although for pensioners a smaller amount was needed. If Housing Benefit recipients needed a weekly entitlement of £5 on average for claiming to be worth while, the 4.1 million claimants could be suffering a disbenefit of more than £1 billion per year—offsetting a quarter of the cash value of the benefits. As with administrative costs (totalling over £200 million in 1989/90; HM Treasury 1990, table 14.2) of running the means test, these costs of claiming are much lower with systems which distribute subsidy automatically.

THE 'POVERTY TRAP'

Figure 10.1 illustrates another side-effect of reliance on means-testing. It shows what net income a couple with two children (one aged under 11, one over) would have ended up with at different earnings levels in 1989/90, taking account of tax, National Insurance, Child Benefit, Family Credit, and Housing Benefit, assuming that their rent was £25 per week and their Poll Tax £6 per week each (and that benefits were, in fact, claimed).

As intended, Housing Benefit goes to those with the lowest incomes, but is withdrawn as income rises. This contributes to the phenomenon that over a wide range changes in earnings have little effect on net income. In this case, an increase in weekly earnings from £32 to £163 only increases net income by £14. As a result of the combination of tax and withdrawal of Family Credit and Housing Benefit, this couple would only keep 10p out of every £1 earned. It is as if they faced a tax rate of nearly 90 per cent—more than twice the top income tax rate of 40 per cent.

In fact over some income ranges, this 'effective marginal tax rate' can reach 96 per cent. Between earnings of £84 per week (where income tax starts) and £126 per week (where the rent rebate would

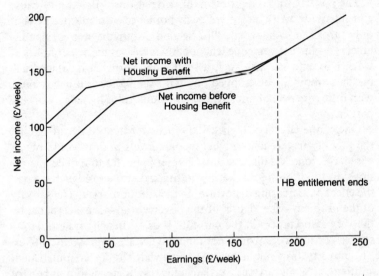

Figure 10.1 The poverty trap, 1989/90
Two-child couple, rent £25/week

drop to zero in this case) the effect of an extra ten pounds of earnings would be as follows:

	Increase in gross earnings:		£10.00
less	National insurance (at 9%):	£0.90	
less	Income tax (at 25%):	£2.50	
gives	Increase in after-tax income:		£6.60
less	Reduction in Family Credit (70% of £6.60):	£4.62	
gives	Increase in income for calculating Housing Benefit:		£1.98
less	Reduction in rent rebate (65% of £1.98):	£1.29	
less	Reduction in Poll Tax rebate (15% of £1.98):	£0.30	
gives	Increase in final net income:		£0.39

On top of the effect of taxation, the Family Credit 'taper' is 70 per cent (i.e. benefit is cut by 70p for every £1 increase in after-tax income), and the rent and Poll Tax rebate tapers are 65 per cent and 15 per cent respectively (calculated on income after allowing for tax and Family Credit).

The poverty trap is a problem for two reasons. First, it may cause a problem for 'work incentives': why bother to earn an extra £10 if it only turns out to be worth 39p? Second, it may be seen as inequitable: is it fair that someone who greatly increases his or her hours of work may end up with such a small change in net income? Such families are, in effect, trapped on their existing level of net income, with little prospect of improving their standard of living by working harder.

One of the effects of higher real rents over the last decade is that the poverty trap reaches higher income levels than it would otherwise have done. As discussed in Chapter 2, moves to reduce 'distortions' in the housing market by cutting general subsidies have had the effect of increasing distortions in the labour market. The severity of the problem—the 'depth' of the poverty trap—is exacerbated by the very steep tapers in the current Housing Benefit system. However, a cut in tapers would not unambiguously improve incentives. The poverty trap might become somewhat shallower, but benefit entitlement would extend further, affecting increasing numbers of people as the trap extended towards average earnings.

'UP-MARKETING'

A less well-known problem of housing benefits is that they can remove any net effect on recipients of a change in gross housing costs. Theoretically this could lead to recipients deciding that, as government would foot the bill, they might as well go 'up-market' and move to more expensive accommodation than they otherwise would. At the bottom of the income scale one of the main intentions of housing benefits and other subsidies is precisely to ensure that even the poorest end up able to pay for accommodation of at least a minimum standard; higher up the income scale encouraging greater housing consumption may be less of a priority.

In the current British system, the phenomenon is most obvious in the case of those either receiving Income Support (IS) or with equivalent incomes and therefore entitled to full rent rebates. As a result of the way benefit is now calculated (see below), it is also true of those only receiving partial rent rebates: even if benefit starts off contributing only a few pounds towards rent, it will cover any rent increase pound for pound—the 'marginal cost of housing' is reduced to zero.

Fully insulating beneficiaries from the effects of changing rents may strike many readers as wholly admirable. For some recipients—those on the lowest incomes—it may well be. Not only would they be worst hit by any rent increase, but many will have no realistic option of choosing their own accommodation: going up-market simply is not an option for those being allocated housing through local authorities or housing associations.

However, those on higher incomes may well have more options. Even if few would actually take advantage of the system (either by moving or through collusion with landlords), the danger that government could face an open-ended bill has led to several measures being taken to tighten up on claims generally, particularly since April 1988 (when the current structure came in). These include the use of rent officers to set 'market' limits to the amount of rent eligible for benefit (strictly speaking, the limits apply to the subsidy which local authorities receive, not to the actual claim itself), and stricter enforcement of existing powers to withhold benefit if the accommodation is 'unnecessarily large'. Concern to avoid the problem may also have contributed towards the steepness of the benefit tapers—restricting the income range affected. It would also stand in the way of extending the current system to help with the costs of owner-occupiers (who have much more realistic options to go up-market). In all four ways the generosity of the system in one sense may make inevitable its lack of generosity in others.

The phenomenon has had the ironic effect that as the Government has increased rents to get closer to an undistorted housing market, more tenants have become eligible for a benefit which makes their gross rents immaterial, putting them even further away from the pressure of market forces. 'Up-marketing' may not have mattered very much when private rents were mostly set by rent officers through the fair rent system; with deregulation, it becomes much more important.

GENERAL REQUIREMENTS FOR HOUSING BENEFITS

Effects on take-up, the poverty trap, and up-marketing are clearly important in evaluating a particular structure for benefit. To them can be added three others:

Treatment of those on the lowest incomes

The most recent government review of housing benefit (DHSS 1985*a*) concluded that it is not possible to include a flat-rate element for housing costs in the state's minimum income safety net—currently known as Income Support (formerly National Assistance and then Supplementary Benefit), echoing Beveridge's admission of failure to solve this 'problem of rent' (1942, pp. 77–84). Instead, recipients have been entitled to assistance with all of their actual rent. The relative treatment of those with incomes just above their IS level is then of importance for two reasons. If they are not entitled to benefit at least approaching 100 per cent of rent, there may be a problem of 'horizontal equity'—those with similar incomes may be treated differently depending on receipt of IS. Others may find themselves having to make a complicated choice between benefits—this was a particular problem with the system applying before 1982/3.

Administration and simplicity

Means-tested benefits tend to have higher administrative costs than other kinds of benefit or subsidy. The more complicated the means test, the higher these will be. Simplicity may not only reduce administration costs and the chance of error, but also make entitlement easier for claimants to understand and improve take-up. On the other hand, greater transparency may make it more likely that recipients will understand and react to any undesirable incentives built into the system.

Distributional effects and revenue cost

Finally—but probably most importantly so far as governments are concerned—there are the questions of the overall cost of any scheme (or modification to it) and of who benefits from it and who gains or loses from any change. Since 1980 the cost of Housing Benefit has risen rapidly (see Chapter 3), provoking a series of cuts to its generosity in an attempt to hold back this growth. Since those who have lost as a result of such cuts had low enough incomes to qualify for benefit before the change at least, the distributional effect of these cuts has been highly controversial.

THE EVOLUTION OF HOUSING BENEFIT

The current system of Housing Benefit can be traced back to three roots. First, since the 1930 Housing Act, local authorities had been permitted (if not particularly encouraged) to charge differential rents to tenants depending on incomes (see Malpass 1990*b*). Rent rebate schemes gradually evolved until the 1972 Housing Finance Act introduced a national 'model scheme' for rent rebates to be applied by all authorities (with limited discretion to make some aspects more generous) for their own tenants and equivalent rent allowances for other tenants. Second, what was National Assistance and later became SB, made up the difference between recipients' 'resources' (net income) and 'needs', the latter calculated as the total of their 'scale rate' (depending on the kind of family), special needs, and their housing costs, including rent, rates, water rates, and mortgage interest. Thirdly, rate rebates were introduced in the late 1960s to mitigate the regressive effect of rates.

1972 TO 1982: RENT REBATES AND SUPPLEMENTARY BENEFIT

Figure 10.2 shows the amount of help with a rent of £10 per week a pensioner couple could have received depending on gross income in November 1981 from either SB or rent rebates (the position was

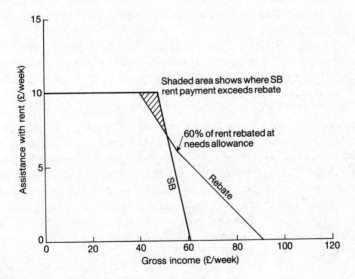

Figure 10.2 The 'better-off' problem, 1981/2
Pensioner couple, rent £10/week

much the same throughout the period from 1972 to 1982). For those entitled to SB (such as pensioners or the unemployed), benefit would cover 100 per cent of rent for net incomes up to the family's scale rate, in this case £47.35 per week. Above this, there would still be entitlement to SB up to the point at which net income equalled the total of the scale rate and housing costs (allowing here for rates and water rates totalling of £3.50 per week). This 'housing only' payment covered part of housing costs, with a 100 per cent taper on additional income.

Alternatively (and for those in employment, the only choice), the family could claim a rent rebate. This was calculated according to different principles. If gross income equalled a certain 'needs allowance' (depending on family composition and only tenuously related to the SB scale rates), a 60 per cent rent rebate would be given, so in the case illustrated in Figure 10.2, if gross income was £55.60, the rent rebate would be £6 per week. If gross income was any higher, the rebate would be reduced by 17 per cent of the excess, until (at an income of £89.72 in this case) the rebate fell below the then minimum payment of 20p. Alternatively, for every £1 by which income fell short of the needs allowance the rebate would be increased by 25p until (for incomes at or below £39.60 here) a £10 rent would be fully rebated. Rate rebates worked on similar principles, but with different tapers.

The rationale for this structure can be found in the problems outlined above. Rebates hinged around payments equal to 60 per cent of rent plus or minus amounts depending only on income, so all recipients had to pay at least 40 per cent of any change in rent—thus avoiding the up-marketing problem. The change in tapers at the needs allowance can be traced back to the shape of the tax and benefit systems in place when the national rebate system was introduced in 1972, when needs allowances were generally below income tax thresholds. The relatively steep 25 per cent taper did not therefore overlap with income tax. At higher incomes the poverty trap was more of a concern, so a shallower taper was used. This rationale disappeared as needs allowances overtook tax allowances, but the 'kink' in the tapers survived in this form until April 1983.

This structure had various shortcomings:

1. The existence of two parallel systems led to confusion for some people—in particular, pensioners with incomes just above their

scale rate—who faced a complicated choice between two benefits based on different principles. Those just above the scale rate would be better off with a 'housing only' payment. After a switchover point (a gross income of £51.29 in the example in Figure 10.2, if rent had been the only factor), rebates would be better. The Supplementary Benefits Commission (SBC) estimated that in 1979 400,000 households were making the wrong choice (quoted in Kemp 1987, p. 173). Getting rid of this 'better-off problem' was one of the reasons behind calls for a 'unified housing benefit' from the SBC and others in the 1970s.

2. The treatment of those receiving SB covering 100 per cent of housing costs involved administrative duplication. In many cases, the local authority sent out a rent demand which the tenant took to the local DHSS office, which eventually paid out cash to cover rent in full (having checked that this was correct). The tenant then paid this over to the local authority (or in some cases did not, running into arrears despite receiving full assistance with rent). The major aim of the 1982/3 reforms was to short-circuit this process.

3. Including housing costs in SB was a barrier to long-term reforms to reduce the numbers dependent on it by increasing the value of non-means-tested benefits like the state pension and Child Benefit. As David Donnison, Chairman of the SBC later put it,

> While [SB] continued to be the main instrument for meeting the housing costs of the poorest people, everyone who claimed the benefit—even for a day or two—had to be put through an elaborate means test, a central purpose of which was to pay for their housing. If that problem could be solved in other and better ways, 130,000 people could be got off supplementary benefit altogether. (1982, pp. 189–90)

4. The system violated horizontal equity, in that different amounts of assistance with identical housing costs could be given to two people with equal net incomes, but where one was entitled to SB and the other was not. The first had the option of (potentially more generous) housing only payments; the second only of rebates.

THE 1982/3 REFORM

Proposals for reform were presented in a consultation document, *Assistance with Housing Costs* (DoE 1981). All four shortcomings of the existing system described above were given as justifications of the proposals, but their overriding objective was to reduce the administrative load on staff in local DHSS offices:

Although because of the 'better-off' and other problems there were good reasons for reforming the system of assistance with housing costs that existed prior to April 1983, the current [pre-1988] housing benefit system was not introduced because of them. Instead, the 1982/83 reform was introduced for other reasons, most importantly the fact that it offered the prospect of civil service job savings while at the same time facilitating a simplification of SB and gave local authorities rent direct for SB recipients (hence savings in arrears and in collection costs). (Kemp 1987, p. 184)

The central point of the reform (eventually carried out in two stages in November 1982 and April 1983) was the introduction of certification and the removal of the need for DHSS staff to know claimants' rents or rates. This saved the DHSS 2,500 staff posts (DHSS 1985*a*, p. 3) at a time when reduction of the size of the civil service was an overriding priority. It also offered local authorities the prospect of cutting collection costs and arrears. To achieve this it was, however, important to establish a cut-off point, below which people would be entitled to SB with full assistance with rent and rates, and above which they would be on rebates. This meant removing the possibility of 'housing only' payments and replacing the 'better-off' problem with a simple choice.

The current Housing Benefit system does indeed achieve this—the IS rates give precisely this clear cut-off. The 1982/3 reforms did not. A main reason for this can be traced to the constraint imposed that the reform should be carried out at 'nil cost'—if any recipients gained, others had to lose an equal amount—combined with a concern to minimise the scale of losses for the losers (later cuts to Housing Benefit displayed less fastidiousness): 'it was not so much the nil cost constraint as such that prevented a unified scheme from being introduced as the likely political opposition that would have resulted if it had been introduced on a nil cost basis' (Kemp 1987, p. 176).

The changes to the rebate formula—illustrated in Figure 10.3— were therefore designed to make the minimum changes to cut down on housing only payments and the better-off problem. As these mainly affected low-income pensioners (whose SB entitlements depended on the more generous 'long-term' scale rates), the benefit formula was made more generous for them. The 25 per cent rent

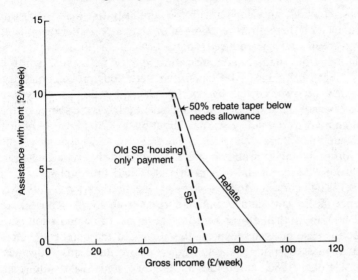

Figure 10.3 The April 1983 reform
Pensioner couple, rent £10/week

taper below the needs allowance was increased to 50 per cent for pensioners (the corresponding rate rebate taper was also raised and a small 'pensioner addition' made to needs allowances), so that a full rebate would be given at a higher income than before. In the case illustrated in Figure 10.3—still with a rent of £10—this did remove the need for a 'housing only' payment for rent. The other changes to the rebate formulae were designed to recoup the cost of this: the tapers above the needs allowance for pensioners and non-pensioners were raised to 21 from 17 per cent for rent and from 6 to 7 per cent for rates.

Even before it was implemented the reform was heavily criticised, for instance as making it necessary 'to create an administrative system of nightmarish complexity' (CPAG 1981). After it happened, *The Times* described it as 'the biggest administrative fiasco in the history of the welfare state' (quoted by Kemp 1986, p. 2). As Berthoud put it, 'Housing benefit . . . never looked liked living up to its advance billing as a "comprehensive" solution. It was just the two old schemes tied together—with red tape' (1989a, p. 90).

The reform failed in two key ways. First, the local authorities had enormous difficulty coping with the administrative load which was dumped on them. In May 1984—more than a year after the scheme had been fully introduced—only a third of local authorities thought they had its administration 'pretty well under control' (Walker 1985, table 2.3). Second, the 'better-off' problem had not, in fact, been solved, but had been replaced by the possibility of a new benefit, Housing Benefit Supplement (HBS), the source of the 'nightmarish complexity' warned about by the Child Poverty Action Group and others.

Both of these problems were heightened by rent increases. Between design of the reform in 1980/1 and full implementation in 1983/4, cuts in Housing Subsidy meant that local authority rents in England and Wales had risen from £7.71 per week to £14.00, more than 50 per cent in real terms. In combination with the increase in unemployment this increased the numbers eligible for rebates, despite the steeper tapers above the needs allowance. In October 1980, authorities in England and Wales had been dealing with about 1.3 million rent rebate and allowance cases. In April 1983 they were coping with 1.7 million equivalent 'standard Housing Benefit cases' plus 2 million 'certificated' rent cases (DoE 1989a, table 11.3; there were similar increases in rate rebate cases). Certification for local authority tenants—where it worked and there were no complications such as 'non-dependants' in the household—did not require any assessment of rent or income by the authority. However, certification for private tenants simply passed the task of rent assessment from the DHSS to the authorities, with the added complication that recipients now had to deal with two different offices—the DHSS for income assessment and payment of the basic amount of SB, and the local authority for rent assessment and payment of cash for the rent allowance. As a result, despite no longer having to collect rent from their own certificated tenants, the new staff taken on by the local authorities—3,500 in 1983/4 (DHSS 1985a, p. 3)—outnumbered the staff savings made by the DHSS.

The second consequence of the higher rents was that the increased taper for pensioners failed to solve the better-off problem. In the example in Figure 10.3—with a rent of £10—there was no overlap between rebate entitlement with the new taper and what would have been the SB 'housing only' rent payment. However, for rents any higher than £11.80 per week there would be an overlap.

Had real rents remained at their 1980/1 levels, the potential problem would only have affected a minority of local authority tenants. By 1983/4, most rents were high enough for there to be a potential overlap.

Where there was an overlap, claimants could have incomes too high to be eligible for SB (under the new rules which abolished 'housing only' payments) but have rebates too small to make up their final resources to the minimum income including housing costs supposedly guaranteed by SB. Under its original proposals (DoE 1981), the Government would have left this hole in the social security 'safety net' open. As the reform was finally implemented, claimants in this position were allowed to claim Housing Benefit Supplement on top of their rebates to make up the shortfall. This was, however, very complicated to work out, worsening both administration and take-up. About 200,000 people were claiming HBS in November 1984 (DHSS 1985a, p. 38). Allowing for those who failed to take it up, as many people were affected by the HBS problem after the reform as had made the wrong choice under the better-off problem before it.

CUTS AND THE HOUSING BENEFIT REVIEW, 1983 TO 1987

During the next four years, the DHSS (which had now taken over full responsibility for the benefit) cut back the generosity of the scheme on every occasion bar one that benefits were 'uprated' for inflation. As Table 10.1 shows, by April 1987 the total of rent and rates tapers for those with incomes above the needs allowance was 46 per cent—double its pre-April 1983 level. As a result, for a given level of rent or rates, assistance extended to incomes roughly half as far above the needs allowances as it would have done before. These cuts gave the DHSS substantial savings and created large numbers of losers at each stage, contrasting with the 'zero net cost but minimise losses' philosophy which had constrained the 1982/3 reforms.

An official review of the whole area was set up virtually as soon as the reform had been carried out, largely in response to the difficulties which authorities were having coping with the new system (see Kemp 1984). The review team did not, however, recommend a return of responsibility for administration from the authorities,

TABLE 10.1 *Housing Benefit means test 'tapers'*

	Rent	Rates	Poll Tax[a]
(a) System before April 1988			
Tapers above the needs allowance[b]			
(% of gross income)			
Up to March 1983	17	6	—
April 1983	21	7	—
April 1984	26	9	—
November 1984	29	9	—
November 1985	29	13	—
July 1986	29	13	—
April 1987	33	13	—
(b) System since April 1988			
Taper on net income (%)	65	20	15
Equivalent taper on gross income (%)[c]	43	13	10

[a] From April 1989 in Scotland and April 1990 in England and Wales.

[b] Tapers below needs allowances were 25% for rent and 8% for rates until March 1988 for non-pensioners and until April 1983 for pensioners, when they became 50% and 20% respectively.

[c] Allowing for 25% income tax and 9% National Insurance Contributions (but not Family Credit).

finding that the original arguments advanced by the SBC for the 1982/3 transfer continued to apply (DHSS 1985*a*, p. 19). Instead, as the review team put it,

Such an early review is an indication of the concern expressed at the complexities of the scheme and the difficulties experienced both by those claiming benefit and those repsonsible for its administration. It is clear to us that these difficulties can no longer be regarded as "teething troubles" or as minor problems capable of solution through further amendments to the regulations. They run deeper than this and point to inherent flaws in the structure and scope of the scheme. (DHSS 1985*a*, p. v)

The evidence submitted to the review (see Kemp and Raynsford 1984) was virtually unanimous in identifying the crucial flaw in the system as being the fact that the formula for 'standard' Housing Benefit did not guarantee 100 per cent assistance with rent and rates for those with incomes at or below SB scale rates, creating the need for Housing Benefit Supplement. Most respondents called for a simplified system, under which entitlement would be based on 100 per cent assistance for incomes equal to the SB scale rates, less amounts depending on a 'single taper' (or one each for rent and rates) applied to any income above this level.

This structure was in fact what the review team recommended and was eventually implemented in April 1988. They also suggested that 'In the longer term, the Government should consider extending the scheme to cover mortgage interest payments and applying a single rate of withdrawal, for all housing costs together, as income rises' (DHSS 1985a, p. vii). This recommendation was carefully balanced—owner-occupiers would have greater costs eligible for assistance, but with a faster rate of withdrawal than had applied to rates alone—although it opened up the possibility of extending 'up-marketing' problems to mortgage costs. In its Green Paper on the overall reform of social security (DHSS 1985b and c), the Government rejected the idea of extension to mortgage costs, but accepted a combined taper. This would have meant very much quicker withdrawal of assistance for owner-occupiers' rates than under the old system, and so large losses for many pensioners. In the event, the Government backed down and retained separate rent and rate tapers (DHSS 1985d).

It kept, however, the proposal that maximum assistance with rates (or the Poll Tax) should be cut to 80 per cent, even for those on what was now Income Support. Its motivation was a version of the up-marketing problem: in the Government's view there was a problem of 'accountability' created by some voters in local elections being unaffected by the level of rates needed to finance high spending because they received full rebates. With a rebate formula based on 100 per cent of rates less an amount depending only on income, this would have been extended to partial rate rebate recipients—they would also have been insulated from all rate increases.

This restriction may—or may not—solve the Government's 'accountability' problem, but it causes problems for claimants. The IS rates are said to include notional amounts for 20 per cent of the average amounts of rates or Poll Tax which claimants face.[2] For those living in authorities where local taxation is much higher than the average this still leaves a problem: a Poll Tax £250 per year above the 'average' would have a net cost to a married couple on IS

of £2 per week, not trivial compared with their IS level of £57.60 in
1990/1. This is, of course, part of the general pressure being applied
to local authority finances, described in Chapter 6.

THE CURRENT HOUSING BENEFIT SYSTEM:
APPRAISAL

Following the general reforms to the social security system in April
1988, the formula for calculating Housing and Community Charge
Benefits has become much simpler. Those receiving Income Support
receive all of their rent and 80 per cent of their Poll Tax (as do those
with incomes at or below the IS allowances for their household
type, even if they are not entitled to IS itself). For others assistance
with rent is given by:

Benefit *equals* Rent *minus* 0.65 (Net income *minus* Applicable
amount)

(subject to a minimum payment of 50p per week and with various
deductions if there are 'non-dependants' in the household), while
assistance for the Poll Tax is given by:

Benefit *equals* 80 per cent of Poll Tax *minus* 0.15 (Net income *minus*
Applicable amount)

(also with a 50p minimum). The 'Applicable amount' equals the IS
allowance for the particular household type, except in the case of
single parents, for whom the Housing Benefit and Poll Tax rebate
allowances are slightly more generous. It should be noted that the
means test is now based on *net* income, after allowing for tax,
National Insurance, half of occupational pension contributions,
and most social security benefits, including Family Credit and
Child Benefit.

In terms of the criteria for assessing housing benefit systems discussed at the start of this chapter, this system is designed to avoid the
need for Housing Benefit Supplement or a 'better-off' problem. The
use of the same income definitions and scales for assessing incomes
as Income Support also has equity advantages: assistance with rent
and the Poll Tax does not depend on eligibility for Income Support,
although assistance with mortgage interest still does (being available beyond tax relief for those on IS but not for others). In one
way—the formula for determining entitlement—the current Hous-

ing Benefit system is very simple. In others—in particular, the assessment of income and needs—it is more complicated than its predecessors, mainly as a result of the moulding of entitlement to match IS rules.

It is too early to tell whether the simpler formula and common means test will have improved take-up (the latest official figures refer to 1985). *A priori* one would expect the overall take-up percentages to have increased simply as a result of the steepening of the tapers and toughening of restrictions on amounts of capital—excluding equity in owner-occupied housing—claimants are allowed to have (a 'cut-off' set at £8,000 of capital in April 1988, but raised to £16,000 in 1990). These measures will have shifted the balance towards those with full rather than partial entitlement, increasing the average entitlement of those left within the system and so making take-up more likely. However, it would not be very convincing to claim an improvement in the effectiveness of a benefit on the grounds that those whom it ought to have reached before had now been removed from its scope. The test to be applied to the take-up figures for the new benefit when they arrive will be the figures for those entitled to partial benefit (the 'standard' cases).

Where the new system can be appraised is in terms of distribution, the poverty trap, and up-marketing. Figure 10.4 illustrates the end result of the changes between 1981/2 and 1989/90 in the treatment of single people with earnings. The lower line shows entitlement to help with a rent of £30 per week under the actual 1989/90 system (for a single person aged 25 or over; under 25s receive less). The higher line shows what entitlement would have been if the 1981/2 system had still been in place, but with the needs allowances and earnings disregards uprated in line with earnings growth. The two lines therefore give a measure of how those with earnings at constant proportions of the average would have been treated in the two periods. The results are dramatic: while at the lowest earnings there is little difference, the 1981/2 system would have extended up to earnings nearly twice as high in relation to the average as the 1989/90 system (for lower rents, the relative generosity of the 1981/2 system would be even greater, but for very high rents there are some earnings ranges where the 1989/90 system would be the more generous). The 1989/90 system is 'better targeted', or 'meaner', depending on one's viewpoint. Indeed, the rent taper in the current Housing Benefit system is so steep that the system is little more than the old

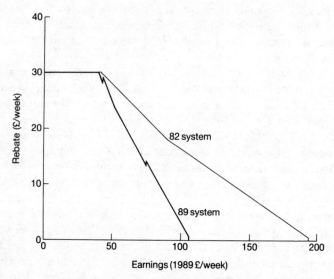

Figure 10.4 Housing Benefit, 1981/2 and 1989/90
Single people over 25, rent £30

SB housing only payments shown in Figure 10.2. The solution to the old 'better-off' problem turns out to have been the effective abolition of the old rebate system!

A further consequence—of some importance in the debate on 'affordable' housing association rents described in Chapter 8—is shown in Figure 10.5. Current Housing Benefit does not prevent net rent absorbing very high proportions of net income in some cases. For the example given—a £30 per week rent for a single person aged 25 or over—the ratio could be as high as 35 per cent (if aged under 25, the figure would be 38 per cent).[3] By contrast, the uprated 1981/2 system would have kept the maximum ratio below 20 per cent. If Housing Benefit had not been cut in the way it was after the DoE handed it over to the DHSS, the increases in gross rents resulting from the changes in housing association finance described in Chapter 8 could have been accomplished without causing the great 'affordability' problems which have in fact arisen.

It is hard to isolate one component of the poverty trap, but the combined 80 per cent taper on rent rebates and Poll Tax rebates would create a poverty trap—over a narrow income range—by it-

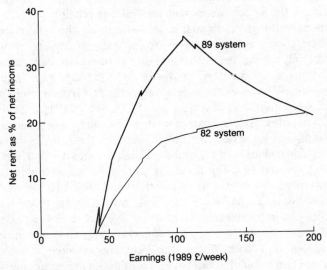

Figure 10.5 Net rent:net income ratio
Single people over 25, rent £30

self. In combination with Family Credit, its effects spread over a wide income range (see Figure 10.1). The April 1988 changes switched the means test for both Housing Benefit and Family Credit (replacing what had been Family Income supplement) to a *net* income basis to remove the possibility that combined effective marginal tax rates could exceed 100 per cent. However, the changes—particularly the structure of Family Credit—left a wide income range over which very high rates apply. Twenty per cent more families were faced with rates of at least 70 per cent in 1989/90 than in November 1985, although the number facing rates of 60 per cent or more was 20 per cent lower (HM Treasury 1990, table 14.19).

Finally, the current benefit calculation depends on 100 per cent of rent less an amount depending only on income. The marginal cost of housing is cut to zero for all recipients unless they fall foul of the restrictions on eligible rents and size of accommodation. The up-marketing potential in this is a problem both for those who want to increase market influences in housing decisions (which are almost entirely removed by it) and for those concerned at the distributional consequences of the restrictions imposed to try to limit its effects (including the 80 per cent maximum Poll Tax rebate).

Up-marketing is a particular problem for those who would like to extend Housing Benefit for low-income owner-occupiers, who at present only receive help with their Poll Tax (unless they are actually receiving Income Support, in which case their mortgage interest payments will be covered—except during the first sixteen weeks of a claim, when only half of them are paid for; the shortfall is made up if the claim lasts more than sixteen weeks). The equity case for such an extension—as suggested for the long term by the Housing Benefit Review and by the Duke of Edinburgh's Inquiry into British Housing (1985*b*)—is that Housing Benefit is more generous to low-income tenants than low-income owners (see Berthoud 1989*b*). However, two qualifications should be noted. First, owner-occupiers derive a benefit—the imputed rent—from being able to live in their homes rent-free. A 'neutral' treatment of owners and tenants would include this in owners' income assessments. Second (as explored in detail in Chapter 11) mortgage interest payments are a poor measure of the true housing costs of owner-occupiers, heavily overstating them for some (whose high interest payments reflect acquisition of an asset) but understating them for others (in particular outright owners whose costs should include the opportunity cost of their equity). Allowing for both of these, it is the treatment of the repair and maintenance costs of low-income owner-occupiers which is the greater source of inequity by comparison with tenants, rather than mortgage interest.

A system which paid all of any additional mortgage costs for people on anything but the lowest incomes would give a strong incentive for mortgage costs to rise, wholly at the expense of government. Similarly, one which refunded all actual repair and maintenance costs would be hard to control.

ALTERNATIVE HOUSING BENEFIT STRUCTURES

The problems of the 'single-taper' structure of the current Housing Benefit system—in particular up-marketing—have provoked a search for alternatives. Some of these were suggested to (and rejected by) the 1985 Housing Benefit Review. Others form part of overall proposals for the reform of housing finance (see Chapter 16). Other systems can be found abroad: for the systems used in France, Germany, and The Netherlands, see Kemp (1989).

RENT PROPORTIONAL SCHEMES

Under these (see Berthoud and Ermisch 1984, and DHSS 1985*a*, p. 8), 100 per cent assistance with rent would be given for incomes at IS levels (as now), but the *percentage* assistance would fall with income, until at some level assistance would fall to zero regardless of the gross rent. Halfway in between, assistance would equal 50 per cent of whatever rent was (and so on). The advantage of such a system is that it gives 100 per cent assistance at IS levels, but does not reduce the marginal cost of housing to zero for any higher income level. In fact, recipients would pay the fraction of a rent increase corresponding to their income level, so the up-marketing problem would diminish with income, removing it from the areas where it might really cause problems. It would also allow the treatment of rent and Poll Tax (and other housing costs) to be combined in one formula.

The bugbear lies in the implied rate of withdrawal of benefit. Suppose that the average rent was £20, and that the net income range over which assistance disappeared was £40 wide, implying an average taper of 50 per cent on net income (more generous than the current system). Someone with a rent of £40 would then lose assistance over the same income range—an effective marginal tax rate of 100 per cent. For a rent of £50, the tax rate would be 125 per cent: people with net incomes just above the IS rates would end up worse off than those receiving IS itself. Avoiding this problem for the highest rents would mean the income withdrawal range would have to be wider—but this would reduce the average taper, and increase the overall cost of the scheme. If rents were uniform, this would not be too great a problem. With rents as they are—with some three or more times the average—it is a very significant one.

LIMITS ON 'AFFORDABILITY RATIOS'

The discussion of 'affordable' housing association rents and the failure of the current Housing Benefit system to set limits to net rent to net income ratios suggest that a benefit system could be designed to achieve precisely that. For instance, it could be decided that enough benefit should be given to reduce net housing costs to no more than 25 per cent of net income. At its simplest, if 100 per cent assistance was to be maintained for those with incomes at IS levels, this would mean setting a maximum to net rent of 25 per cent of the excess of net income over the appropriate IS rate. On examination, however, this is simply the existing single-taper structure, but with a taper of 25 per cent rather than 65 per cent. It therefore suffers just as much from up-marketing—inescapably so as net rent is still determined by income alone—and would have a far greater cost and scope than the existing system.

More sophisticated formulae can be devised to try to get round this problem. In West Germany housing allowances are structured so that a limit is placed on the proportion of net income which a *given* gross rent can imply after deducting the allowance, but with that proportion rising with the rent. Allowances are given on the basis of tables issued by the relevant ministry. The formulae underlying these tables are not, however, published, and—in so far as they can be discerned—are much more complex than either the pre-1988 British scheme or the other alternatives discussed here (see Hills, Hubert, Tomann, and Whitehead 1990).

DUAL-TAPER SCHEMES

An alternative approach, originally suggested by Hemming and Hills (1983) is illustrated in Figure 10.6. This works on the principle that benefit equals whichever of two alternative schedules is the more generous. One of these—like the current single taper—is based on 100 per cent of rent, less an amount calculated by applying a steep taper to the excess of net income over the appropriate Income Support rate. The alternative schedule is based on a lower percentage of rent, but a shallower taper. For people with relatively low incomes the schedule based on 100 per cent of rent is more generous, but once income exceeds a switchover point, the schedule with the shallower taper becomes more generous.

In the example illustrated, the high taper is 60 per cent and the shallow taper 20 per cent, with the latter based on 60 per cent of rent. It is important to note that the two schedules do *not* create a better-off problem as existed before 1982/3. What made that so difficult was that the definitions of income and needs for the two systems were completely different and that a fresh calculation had to be made every time to see which benefit was more generous. In this proposal exactly the same definitions of net income and needs are used for the two schedules as are currently used for Housing Benefit. Moreover, with the particular schedules used, the switchover point

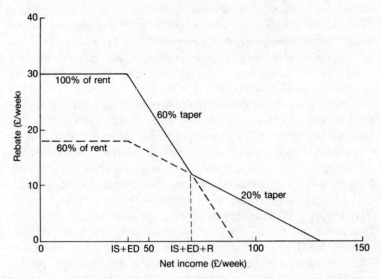

Figure 10.6 A dual-taper scheme
Single person over 25, rent £30, 1989/90

between the two schedules will *always* be the point where the excess of net income (less any disregards) over the appropriate Income Support rate exactly equals the rent.[4]

This structure has four key advantages. First, the steeper taper guarantees a full rent rebate for incomes at Income Support levels, avoiding any better-off problem. Secondly, those with higher incomes will be on the shallower taper, so that although Housing Benefit is extended to more people, widening the poverty trap, its 'depth' or severity is mitigated. Thirdly, for those with higher incomes, benefit only changes by 60 per cent of any rent change (unless a rent increase moves the claimant on to the steeper schedule). This substantially reduces the upmarketing problem. Fourthly, the peak of affordability ratios resulting from the current system is avoided.

The scheme in Figure 10.6 would be more expensive than current arrangements. According to TAXMOD, the simulation model of the tax and benefit system developed at the London School of Economics by A. B. Atkinson and Holly Sutherland (see Atkinson and Sutherland 1988 for an account), it would have increased the cost of 'standard' rent rebates and allowances (i.e. non-IS cases) by

16 per cent (about £200 million) if it had been in operation in 1989/90. For comparison, the single taper in the current system could be cut from 65 to 47.6 per cent at the same cost. The two systems can thus be compared on a revenue-neutral basis by looking at the effects of introducing the dual-taper scheme and of cutting the single taper to 47.6 per cent.

Retaining the single taper would concentrate the gains from the change more on those with lower incomes—90 per cent of the extra benefit would go to the bottom 40 per cent of the income distribution (adjusted for family size), as opposed to only two-thirds with the dual-taper. However, there would be about one-sixth more gainers from introducing the dual-taper than from cutting the single taper.

Cutting the single taper would reduce the worst of the poverty trap, reducing the numbers facing effective marginal tax rates over 70 per cent, but would increase the numbers facing over 60 per cent, whereas the dual-taper scheme would have little effect on either. The shallow part of the dual taper would extend to more people than the single taper, so the dual-taper scheme would be worse for overall 'incentives' (as measured by the 'average marginal tax rate' facing all earners).

Where the dual-taper scheme is decisively better is in respect of up-marketing. Compared with the actual 1989/90 system it would *cut* by 20 per cent the number of those receiving partial rebates but facing a zero marginal cost of housing (as they—and those newly brought into the system—would be on the shallower taper based on 60 per cent of rent). By contrast, the cut in the single taper would increase this number by more than 25 per cent. The dual-taper system would also have advantages for those concerned about 'affordability ratios', as shown in Figure 10.7. Both reforms would cut the maximum ratio generated by a £30 rent for a single person from the 35.2 per cent in the actual 1989/90 system, but to 25.8 per cent with the dual taper, compared to 29.4 per cent with the single taper.[5]

In summary, while simply reducing the single taper has some distributional advantages, the dual taper offers a way of avoiding the constraints of the up-marketing problem and of reducing affordability ratios more effectively. When the proposal was put to the Housing Benefit Review it was met with the response that, 'This is an ingenious scheme .... But whilst the principles of the scheme are both clear and evidently sensible we could not dispel the impression that it would not be understood in practice' (DHSS 1985*a*, p. 9). It

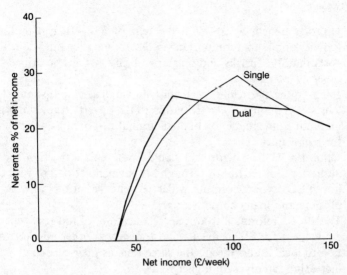

Figure 10.7 Alternative reforms: affordability
Single person over 25, rent £30, 1989/90

was therefore rejected on grounds of complexity. It is, however, worth recapitulating what this complexity is. To work out entitlement, the difference between net income (less any disregards) and someone's Income Support rate would have to be worked out just as now. If this was less than rent, benefit would equal all of rent less 60 per cent of the excess. If the excess was more than rent, benefit would be 60 per cent of rent less 20 per cent of the excess. To be sure, this would add a line or two to manuals describing benefit and to computer programs calculating it. This compares with the *ninety-seven* pages needed to explain all the rules connected with assessing net income, eligible rent, entitlement, and so on in the 1989 *National Welfare Benefits Handbook* (Lakhani, Read, and Wood 1989). The true source of complexity in the current scheme does not lie in the benefit calculation itself but in the regulations surrounding it— many of which are there to try to limit the effects of the up-marketing problem, which the dual-taper proposal would tackle at source. Chapter 17 discusses the place of such a scheme in the context of an overall reform of housing finance.

SUMMARY

- Housing Benefit assists with the rent of more than 4 million families and is more important in determining tenants' housing costs than the 'bricks and mortar' subsidy systems described in other chapters.
- It has three particular problems: incomplete take-up and the 'costs of claiming'; its contribution to the poverty trap; and 'up-marketing', the reduction of the marginal cost of housing to zero for recipients.
- Until 1982/3 help with rent could come either through local authority rent rebates or through SB payments for all or part of housing costs. To work out which left one 'better off' was complicated and many chose wrongly.
- The 1982/3 reforms introduced 'certification' of full rent rebate entitlement for SB recipients and transferred other administration to local authorities at the same time as their case-load was increasing rapidly with higher rents.
- The higher rents also meant that the 1982/3 taper changes for pensioners failed to solve the 'better-off' problem and so required the very complicated Housing Benefit Supplement.
- Following the 1985 Housing Benefit Review, a simpler benefit formula was introduced in April 1988, with benefit equal to 100 per cent of rent less 65 per cent of the excess of net income over the Income Support rate.
- The steepness of the taper makes the system far less generous than pre-1982/3 arrangements and contributes to the poverty trap. The system fails to prevent net rent from absorbing very high proportions of net income in some cases. The single-taper formula means that all recipients have extra rent met pound for pound by benefit. This has led to restrictions on its generosity in other ways, and blocks extension to owner-occupiers.
- Housing Benefit could be made more generous while reducing up-marketing by introducing a 'dual-taper' scheme, with an alternative shallower taper based on less than 100 per cent of rent for those on higher incomes.

NOTES

1. 'Housing Benefit' is used to describe means-tested assistance with rent (and rates in the past), including for those on Income Support. Those on

Income Support receive 'certificated Housing Benefit' (so called because the DSS certifies to the local authorities running the scheme that someone is entitled to benefit without a further means test). Others receive 'standard Housing Benefit'. Housing Benefit towards rents of local authority tenants is sometimes known as 'rent rebates', for the rents of other tenants as 'rent allowances'. 'Community Charge Benefit' for the Poll Tax of tenants and owner-occupiers has replaced what were their 'rate rebates'. This chapter is primarily concerned with assistance with rent, not with the Poll Tax or rates.

2. Even this is disputed, as the IS rates set in April 1988 were not high enough both to allow for the need to uprate the previous SB scales fully for inflation and to include this notional amount as an addition.

3. Given that Housing Benefit is now calculated on the basis of net income, the maximum 'affordability ratio' for a particular rent and household type is given by a straightforward formula. This ratio occurs at the point where income is just too high for the tenant to be entitled to benefit. This is where 65 per cent of the difference between net income excluding any earnings disregard (ED) and the relevant Income Support rate (IS) equals the gross rent (R) minus the minimum payment (Min). This critical net income level (NI^*) is therefore given by:

$$NI^* = IS + ED + (R - Min)/0.65$$

and the maximum 'affordability' ratio (AR^*) of net rent to net income is then:

$$AR^* = R/(IS + ED + (R - Min)/0.65)$$

4. If the two schedules have the formulae:

$$HB_1 = R - \beta_1 (NI - ED - IS)$$

and

$$HB_2 = aR - \beta_2 (NI - ED - IS)$$

where a is the proportion of rent used for the shallow taper, and β_1 and β_2 are the two tapers, the net income where the two are equal is given by:

$$NI^{**} = IS + ED + [(1 - a)/(\beta_1 - \beta_2)] R$$

In this case, with $a = 0.6$, $\beta_1 = 0.6$, and $\beta_2 = 0.2$, it follows that $NI^{**} = IS + ED + R$.

5. In the dual-taper system the maximum ratio in most cases occurs at the switchover point between the steeper and shallower tapers, at which point it is given by:

$$\beta_1 \left[(1 - a)/(\beta_1 - \beta_2) \right] R/NI^{**}$$

With the values in Figure 10.6 this is simply $0.6R/(IS + ED + R)$.

PART IV

Taxation

11

Principles of Housing Taxation

A backdrop to the description of British housing taxation in the next chapter is needed for two reasons. First, the actual system follows little discernible principle other than that of letting sleeping dogs and existing concessions lie. Second, analysts and would-be reformers disagree over precisely what constitutes the tax concessions to housing. This disagreement stems from different ideas about what benchmark or 'neutral' tax system, free of concessions for particular activities, to use to measure the concessions. The UK tax system contains many different—and conflicting—principles, from which a wide variety of benchmarks can be derived. Some are described below; for a more general description of the tax system see Kay and King (1990) or Hills (1988*b*).

HOW HOUSING ENTERS THE TAX SYSTEM

Taxes can be divided into those on income, consumption, wealth, and transactions. Housing could enter each of these 'tax bases'. Landlords receive income from rent. Owner-occupiers derive a benefit—the imputed rent—from being able to live in their property rent-free. Both may receive capital gains. All households consume 'housing services' either paid for through rent or received in kind. Residential buildings are the single largest component of net personal wealth, net of mortgages representing 41 per cent of the total in 1987 (Board of Inland Revenue 1989, table 10.3), and would thus be an important part of the base for any wealth tax. Large amounts change hands every year in the housing market, making it a tempting target for transactions taxes like stamp duty.

What makes the taxation of housing particularly difficult is that its true economic costs are so poorly measured by cash flow payments, as already explored in Chapter 5. Returns often come in kind (as imputed rents) or accrue over long periods (as capital gains) with only infrequent transactions. Meanwhile, the cash flow costs of housing may combine the purchase of both current consumption and

TABLE 11.1 *Taxation of owner-occupiers and other benchmarks*

	Interest payments	Return (cash/ imputed)	Capital gains
Owner-occupiers	Tax relief (up to £30,000)	Tax-free	Tax-free imputed rent
Private landlords	Interest tax deductible	Rents taxed (no deduction for depreciation)	Real gains taxable
Other business investment	Interest tax deductible	Income taxable (after depreciation)	Real gains taxable
Other consumption	No interest relief	No tax	No tax
Personal Equity Plans	No interest relief	No tax	No tax
Pensions	No interest relief	Advantage from contribution relief and tax-free lump sums	(Not applicable)
Shares	No interest relief	Dividends taxed	Real gains taxable
Building society and bank accounts	No interest relief	Nominal return taxed	(Not applicable)
Real Comprehensive Income Tax	Relief on real interest payments	Taxable (real return)	Real gains taxable

of an asset. Housing costs may also be hidden—the opportunity cost of an owners' equity stake in a house, or depreciation which only becomes apparent over a long period.

THE LACK OF A CONSISTENT BENCHMARK

To anticipate the next chapter, the key features of the tax treatment of owner-occupiers are that interest payments on the first £30,000 of a mortgage receive income tax relief, and that imputed rents and capital gains are untaxed. While there is general agreement that this combination gives substantial benefits, there is little agreement on what exactly constitutes the benefit. It all depends—as can be seen from Table 11.1—on what benchmark is taken. As other forms of saving or consumption are taxed in such widely varying ways, the advantages of owner-occupiers *relative* to those other activities also vary widely.

Compared with other forms of consumption, the advantage is interest relief—since 1974 tax relief has not been given for other personal interest payments (nor has there ever been any tax on the 'imputed benefit' from owning other consumer durables like cars). However, by comparison with private landlords—who can deduct all interest payments—the restriction of interest relief to the first £30,000 of a loan is a disadvantage. Here the relative advantage of owner-occupiers is given by the lack of tax on imputed rents and capital gains. The position relative to other forms of unincorporated businesses would be much the same (except that they—unlike private landlords—are given depreciation allowances).

The variation is as wide if one looks at personal saving. In each case, interest relief is a clear advantage—there is none for loans taken out to buy shares, for instance. However, some savings instruments actually receive a bonus from the tax system (pension contributions), others produce tax-free returns (Personal Equity Plans or, from 1991, Tax Exempt Special Savings Accounts), while others are taxed on their real return (share ownership) or even the nominal return (interest-bearing accounts). The advantage of owner-occupation is greatest relative to the latter—for equality of treatment, imputed rents plus *nominal* capital gains would have to be taxed.

A COMPREHENSIVE INCOME TAX

In the last few years the basis of the UK tax system has been moving somewhat erratically from taxing nominal returns towards taxing real returns. Notably, only real capital gains are now subject to tax, and the rate of Capital Gains Tax now equals the recipient's marginal tax rate on other income. The final line of Table 11.1 summarises what would happen if this principle was applied consistently to all forms of income, that is, if there was a 'Comprehensive Income Tax' (CIT) on real income.

Under a Comprehensive Income Tax income of all kinds would be treated equally (see Pechman 1977 or Meade Committee 1978).

Tax would be applied to cash receipts (such as earnings, dividends, rents, and gifts received), to income in kind (such as the benefits from company cars or owner-occupiers' imputed rents), and to capital gains. Examining the treatment of housing under a such a tax provides a consistent benchmark against which to measure the actual tax treatment of housing (as is done in Chapter 14). It does not imply—any more than did the construction of an economic rent in Chapter 5—that it would necessarily be desirable to adopt it.

One rationale for a CIT is that failing to tax these different flows equally is unfair between those who can receive income in the most favourably treated form (such as executives opting for fringe benefits rather than cash, or unit trusts being structured to give 'capital growth' rather than income) and those who are not. A second is that substantial differences in tax treatment may induce changes in behaviour which are not justified by the underlying economic returns—thus it has often been suggested that its unfavourable tax treatment relative to owner-occupation has contributed to the collapse of the private rented sector in Britain, and the generally favourable treatment of housing has diverted resources into investment in housing rather than industry (not that British investment in housing has been high by international standards in recent years— see Greve 1990, p. 22).

There are, however, practical and conceptual problems with a CIT. First is the problem of measurement: how much are fringe benefits or imputed rents worth? With cash, there is not much room for argument about its value; measuring the value of an owner-occupier's imputed rent in the absence of a functioning rental market is much more controversial.

Second, there is the problem of ability to pay in the absence of a cash flow. Short of inviting tax inspectors to live in their spare rooms, owners could not pay a tax on imputed rents in kind, but payment out of cash incomes could be hard for some. Similarly, the value of a capital asset may rise for some reason and a capital gain accrue to its owner at that moment, but there may be no cash with which to pay tax until the asset is eventually sold and the gain realised. Practical capital gains tax regimes recognise this by levying tax only at realisation, rather than accrual, but a tax payment to be made in several years' time is less onerous than one which has to be made today (in the delay, the money could be set aside to earn interest). As a result the effective burden of capital gains tax is usually much less than that on ordinary income, even if the notional tax rates are the same.

Nor is income such a clearly defined concept. As a starting-point one could take the 'Haig–Simons' definition: 'According to this definition, income is the accretion of the power to consume. It consists of a person's actual consumption plus or minus any increase or decrease in the value of his power to consume in the future as measured by his net worth' (Goode 1980, pp. 50–1). Thus, if someone starts the year with an investment of £1,000 which by the end of the year is worth £1,100, the investment has contributed £100 to income regardless of whether this came by way of interest or capital gain.

A first point to note is the effect of inflation. The 'value of his power to consume in the future' is a real, not a nominal, concept. In the example just given, if prices rose by 5 per cent, £1,050 would be needed at the end of the year to maintain future consumption power, so that the contribution to real income would only be £50. If prices rose by 10 per cent, there would be no contribution to real income at all. Systems based on nominal returns may end up taxing 'paper gains' which do not correspond to any increase in spending power at all. In what follows it is assumed that, to avoid this, it is *real* income which would be taxed under a CIT.

A second point relates to interest payments. If someone borrows £1,000 at an interest rate of 10 per cent and invests it in something yielding a 15 per cent return, net income over the year will be £50: during a year starting with zero net worth (the debt and asset being of equal value), the amount he or she can consume and remain in that position is the £150 return less the £100 interest payment. In principle therefore, a CIT would allow interest payments as a deductible expense in calculating taxable income. Without it, inequities could clearly arise: if someone borrows and lends at identical interest rates, the power to consume is completely unaffected. Only if interest payments are allowed as a deduction is this also true of taxable income. However, for analogous reasons to those discussed above for receipts, it is *real* interest payments which should be deductible, not the full nominal payments when real debt burdens are eroded by inflation.

It is sometimes suggested that interest payments should only be deductible if investment is being financed, but as White points out, consider a vacation trip; if the vacationer finances the trip by drawing down his assets he thereby forgoes interest earnings, which reduces his taxable income, and the deduction of the interest payment is implicit; if he finances the trip by borrowing, the interest payment is explicit. In general, consumption today implies lower Haig–Simons income in future, regardless of how the consumption is financed. (1977, p. 202)

Thus, the *lack* of interest deductibility for non-housing borrowing in the British tax system since 1974 is a divergence from a CIT, under which real interest payments for all types of borrowing would be deductible.

But this leaves a major problem with Haig–Simons income, elided in Goode's 'value of his power to consume in the future as measured by his net worth'. The two are not necessarily the same thing. In the Meade Committee's example (1978, p. 31), a millionaire could have an asset which was expected to yield an income flow of £100,000 in perpetuity. With 10 per cent interest rates, the asset would be valued at £1 million. But if they rose to 11.11 per cent, the asset's market value would fall to £900,000. Unless expected future inflation had also changed, in terms of the 'power to consume in the future' nothing has changed. In terms of net worth, however, the millionaire has suffered a capital loss of £100,000, reducing that year's net income to zero.

More pertinently for the taxation of housing, is an owner-occupier whose house's value rises from £50,000 to £75,000 in a house price boom really £25,000 better off, given that he or she expects to continue to occupy exactly the same property—and receive identical 'housing services'—albeit more highly valued by the market—in the future?

In practical terms, there is no alternative but to use changes in the valuation of net worth in calculating real income, recognising that this may not be the same thing as changes in future consumption streams if expectations or interest rates change. This is one of the reasons which have led to suggestions that expenditure is a more satisfactory basis for taxation than income (see Kay and King 1990; for a general account of the debate, see Aaron, Galper, and Pechman 1988).

HOUSING IN A COMPREHENSIVE INCOME TAX

With this background, it is clear how housing would be treated in a comprehensive tax on real income:

1. Private landlords would be subject to tax on their net rental

income, with management and maintenance expenses, depreciation, and real interest payments deductible from gross rents.

2. Owner-occupiers would be subject to tax on the imputed net rental value of their dwellings, and would be able to deduct real interest payments from taxable income.

3. Both landlords and owner-occupiers would be taxed on real capital gains (either on accrual, or with some adjustment to the rate of tax to offset the benefits of taxation on realisation only).

A fable

The need for the first two of these provisions can be illustrated by the following example, which takes place (for simplicity) in a mythical land without inflation, and with a uniform proportional 25 per cent CIT.

Androcles, an entrepreneur, is on good terms with Leo, a lion. Androcles has recently inherited £100,000. He invests his inheritance in a luxurious lion's den, knowing that people will pay £10,000 per year to come and visit the den. Feeding Leo costs £2,000, and repairs and maintenance plus provision for depreciation cost £4,000 per year. This leaves Androcles with a net income of £4,000, identical to the return which he could have received from investing in government bonds at the 4 per cent real interest rate available. The Inland Revenue also allows deduction of these costs, and leaves him with a net income of £3,000 after £1,000 CIT.

After a few years, Leo's fame spreads and he is offered a salary of £20,000 to act as presenter of the TV improvisation game, 'Whose Lion is It Anyway?' He takes the job and decides to rent his old den from Androcles for £8,000 per year. Androcles still pays £4,000 for repairs, maintenance, and depreciation, leaving him with an unchanged net income before tax of £4,000. As the costs are still deductible, his taxable income is unchanged by the transition from businessman to landlord (in Britain he would have lost the depreciation allowance).

Leo now accepts a leading role in the film 'Out of Africa II' and ends up with £100,000 to invest. If he bought bonds, he would receive £4,000 interest each year and pay £1,000 in tax on it. On the other hand, he could just afford to buy the den outright, saving £4,000 each year (the £8,000 gross rent less the expenses he will now have to pay). His taxable income would then include £4,000 imputed rent, on which he would pay £1,000 tax, leaving a net return of

£3,000 as before. Taxation of owner-occupiers' imputed income means that the net return on capital is the same whether the property is owned by a landlord or by its occupier (in Britain, without tax on imputed rents, the return to owner-occupation is higher).

Alternatively, Leo could buy the den with a 4 per cent £100,000 building society mortgage and invest his savings in bonds. He would still be imputed a rent of £4,000, but would set his £4,000 interest payments against it. His total taxable income would still only have risen by £4,000 and the net outcome would be the same. Interest deductibility ensures that the return on home ownership is independent of how it is financed (in Britain, only part of the interest would be deductible, but relief would be given on nominal, rather than real, interest).

The moral of this story is that full 'neutrality' in the tax system requires both interest deductibility and taxation of imputed rents; the former to prevent distortions in the return to investments financed in different ways, and the latter to prevent distortion of the relative rates of return on owner-occupation as opposed to other investments. Having *neither* results in neutrality only in very restrictive circumstances.

TAXES ON CONSUMPTION

While most discussion has surrounded the treatment of housing income, consumption taxes, like Value Added Tax (VAT), are of growing importance. If VAT was uniformly applied to all forms of consumption, it would apply to both actual and imputed rents (in this case it would be *gross* rents which would be taxed—including payments for services like management and maintenance and payments to cover depreciation). If owner-occupiers were subject to VAT on gross imputed rents (a more unpopular tax is hard to imagine), any VAT paid on repairs or other inputs could be set against this liability. Given that the flow from housing investment was being taxed, VAT would not be charged on new construction or improvement which raised future actual or imputed rents.

In reality, housing is mostly free from VAT. Again, whether this is classified as a tax concession to housing depends on the comparison being made. Compared with most commodities, the lack of VAT certainly is an advantage, but compared with other essential items on which VAT is not charged, like food, it is not. Until 1989/90, however, housing—unlike other forms of consumption—was subject to local authority rates. Their size varied in proportion to 'rate-able values', based on (outdated) assessments of the (net) rental values of property. Although rates were in part a tax on location, the fact that their size also varied with assessed rental values meant that they—and their abolition—should at least partly be taken into account in any assessment of the relative position of housing.

INCIDENCE PROBLEMS AND CAPITALISATION

It is one thing to measure differences between the actual and idealised treatment of housing for a particular individual or group, but quite another to argue that they really 'benefit' or 'lose' as a result of them. If the supply of new housing does not respond very much to price changes (if it is 'inelastic'), the result of tax conces-sions to owner-occupiers will have been to raise house prices above what they would otherwise have been—the concessions will have been 'capitalised'. New purchasers may receive the tax concessions, but they need them to pay the inflated purchase costs and may (in the extreme) be no better off than they would have been if the tax con-cessions had never existed in the first place.

An equivalent problem would occur if the availability of low-rent accommodation in an area meant that employers could attract labour at lower wages than they would otherwise have to pay. In that case the employers (or their customers) could end up as the beneficiaries of the subsidy—its true 'incidence' would be on them, not the tenants.

As well as such effects, the price changes caused by subsidies or tax expenditures may result in consumption changes which are not as valuable to the recipient as the equivalent amount of cash. One problem with valuing subsidies to local authority tenants is that they come tied to a particular range of accommodation (access to which is rationed) with a particular standard of management and maintenance service. This standard of accommodation is not neces-sarily what the tenant would have chosen given an equivalent cash subsidy and a free choice on how to spend it (even if that choice was restricted to housing).

These problems limit the inferences which can be drawn once a tax concession or subsidy has been identified. Even if the intended end-result was to produce a 'level playing field' for all, immediate removal of the concession or subsidy would not necessarily be appropriate.

SUMMARY

■ To assess the tax advantages of housing, a benchmark is needed against which to measure them. The UK tax system treats different forms of saving and consumption in widely varying ways, so no consistent benchmark is available. One of the reasons for disagreement over the value of tax concessions to owner-occupiers is that different benchmarks have been used.

■ Under a Comprehensive Income Tax (a consistent tax on real income of all kinds) the following would apply:
  – private landlords would be taxed on net rents after deducting expenses including real interest and depreciation;
  – owner-occupiers would be taxed on net imputed rents, also with all real interest payments deductible;
  – both would be taxed on real capital gains.

■ If all commodities were subject to consumption taxes like VAT, actual and imputed rents would be included. However, in the past local authority rates acted partly as an indirect tax on housing of this kind.

■ The effects of tax concessions or subsidies may have been capitalised in house prices. This may mean that current recipients are not the true beneficiaries from them.

12

Housing Taxation in Britain

INCOME TAX AND OWNER OCCUPIERS

Originally, owner-occupiers were treated in a way roughly equivalent to private landlords. The return on their investment—the imputed rent—was taxed (under 'Schedule A' of the income tax system). Against this income they could deduct expenses, including interest payments and maintenance costs. Over the years the tax system changed, with the changes usually improving the tax position of owner-occupiers relative to private landlords and their tenants.

First, the estimates of imputed rents fell behind inflation. By 1963 they were twenty-seven years out of date. Rather than bring the values up to date (prices in general had trebled since 1936), the Conservative Government abolished taxation of imputed rents in what Mr Harold Lever described as 'a piece of unprincipled Poujadeism on the part of a government desperately wooing the Orpington electorate' (*Official Report*, 6 May 1963, quoted in Shelter 1975). The by-election was lost, but the concession has remained. Second, when Capital Gains Tax was introduced by the following Labour Government in 1965, owner-occupied housing was exempted (while private rented property was subject to the tax, originally charged on nominal gains, including the effects of general inflation). Finally, when income tax relief for most forms of personal borrowing was ended from 1974/5, relief for mortgage interest on 'principal private residences' stayed (but not for second homes), subject to a £25,000 limit on the amount of a mortgage eligible for relief (relief for other personal borrowing had also been suspended between 1969/70 and 1971/2, but without a mortgage limit).

Since then income tax concessions to owner-occupiers have been reined back in several ways. Most importantly, the interest relief limit has only been raised once, to £30,000 from 1983/4. Had it kept up with general inflation since 1974/5, it would have been over £100,000 in 1989/90. Second, relief for new loans for improvements was ended in April 1988. This was done in a bid to prevent 'leakage' of the relief on to loans that were effectively paying for other spending. It has the curious effect in housing policy terms that relief is now given for purchase of existing dwellings, but not for improvement of the housing stock. Third, as part of general moves to ensure that the income tax system never favours unmarried couples relative to married ones, since August 1988 the £30,000 limit applies (for new loans) to each *property* (before that unmarried people could each receive relief on loans of up to £30,000, including more than one on the same property). This restriction was advertised five months in advance and was a contributory factor to the overheating of the housing market in 1988. Finally, falling income tax rates since 1979 (resulting from the shift to indirect taxes like VAT) have reduced the relative advantage of owner-occupation over other kinds of housing.

The main way in which income tax now affects owners is thus that mortgagers receive tax relief on the interest on the first £30,000 of a mortgage. Relief at the basic rate of tax (currently 25 per cent) is actually paid through the Mortgage Interest Relief at Source (MIRAS) system, under which the lender—usually a building society or bank—charges the borrower 75 per cent of the gross interest due (plus any principal repayment) and claims the balance—the tax relief—from the government. Basic-rate taxpayers thus receive the correct amount of relief automatically, without—as until 1982/3—their employer having to make adjustments to tax collected through the Pay as You Earn (PAYE) system or themselves filing a tax return to the Inland Revenue. From 1969/70 an equivalent subsidy—'Option Mortgage Subsidy'—had been available for non-taxpayers. This was subsumed into the MIRAS scheme in 1983/4, so that they also receive the correct amount of subsidy automatically. For the minority liable to tax at the higher rate (only about one in twenty taxpayers), additional relief is given through the tax system to take the total up to the appropriate rate (40 per cent since 1988/9).

Thus the interest on a mortgage of £30,000 would be £4,500 per year if interest rates were 15 per cent. Relief of £1,125 would be given to all borrowers through MIRAS, leaving them to pay £3,375. However, higher rate taxpayers would receive a further £675 through the tax system, bringing their total relief to £1,800, and reducing their net cost to £2,700.

If relief was to be restricted to the basic rate only, the administrative complications of granting the additional higher-rate relief would end and all borrowers would receive relief at an equal rate. Relief would—in effect—have been divorced from the tax system, and would have more of the character of an explicit mortgage interest subsidy. Such a restriction would not only affect those currently actually paying tax at the higher-rate, but also those who would pay at the higher rate if it was not for the additional relief: higher-rate liability starts from *taxable* income of £20,700 (in 1989/90), so mortgage interest (like other allowances) increases the gross income to which this corresponds.

THE EFFECTS OF THE £30,000 LIMIT

Between 1958/9 and 1973/4, the real cost of mortgage interest relief (including Option Mortgage Subsidy) at 1988/9 prices rose from about £0.4 billion to £2.6 billion (derived from Board of Inland Revenue 1989, table 5.1). Table 12.1 shows the growth in the cost of the relief since then, together with some of the factors driving it. Between 1973/4 and 1982/3, the cost grew relatively modestly, fluctuating with changes in interest and tax rates as well as the real value of the average mortgage (note that the available figures are for new mortgages—the cost of the relief depends on the stock of all mortgages, the value of which moves somewhat differently). Since 1982/3, the cost has risen much more rapidly—almost doubling within seven years. The number of recipients has risen rapidly with the growth of owner-occupation and the Right to Buy (although a part of the rise in 1983/4 reflects reclassification of Option Mortgage Subsidy). The real value of new and existing mortgages has risen substantially. Interest rates were higher at the end of the period than they had been at the start. Only the fall in tax rates had a restraining effect: if the basic rate had remained at 30 per cent, the cost of the relief would have been nearly 20 per cent higher in 1988/9 and 1989/90.

Given that the average new bank and building society mortgage had reached £34,800 by 1988, it may seem surprising that the £30,000 limit has not produced a levelling off in the cost of the relief. However, the limit's effect lags well behind the size of new mortgages, as Table 12.2 shows. While more than half of new mortgages exceeded £30,000 in 1988, less than 30 per cent of their value was accounted for by amounts in excess of the limit and hence disallowed from

TABLE 12.1 *The cost of mortgage interest tax relief, UK*

	Cost of relief at 1988/9 prices[a] (£bn.)	Numbers of recipients (million)[b]	Average new mortgage at 1988 prices (£)[c]	Mortgage interest rate (calendar year aver-age, %)	Basic rate of income tax (%)
1973/4	2.6	n.a.	29,200	9.6	30
1974/5	3.0	5.1	26,000	11.1	33
1975/6	3.2	n.a.	23,100	11.1	35
1976/7	3.4	n.a.	23,000	11.1	35
1977/8	2.9	n.a.	21,500	11.1	34
1978/9	2.7	5.6	22,300	9.6	33
1979/80	3.1	5.9	21,800	11.9	30
1980/1	3.5	5.9	20,900	14.9	30
1981/2	3.4	5.9	21,600	14.0	30
1982/3	3.3	6.1	21,800	13.3	30
1983/4	3.6	7.5	24,300	11.0	30
1984/5	4.4	7.8	25,800	11.8	30
1985/6	5.5	8.1	26,800	13.5	30
1986/7	5.3	8.5	30,100	11.9	29
1987/8	5.2	8.8	31,700	11.6	27
1988/9	5.5	9.1	34,800	11.0	25
1989/90	6.5	n.a.	n.a.	13.6	25

[a] Including Option Mortgage Subsidy until 1982/3. Adjusted by GDP deflator.
[b] Beneficiaries from tax relief (excludes OMS recipients from 1978/9 to 1982/3).
[c] New building society mortgages completed, plus bank approvals from 1983/4. Figures are for calendar year in which financial year starts. Adjusted by GDP deflator.

Sources: DoE (1989*a*), tables 10.11 and 10.25 and earlier equivalents;
  Board of Inland Revenue (1989), tables 5.1 and 5.2;
  HM Treasury (1990), tables 21.2.1 and F1;
  DoE (1977*b*), table IV.34;
  CSO (1990*a*), table 13.12 and earlier equivalents.

relief. Furthermore, the cash value of the total stock of mortgages lags behind that of new ones. Figures for the value of the mortgage stock as a whole are scarce, so the figures in Table 12.2 are based on a simple model of the mortgage stock in which there is constant attrition of old mortgages (at a rate independent of their age) and where new mortgages represent 15.31 per cent of the total stock at any time.[1] This model suggests that by the end of 1988 only about 22 per

TABLE 12.2 *Mortgages and the £30,000 limit, UK*
(Building society advances and bank approvals)[a]

	Average new mortgage (£)	New mortgages over £30,000		Mortgage stock over £30,000[b]	
		Percentage (number)	Percentage of amount[c]	Percentage (number)	Percentage of amount
1978	10,100	—	—	—	—
1979	11,600	—	—	—	—
1980	13,200	0.3	—	0.1	—
1981	14,900	1.2	0.1	0.3	—
1982	16,100	3.6	0.3	0.8	0.1
1983	18,800	10.6	2.5	2.3	0.4
1984	21,000	17.1	4.0	4.5	1.0
1985	23,000	24.0	7.2	7.5	1.9
1986	26,600	35.4	13.8	11.8	3.8
1987	29,500	42.0	19.7	16.4	6.2
1988	34,800	52.4	28.7	21.9	9.7

[a] Building society advances only up to 1982.
[b] Estimated using continuous attrition model of mortgage stock, with new mortgages representing 15.31 per cent of end-year stock. Figures estimated for end of calendar year.
[c] Estimated.

Sources: DoE (1989a), tables 10.4, 10.10, and 10.20, and author's calculations.

cent of the stock of mortgages exceeded £30,000, and that only 10 per cent of the stock's value was made up of amounts above the limit. As those receiving relief at the higher rate have larger mortgages than average, the effect of the limit on the total value of relief would have been somewhat greater. By 1989/90 official estimates suggest that the limit was reducing the cost of tax relief by something over £1 billion, or about 12.5 per cent of the cost if there had been no limit (Official Report 22 January 1990, col. WA 541; the cost of raising the limit to £50,000 was put at £900 million).

This relatively undramatic effect by the late 1980s does not mean that the limit is insignificant. Figure 12.1 projects the figures forward on the assumptions that the overall distribution of new mortgages in relation to the average stays as it was in 1988, and that the cash value of the average new mortgage grows by 10 per cent each year. Over the 1990s, the effect of the limit—if it is maintained—will become much

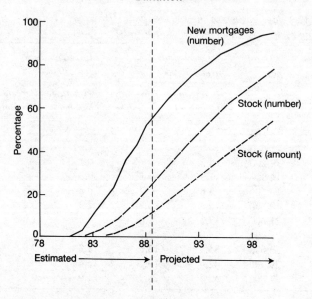

Figure 12.1 Mortgages above the £30,000 limit

more important. With these particular assumptions three-quarters of the stock of mortgages would be larger than £30,000 by 1999, and half of their value would be ineligible for relief.

There are great advantages to withdrawing a tax concession by setting a cash limit and letting inflation erode its value (see Whitehead 1978 for a discussion). In particular, it avoids the pain and unpopularity of a sudden jump in outgoings if there were a sudden explicit cut. The idea that the limit is fixed can also gradually sink into people's expectations, so that its eventual effects do not come as a nasty shock. The disadvantage of such a strategy is that it is very vulnerable: a relatively small increase could reverse the effects of several years of inflation.

THE COMPOSITE RATE OF TAX

A further feature of the tax system up to 1990/1 of importance to owner-occupiers has been the 'composite rate of tax' charged on building society and (since 1985/6) bank accounts. Under this, the interest depositors receive is deemed to be net of basic rate tax, so that—except for higher-rate taxpayers—no further tax is due. The amount which the institutions have had to pay on their depositors' behalf is based on the composite rate—calculated so that roughly the correct amount of tax is collected in total. As some depositors are non-taxpayers, the composite rate is worked out as the proportion of the basic rate corresponding to the amount of interest which goes to taxpayers. This is done on the basis of survey evidence and a year in arrears. Thus in 1989/90, the composite rate was 21.75 per cent, as 87 per cent of the interest in the previous year—when the basic rate was also 25 per cent—went to taxpayers.

It is clear who lost from this administrative short-cut—the non-taxpayers who had money on deposit with banks and building societies and who paid tax which they should not. As their numbers grew rapidly with the introduction of independent taxation for married women in April 1990, it was decided in the 1990 Budget to abandon the system from 1991/2 and replace it with a fairer (but administratively more complicated) system under which tax will be withheld at the basic rate, but will be reclaimable by non-taxpayers.

It is less clear who gained from the system and who will lose in April 1991. The most straightforward answer would be the tax-paying depositors, paying tax at 21.75 per cent rather than the 25 per cent basic rate, or 37.4 per cent rather than 40 per cent if they pay at the higher rate (allowing for the way in which net interest is 'grossed up' to calculate higher-rate tax). However, the main beneficiaries may well have been mortgagers. This would happen if building society deposit interest rates were set by competition in the *net* interest rate which they could offer basic-rate taxpayers (which seems likely, a conclusion shared by Foster 1975). Suppose that the gross return which savers could obtain elsewhere was 12 per cent, translating to 9 per cent net after basic-rate tax. Then, with a 21.75 per cent composite rate, building societies would only have to offer 11.5 per cent gross to give the same net return. As the bulk of building societies' lending all goes to finance mortgages, they could set gross mortgage interest rates half a percentage point below what they would otherwise have been.

The actual effect may have been something of a mixture, but it is plausible to assume that the main effect was that non-taxpayers—by definition those with very low incomes—were subsidising mortgagers, the tenure group with the highest incomes. The net result of abolition in April 1991 may well therefore be to raise mortgage rates above what they otherwise would have been.

INCOME TAX AND PRIVATE LANDLORDS

The general income tax treatment of private landlords has much more in common with that of other unincorporated businesses, although even on that comparison they suffer disadvantages. While rents received are taxable and explicit payments for interest, maintenance, and repair are tax-deductible, depreciation and imputed expenses are not. The first of these affects all landlords and is not insignificant: if the true real return being obtained was 5 per cent, failure to allow deduction of, say, 1 per cent of the current value of the property for depreciation would overstate taxable income by 20 per cent. The treatment of imputed expenses is a significant disadvantage to small landlords carrying out their own repairs and maintenance. Finally, losses on property income cannot be set against other kinds of taxable income (as would be the case for other business costs).

THE BUSINESS EXPANSION SCHEME

Apart from a short-lived depreciation allowance for new construction of property to be let as assured tenancies (introduced in the 1982 Budget, but phased out as part of the general Corporation Tax reforms of 1984), the first significant attempt to give a tax break to private landlords came with the extension in 1988 of the Business Expansion Scheme (BES) to cover new equity investment in companies providing residential lettings. Under the BES, investors can receive tax relief at their marginal rate on up to £40,000 subscribed each year for new shares in qualifying companies (each residential letting company can raise up to £5 million in this way). Investors must hold the shares for a minimum period of five years, after which they can be sold free of Capital Gains Tax. Any dividends paid out are taxed in the normal way. Overwhelmingly, investors in BES schemes have not only been higher-rate taxpayers, but those with very high incomes indeed: in 1982/3 85 per cent of those investing directly in BES schemes and 92 per cent of those using 'Approved Investment Funds' to do so had incomes putting them in the top 3 per cent of taxpayers (Board of Inland Revenue 1985, table 3.21). One attractive feature for investors is that they can 'carry back' part of the relief to a previous tax year. Thus those subscribing for shares in 1988/9 could carry back up to £5,000 to set against their 1987/8 tax bill—when marginal tax rates could have been as high as 60 per cent. Someone subscribing for £10,000 of new shares in a BES residential letting company in 1988/9 might only have faced a net cost of £5,000 (as half could have received tax relief at up to 60 per cent, and half at up to 40 per cent).

If judged simply in terms of the rented housing created, this is an expensive exercise. It is perfectly possible for a BES lettings company to be established, let out property until five years after the shares were issued, and then sell the units to owner-occupiers, with most of the profit coming by way of tax-free capital gain at the end. The government, through tax relief, could have provided up to half of the original equity. It would also have lost any tax which it would have collected on any alternative use of the same funds. It might gain Corporation Tax if the company made any taxable profits, but this can be avoided if the company borrows to add to its equity and so has interest payments to deduct against rental income.

A plausible result could be that the government would pay for a third of the capital cost (if borrowing was equal to half the equity) of units which were let out at market rents to people on relatively high incomes for about four years (allowing for a lag between share issue and the first lettings). The direct benefits of this seem small compared with, say, Housing Association Grant at 75 per cent of capital cost to create rented units available for thirty years or more at 'affordable' rents to those with low incomes.

What the Government would stress is the possible 'demonstration effect'. For sixty years or more the private rented sector has been in decline. The result of the scheme could be to lead not only to BES investment in the private rented sector, but also to change the climate of opinion towards general investment in the sector, resulting in the provision of many more rented units and revival of the sector as a result of this 'pump priming' (combined with rent deregulation for new tenancies). Whether this occurs—and whether BES-financed units remain in the rental sector after the five-year minimum—remains to be seen.

OTHER TAXES ON HOUSING

VALUE ADDED TAX

VAT is currently charged at 15 per cent on most spending. 'Land'—which includes rents (actual and imputed)—is one of the categories 'exempt' from VAT. New residential construction is 'zero rated' for VAT. This does not mean that housing is completely free of VAT.

First, being 'exempt' from VAT means that no tax is charged on sales (in this case, on rents), but VAT paid on inputs cannot be reclaimed. Thus VAT paid by a landlord on a plumber's bill (if declared to the VAT-man) cannot be reclaimed; nor can owner-occupiers reclaim the VAT they pay at Do-It-Yourself stores. Part of the cost of providing housing is thus subject to VAT (in contrast to the position for 'zero rated' items like new construction, where VAT on inputs can be reclaimed).

Second, spending on repairs and improvements to housing are charged VAT at the standard rate. Until March 1984 'improvements' were zero rated like new construction. This reflected the theoretical but impractical distinction between an 'improvement'—creating an addition to the capital stock (and hence a larger flow of 'housing services' in the future)—and a 'repair'—required to provide a constant level of service. If rents were liable to VAT the distinction would not matter much (since any VAT paid on either repairs or improvement would be set against that due on rents); as it is, there is now an artificial bias in favour of new construction as against improvement of existing dwellings.

CAPITAL GAINS TAX

Since 1988/9 Capital Gains Tax has been levied on realised gains in excess of inflation which have accrued since 31 March 1982 (for assets bought before then an estimate of their market value then is used). Tax is charged at the individual's top income tax rate—25 per cent or 40 per cent. However, each taxpayer (including each of a married couple from 1990/1) is allowed £5,000 of untaxed gains. This last provision is very generous—a couple could, for instance, own shares worth £200,000 which were growing in value at 5 per cent above inflation and avoid the tax altogether. Furthermore, as discussed in the last chapter, the effective rate of tax is reduced because it is charged on realisation rather than accrual. 'Realisation' in this context does not include transfer of assets on the death of their owner, so property on which large gains have accrued can be inherited without any tax payable until the heir decides to sell.

All these features have reduced the relative value of owner-occupiers' exemption from the tax: while owner-occupiers are completely exempt, private landlords pay tax on their real gains at a lower *effective* rate than their ostensible income tax rate (in the past they might have paid tax on nominal gains well in excess of any real return, so the reverse could have been the case).

INHERITANCE TAX

There are no special provisions relating to housing for what is now called Inheritance Tax (although it is one of the categories where payment can be made in instalments over ten years). However, as tax (at a rate of 40 per cent) is only payable on transfers exceeding a substantial threshold (£128,000 in 1990/1), estates consisting solely of a family house will usually escape tax (which is not charged in any case on transfers to a surviving spouse).

STAMP DUTY

Stamp duty is charged at 1 per cent of the price whenever land or buildings are bought and sold, unless the price is below a threshold (most recently revised in March 1984) of £30,000, in which case there is no liability.

Taxes like stamp duties are generally held by economists to be undesirable by comparison with those like income tax or VAT (for more detailed discussion see Whitehead 1980 and Hills 1983). This is because the amount charged depends on the number of trans-actions made, rather than the flows of income or consumption derived. First, this could be unfair: someone who has to move house every year will pay ten times as much as someone who only has to move once every ten years. Second, the tax adds to the already large transactions costs in the owner-occupied housing market, adding to barriers to movement and more efficient use of the house stock. Third, the particular form of the tax—its 'slab' structure—can have odd effects. Someone thinking of buying a flat for £31,000 would be better off agreeing with the seller that the flat was only worth £29,999 while its curtains were worth £1,001, thus avoiding £310 of duty.

The simple argument in its favour is that it is one of the very few offsets to the other tax advantages of housing in general and owner-occupation in particular. In 1988/9, the duty on all land and property raised £1.4 billion (Board of Inland Revenue 1989, table 12.1). On the basis of figures for conveyancing in England and

Wales, residential property accounted for 77 per cent of transactions in land and buildings in 1988 (ibid. table 15.1). This suggests that nearly £1.1 billion of the total came from residential property.

What is remarkable is that this very old-fashioned tax—originally designed in the reign of William and Mary—has only recently been charged on housing on this kind of scale. Back in 1974/5 the amount raised from residential buildings was equivalent to about £150 million at 1988/9 prices (adjusted by the GDP deflator and with the same methodology for apportioning the duty), so that its real yield from this source rose more than sevenfold over fourteen years.

The reason for this increase lies in the familiar process of failure to uprate thresholds for inflation. In May 1974 the stamp duty threshold was £15,000, with duty of 0.5 per cent payable at that point, rising to 2 per cent for transactions worth over £30,000 (with the slab structure and jumps in liability at each of the four points where the rate changed). As house prices quadrupled between 1974 and 1988 (DoE 1989*a*, table 10.8 and earlier equivalents), the fact that the threshold only doubled in cash terms meant that a much greater proportion of transactions became liable. In 1974/5 only about 13 per cent of sales of residential property were liable to duty; by 1988/9 this had risen to 68 per cent (Board of Inland Revenue 1989, table 12.2 and earlier equivalents; 1988/9 figure excludes Scotland).

Given its undesirable structure and effects, stamp duty on housing is an obvious candidate for abolition—but only in the context of any reform of housing finance which addressed the tax advantages to which it is an offset.

HOUSING ASSOCIATIONS

While charitable housing associations are exempt from Corporation Tax, non-charitable associations are not. However, under the 1965 Finance Act registered non-charitable associations receive an offsetting grant from the government, effectively putting the two groups in the same, tax-free, position.

LOCAL AUTHORITY RATES

Rates were a tax levied at tax rates ('rate poundages') set by local authorities to finance part of their spending (the rest being paid for from the system of grants from central government described in Chapter 6). They were charged on the 'rateable values' of domestic and non-domestic properties, estimates of the rent (net of expenses) which could be charged for them at a particular date. In between rating revaluations, rate poundages had to rise to keep up with inflation, and the relativities between different properties became progressively out of date. Following the political pain when reassessed rateable values were introduced in Scotland in 1985/6, the Government decided to replace domestic rates with the Community Charge or Poll Tax (DoE 1986).

Traditionally rates were regarded as a charge for local services rather than a tax on housing. While the value of property may have been a good proxy for the use of local services in Tudor England when they were first introduced, the provision of services like education is less obviously related to property values.[2] By the time the Layfield Committee considered the issue, they found that, 'In its developed form rating is properly regarded as a tax on the benefit of occupation of land and buildings' (1976, p. 147). A tax on the 'benefit of occupation' is, of course, very close to the tax on owner-occupiers' imputed rents which would be part of a Comprehensive Income Tax, so rates on owner-occupiers could be regarded as having been a kind of proxy for this. However, the rates paid by tenants could not be regarded this way—for local authority and housing association tenants they could be seen as an offset to the subsidies they received, but for private tenants they were a straight-forward penalty. The distributional effects of rates are discussed in Chapter 14. Whether one regarded rates as an indirect tax on housing or as an offset to direct tax concessions and other subsidies, it is clear that their abolition has substantially improved the position of housing relative to other forms of investment or consumption.

THE COST OF TAX EXPENDITURES TO OWNER-OCCUPIERS

As will be apparent, the tax treatment described above differs greatly from any idealised 'neutral' treatment of the kind described in the last chapter. A first difficulty with measuring these differences or 'tax expenditures' is that they can only be measured on the assumption that nothing would change if they were removed. This is clearly untrue: if Capital Gains Tax applied to owner-occupiers, for instance, house prices and the gains themselves would be lower. The size of a tax expenditure does not, therefore, necessarily measure the tax which *could* be collected if the tax system was actually changed.

A second problem is that their value depends on the benchmark used to represent a tax system without concessions. As the last chapter showed, there is no consistent benchmark to reach for in the UK tax system. The Public Expenditure White Paper (HM Treasury 1990, table F1) lists the following amounts as tax expenditures in 1989/90:

Mortgage interest tax relief	£7.0 billion
Capital Gains Tax exemption of owner-occupiers	£7.0 billion
Stamp duty threshold	£80 million.

Implicitly, these assume that a neutral tax system would give no mortgage tax relief, would not charge tax on imputed rents, but would levy Capital Gains Tax (according to the structure described above) on owner-occupied housing. It would also include a stamp duty of 1 per cent with no threshold (about £5 million of the value of the stamp duty threshold went to non-owner-occupiers). In addition to these items, relief for BES residential lettings schemes cost about £110 million in 1988/9 (*Official Report*, 8 March 1990, col. WA 749). The total real value of these expenditures was double the equivalents listed for 1978/9 (HM Treasury 1979, table 16), while the number of owner-occupied dwellings in the UK had risen by a third.

This listing gives a comparison with a strange tax system, however. It would not be neutral in any meaningful sense between owner-occupiers and private landlords, nor between those financing their housing in different ways. The conclusions which can be drawn as to the relative advantages of owners are therefore limited.

If instead the comparison was with a real Comprehensive Income Tax, the estimates described in Chapter 14 suggest that the key tax expenditures on owner-occupiers in particular (as opposed to housing in general) totalled £10.7 billion in 1988/90 (£7.5 billion from the lack of taxation of the combined value of imputed rents and real capital gains, plus £3.2 billion from the value of tax relief in excess of that which would be given on real interest alone, after allowing for the offsetting effects of removing the £30,000 limit).

THE COST OF CAPITAL TO OWNER-OCCUPIERS

The answer to the question 'what are tax subsidies to owner-occupiers worth?' therefore depends on the benchmark used to make the comparison. As the last chapter discussed, the UK tax system provides no consistent benchmark. However, a direct comparison can still be made between the effects of taxation on owner-occupiers and the value of subsidies to tenants without having to establish a definitive benchmark of a 'neutral' tax system.

This starts with the observation that neither the day-to-day maintenance costs nor the depreciation costs of owners are subsidised. What the tax system affects is the third element of their housing costs, the 'cost of capital'. The relative positions of tenants and owners can then be compared by deducting management, maintenance, and depreciation costs from rents, to give the amount which tenants contribute towards the cost of capital (taking account of capital gains or rising future rental streams). The result of this kind of exercise for local authority tenants is explored in Chapter 13.

Calculating what Atkinson and King (1980) refer to as the 'true capital cost of housing services' to owner-occupiers is relatively straightforward. An owner has a certain amount of capital tied up in his or her house. Part of this may be financed by a mortgage, in which case the relevant cost is the net rate of interest after allowing for tax relief. The rest is the owner's equity. The 'opportunity cost' of this is the amount forgone by not investing it elsewhere. Here some uncertainty does enter the equation—is the relevant 'elsewhere' a building society account taxed on its nominal return, shares taxed on their real return, or something tax exempt like a Personal Equity Plan?

In return for these actual or imputed outgoings, the owner receives two returns. One is the untaxed capital gain which accrues on the value of the whole property. The other is the value of living in the dwelling—the 'housing services'. The true capital cost of housing services to owner-occupiers is therefore measured by the net interest rate on any mortgage (part of which may be above the ceiling for relief), plus the net opportunity cost of equity, less the annual capital gain to be expected.[3] Table 12.3 shows how this depends on the proportion of the property's value covered by a mortgage, the owner's marginal tax rate, the treatment of alternative investments, and the rate of inflation. The table is based on the assumption that

TABLE 12.3 *Capital cost of housing services to owner-occupiers*[a] (%)

Alternative investments	Basic-rate taxpayers			Higher-rate taxpayers		
	Taxed on nominal return	Taxed on real return	Untaxed	Taxed on nominal return	Taxed on real return	Untaxed
(a) Inflation 5%						
80% mortgage (with relief)	0.38	0.63	0.80	−0.90	−0.50	−0.22
80% mortgage (half relief)	1.23	1.48	1.65	0.46	0.86	1.14
No mortgage	0.38	1.63	2.50	−0.90	1.10	2.50
(b) Inflation 10%						
80% mortgage (with relief)	−0.87	−0.37	−0.20	−2.90	−2.10	−1.82
80% mortgage (half relief)	0.48	0.98	1.15	−0.74	0.06	0.34
No mortgage	−0.87	1.63	2.50	−2.90	1.10	2.50

[a] Assuming 3.5% real interest rate (gross) and 1% expected real capital gain on housing.

Source: Author's calculations.

the real rate of interest is 3.5 per cent and that house prices can be expected to increase by 1 per cent more than general inflation each year (see Chapters 4 and 5 for a discussion of these assumptions).

If there was no tax system, the capital cost of housing services to all owner-occupiers would equal 2.5 per cent (the real interest rate minus the real rate of capital gain) on these assumptions. As the table shows, given the actual tax system, the cost is only as high as this for outright owners whose alternative investments are untaxed. In all the other cases shown, the cost is lower—indeed, in some cases it is negative. The variation between the different cases is large, ranging from minus 2.9 per cent up to plus 2.5 per cent. The benefits of the current system thus vary widely between different owner-occupiers. In nearly all cases, the cost is lower for higher-rate tax-payers. As one would expect, the cost is higher the more favourably alternative investments are taxed (as this raises the cost of equity) and the cost is also raised if part of a mortgage is above the ceiling for relief. In most cases the cost is higher the greater the equity stake (unless only part of the mortgage benefits from relief and alternative investments are heavily taxed). The cost also tends to be lower, the faster the inflation rate.

Given this variation, there is no unique cost of capital for owners to compare with the equivalent component of rents. However, it is possible to estimate a rough average for the sector based on current long-run expectations. Mortgages cover about a third of the value of the owner-occupied stock as a whole. As discussed above, by 1989/90 about one-eighth of mortgage interest relief was disallowed because of the limit. The average tax rate of owner-occupiers is just above the basic rate, say 26 per cent. Looking at current (early 1990) yields on government stock suggests a long-run real interest rate of 3.5 per cent and expected inflation of around 7 per cent, to which can be added a further 1 per cent for expected house price inflation. If one then takes the opportunity cost of equity as being given by an equal mix of investments taxed in the three ways listed in the table, these assumptions suggest an average capital cost of housing services to owners of 0.94 per cent. If it was intended to achieve rough equivalence of treatment—or 'neutrality'—between the tenures, rents (net of management, maintenance, and depreciation) would then have to yield a return of about 1 per cent. If—as may happen within the next ten years—only half the mortgage stock received relief, the cost to owners would be raised to 1.23 per cent.

Finally, it should be noted that if the tax system for both housing and other investments followed real Comprehensive Income Tax principles with imputed rents and real capital gains taxable (but relief only given for real interest payments), this cost would equal 2.5 per cent (as it would in the absence of taxation) regardless of the owner's tax rate, equity share, or the rate of inflation. Rents which acheived 'tenure neutrality' would then be correspondingly higher than are needed with the current divergences from real CIT treatment.

SUMMARY

- Owner-occupiers in the UK have not paid tax on their imputed rents since 1963, nor have their capital gains ever been taxed. Interest on the first £30,000 of a mortgage receives relief at the owner's marginal tax rate (at the basic rate for non-taxpayers).
- For new loans since 1988, those for improvement have not received relief, and the £30,000 limit applies to each property, not each tax unit.
- The limit was originally set at £25,000 in 1974. Since then its value has been eroded by inflation. By 1988, the majority of new mortgages exceeded it, but only about 10 per cent of the stock of mortgages was made up of amounts in excess, and hence in-eligible for relief. If the limit is maintained in cash, this could rise to 50 per cent by 1999.
- The main effect of the composite rate of tax applied to bank and building society accounts until 1990/1 was probably to benefit mortgagers at the expense of non-taxpaying investors. Its abolition could raise the mortgage rate by up to 0.5 percentage points.
- Private landlords cannot deduct depreciation or imputed expenses, nor set losses on property income against income from other sources for tax purposes. This puts them at a disadvantage to other businesses, as well as to owner-occupiers.
- The Business Expansion Scheme, which gives income tax relief on investment and freedom from Capital Gains Tax, was extended to new shares in residential letting companies in 1988.
- Housing is largely free from Value Added Tax, although it is charged on spending by owners and landlords on repairs and improvements (with no subsequent refunds). New construction is completely free from VAT.
- Stamp duty—charged at 1 per cent of any transactions of £30,000

or more—raised about £1.1 billion from residential property in 1989/90, seven times more in real terms than in 1974/5. As a transactions tax it has undesirable effects, but it acts as an offset to the other advantages of housing.

■ The abolition of local authority rates has substantially improved the position of housing relative to other activities.

■ The positions of tenants and owners can be judged by comparing rents net of management, maintenance, and depreciation with the capital cost of housing services to owner-occupiers.

■ This cost varies between owners depending on their tax rates, their equity share, and other factors. On plausible assumptions for long-term expectations of rates of return and inflation, the average figure for the sector as a whole is about 1 per cent (compared with the 2.5 per cent it would be without taxation or under a real CIT).

NOTES

1. This model is consistent with the average age of the mortgage stock being just over six years, in line with the average length of residence for owners with mortgages found in surveys in 1983, 1986, and 1989 (Coles 1989). The constant attrition rate is clearly not accurate as an assumption to predict year-to-year changes, but seems relatively plausible to produce reasonable estimates over the medium term.

2. However, Bramley, Le Grand, and Low (1989) suggest on the basis of the use of local services in Cheshire that rates were better matched to service use by those with different incomes than either the Poll Tax or than a Local Income Tax would be.

3. That is,

$$k = [m_1(1 - t) + m_2] R + (1 - m_1 - m_2) R^* - h$$

where k is the capital cost of housing services, m_1 is the proportion of the property's value covered by the mortgage receiving tax relief, m_2 the proportion covered by a mortgage above the limit, R the gross mortgage interest rate, t the owner's rate of tax relief, R^* the net opportunity cost of equity, and h the expected growth in (nominal) house prices.

PART V

Evaluation

13

The Economic Return on
Local Authority Housing

The previous chapter concluded that the current tax treatment of owner-occupiers reduces the 'capital cost of housing services' to them below what it would be in the absence of taxation (when it would equal the real interest rate less the annual real capital gain on housing). Given the current tax system, the cost varies with inflation, the owner's marginal tax rate, and the equity share in the house (see Table 12.3). On average, with conditions and expectations as they were in 1989/90, the cost was somewhere just below 1 per cent in real terms, suggesting that broad 'tenure neutrality' would be achieved if local authority rents were set to achieve a comparable real yield after allowing for management, maintenance, and depreciation. This chapter examines the return actually achieved on local authority housing in the recent past.

PROSPECTIVE RETURNS ON LOCAL AUTHORITY HOUSING

Atkinson and King (1980) used data from the national accounts to estimate a net real return (after allowing for management, maintenance, depreciation, and an annual real capital gain of 1 per cent) of around 2.8 per cent between 1968 and 1973, falling to around 2 per cent between 1974 and 1978. Using more recent data (from CSO 1989b), the same method yields a net return of 2.8 per cent between 1979 and 1987.

At face value, this appears to suggest that local authority housing was receiving relatively little subsidy in economic terms (compared with an 'unsubsidised' real return of 3.5 per cent needed to match indexed gilt yields—see Chapter 4) and that tenants were paying far more than the 1 per cent currently paid by owners (the equivalent figure for which would have been negative during the higher inflation of the 1970s). However, there are three problems which cast doubt on such conclusions:

1. Atkinson and King assume management and maintenance costs of only 0.5 per cent of the Central Statistical Office's (CSO) estimate of the net capital value of local authority dwellings at current replacement cost, for instance, implying a cost of about £200 million in 1978, compared with actual spending by local authorities in Great Britain of £1.1 billion in 1978/9 (DoE 1989*a*, table 10.26; Scottish Development Department 1987; and earlier equivalents). By itself, correcting this underestimation removes most of the calculated net return.

2. Their return is measured on the replacement cost of buildings, with a relatively crude adjustment for land, assuming that it would represent a quarter of the total value of the stock, and that this would be constant from year to year. The CSO now publishes balance sheet estimates giving current market values, including land, which allow a more sophisticated approach.

3. They include the whole of the trend real capital gain in the net return, but if property is—and will continue to be—let at sub-economic rents, this is questionable, as discussed below.

Table 13.1 shows the results obtained from an analysis which attempts to avoid these problems. The first column shows gross local authority rents (as this analysis is concerned with general subsidies, rather than the effects of Housing Benefit, this includes those actually paid by rebates) in each financial year as a percentage of the CSO's estimate of the vacant possession market value of local authority dwellings at the end of each December.[1] The pattern matches the movement of rents in relation to average earnings shown in Figure 4.1(b), with the gross return falling to 2.5 per cent by 1979/80, jumping to over 4 per cent by 1982/3, but then falling back to just over 3 per cent by 1987/8 (after 1982 rents rose roughly with prices in general, but capital values rose more rapidly).

The second column shows the net return, allowing for actual management and maintenance costs.[2] These represented just over 2 per cent of capital value on average over the period, producing a net return which fell below 1 per cent in 1979/80, rose to 1.7 per cent in the early 1980s, but fell back to 1.2 per cent by the end. The next column deducts the CSO's estimate of capital consumption (depreciation) of local authority dwellings. In the 1970s, net rents after allowing for management and maintenance failed to cover all of this, so the net return on this basis was negative, but rose to a maxi-

TABLE 13.1 *Real rate of return on local authority housing (prospective),*
GB (%)

	Gross return[a]	Return net of management and maintenance	Return net of deprec-iation[b]	Total return, adding 1% capital gain	Total yield, allowing for 1% real rent rise[c]	Total yield, with lower deprec-iation[d]
1975/6	3.1	1.3	−0.1	0.9	−0.1	0.1
1976/7	3.2	1.4	0.0	1.0	0.0	0.2
1977/8	3.3	1.4	0.0	1.0	0.0	0.3
1978/9	2.9	1.1	−0.2	0.8	−0.3	0.0
1979/80	2.5	0.7	−0.4	0.6	−0.6	−0.4
1980/1	2.8	0.8	−0.5	0.5	−0.7	−0.4
1981/2	3.9	1.7	0.3	1.3	0.4	0.8
1982/3	4.1	1.7	0.4	1.4	0.5	0.9
1983/4	4.0	1.6	0.3	1.3	0.4	0.8
1984/5	3.9	1.5	0.2	1.2	0.3	0.7
1985/6	3.7	1.4	0.2	1.2	0.3	0.8
1986/7	3.5	1.4	0.3	1.3	0.4	0.8
1987/8[e]	3.2	1.2	0.2	1.2	0.2	0.6
ANNUAL AVERAGE	3.4	1.3	0.0	1.0	0.1	0.4

[a] Gross rents as percentage of CSO's estimate of market value of local authority stock at end of calendar year (without discounting to 'tenanted market value').
[b] Deducting CSO estimate of capital consumption of local authority dwellings (adjusted to financial years).
[c] Assuming that net rents would rise at 1% per year in real terms and with 3.5% real discount rate.
[d] Deducting depreciation at 1.2% of net replacement cost of local authority dwellings.
[e] GB figures for rents and management and maintenance estimated by grossing up England and Wales totals (using 1986/7 proportions).
Sources: DoE (1989*a*), table 10.26 and SDD (1987) and earlier equivalents; CSO (1989*b*), tables 12.8, 14.3, and 14.7 and information supplied by CSO.

mum of plus 0.4 per cent in 1982/3, before falling back again, averaging roughly zero over the period as a whole.

This does not allow, however, for the part of the return which accrues as a real capital gain. The next column, following Atkinson and King, adds a trend rate of 1 per cent to allow for this. It is because this allowance for capital gains reflects a long-term average, that is, what might be expected in advance on average for any particular period, that the returns calculated in this section are described as 'prospective' (or *ex ante*). This produces a total return averaging 1 per cent over the period as a whole, coming wholly from the capital gain. On this basis, rents on average over the period would have given neutrality with the *current* treatment of owner-occupiers (but less favourable treatment than that of owners over the period as a whole, allowing for the advantages to owners from negative short-term real interest rates in the 1970s).

At this point, however, it is worth reflecting on the meaning of this addition. Suppose that rents exactly covered depreciation, management, and maintenance—as these calculations suggest they did between 1975 and 1987—and would continue to do so in perpetuity. Unless at some point landlords gain vacant possession and sell the property (or let it at a market rent from that point), the rising real vacant possession capital value of the property is of no benefit to them, so including it in the 'return' generated is misleading. In general, if property will continue to be let at sub-economic rents in perpetuity—which is what policy hitherto has been for local authority housing—only part of any real capital gain can be credited to the landlord. In this situation what is important to the landlord is the future rental stream. If there is a positive net return after these costs *and* this stream is rising in real terms, for instance because rents stay in proportion to rising real capital values, then the total yield does exceed the net return of the kind shown in the third column of the table, but only by *part* of the gain in vacant possession value, unless economic rents are being charged. If one allows for a 1 per cent real rise in net rents from year to year (with a 3.5 per cent real discount rate), the total net yield to the landlord works out at 140 per cent of the net return before allowing for capital gains.[3]

An alternative way of looking at this would be to consider tenanted market values, incorporating a discount to vacant possession values reflecting the sub-economic rents. If rents (net of management, maintenance, and depreciation) stayed in proportion to vacant possession capital values in perpetuity, tenanted values would remain as a constant proportion of vacant possession values. The landlord could then be credited with the *full* capital gain on *tenanted* market value—which would give the same result as the calculation outlined above. If rents only just covered management, maintenance, and depreciation in perpetuity, tenanted market value—and any capital gain in it—would be zero.

The fifth column of the table shows the results of a calculation on this basis. Overall—given the very low net returns—the adjustment makes little difference. At these rent levels the majority of the capital gain effectively benefits the tenants. The highest total yield on this basis was 0.5 per cent in 1982/3, since when it has slipped back. Over the period as a whole, the yield was only just above zero.

However, this calculation is very sensitive to the depreciation estimate. The CSO's figures are equivalent to about 1.3 per cent of capital value (including land), or about 1.5 per cent of (mid-year) net capital stock (excluding land). This seems rather high for instance by comparison with the major repairs provisions currently being recommended for housing associations (up to 1 per cent of rebuilding cost). To show the sensitivity of the findings to this, the final column gives the total yield (again apportioning only part of the vacant possession capital gain to the landlord), allowing for depreciation equal to 1.2 per cent of the net capital stock at current replacement cost. On this basis, the yield very nearly reached 1 per cent in 1982/3, and averaged 0.4 per cent over the period as a whole. Rents in 1987/8 would have had to be 17.5 per cent higher to achieve a 1 per cent yield on this basis.

RETROSPECTIVE RETURNS ON LOCAL AUTHORITY HOUSING

Even with the use of actual management and maintenance spending, these calculations are heavily dependent on assumptions about capital gains and depreciation. They also ignore any benefits—or penalties—which might have accrued to authorities as a result of other factors, such as the effect on their debt structures of changing interest rates. Data are available which allow an alternative approach to examining the rate of return actually achieved—*ex post*—by local authorities over the period as a whole.

The principle behind this can be seen from what would happen if a local authority's Housing Revenue Account (HRA) was a sealed system, with no subsidies going into or out of it, and no complications like the Right to Buy. In this case, one could look at the value of the authority's stock at the start of a period, subtract the

TABLE 13.2 Authorities included in the sample

Region	No.	Stock size ('000)[a]		Coverage (%)		Average value (£, unadjusted)[a]	
		1975	1988	1975	1988	1975	1988
Greater London[b]	14	223	195	32	27	9,280	58,690
Rest of South-East	31	207	217	27	31	8,600	50,350
South-West	13	128	120	40	40	7,050	38,410
East Anglia	2	18	17	11	11	6,110	35,740
East Midlands	15	182	178	52	53	5,410	25,050
West Midlands	21	471	440	84	86	5,530	24,020
Yorkshire & Humberside	13	240	229	44	44	5,330	22,000
Wales	9	97	93	37	38	5,260	21,970
North-West	18	392	361	60	62	5,460	21,910
North	10	216	215	51	55	5,760	21,060
All sample authorities	146	2,174	2,065	46	47	6,270	30,100
England & Wales	403	4,750	4,439	–	–	6,670[c]	34,300[c]

[a] Figures refer to end of March.
[b] 1975 figures include 20% of Greater London Council stock.
[c] Weighted by actual regional distribution of stock.

Sources: Stock figures from CIPFA (1988b) and earlier equivalent.
Average values for 1988 from author's calculations based on data from DoE 5% survey of building society mortgages for first quarter of 1988 (see text).
1975 values derived from those for 1988 using regional mix-adjusted indices from DoE (1989a), table 10.8 and earlier equivalents.

debt carried on the HRA at that point to give the authority's equity in the stock, and compare this with its equity at the end. Any return earned over the period in excess of management, maintenance, and depreciation would have had to be ploughed back into its net assets—either through a rise in the value of the stock or a fall in the value of its debt. Conversely, any failure of rents to cover costs would show up as a fall in the stock's value or as an increase in debt. A great advantage of this approach is that it avoids the need to monitor actual investments over the period or flows of management and maintenance costs in relation to rents—it all 'comes out in the wash'. In reality, of course, life is not so simple. In particular, there have been flows into HRAs from Exchequer subsidies and Rate Fund Contributions, and flows out in the forms of 'negative RFCs' and of the discounts given to tenants under the Right to Buy (if property was bought or sold at market value, the rate of return would not be affected). These can be allowed for, as explained below.

This 'balance sheet' approach also allows a disaggregated analysis, using data on individual local authorities collected annually by the Chartered Institute of Public Finance and Accountancy (CIPFA). The crucial information is for outstanding debt and on stock size and composition (needed to estimate its value). Unfortunately not all authorities complete their returns to CIPFA each year, but there were 146 authorities in England and Wales for which both debt and stock information was available for the ends of March 1975 and 1988, that is the start and end of the 1975/6 to 1987/8 period (the others failed to provide information in at least one of the four returns).[4]

Table 13.2 gives the regional breakdown of these authorities and information on their stock. The sample covered just under half of the total local authority stock in England and Wales. Information is also available for England and Wales as a whole (estimated by CIPFA allowing for missing returns). There is, of course, a bias in this sample—it consists of authorities which are diligent in compiling statistics. However, the authorities are not out of line with their regions as a whole (as judged, for instance, by April 1988 rents), except in the case of London. Here the authorities which could be included are either in Outer London or are relatively high-rent Inner London boroughs. The rates of return estimated for Greater London are almost certainly overestimated as a result of

TABLE 13.3 *Stock value and outstanding housing debt of sample authorities, 1975 and 1988 (£bn. at 1988/9 prices)*[a]

	End March 1975			End March 1988		
	Stock value (unadjusted)	Debt (nominal)	Equity (unadjusted)	Stock value (unadjusted)	Net debt[b] (nominal)	Equity (unadjusted)
Greater London[c]	7.1	4.0	3.2	11.9	1.3	10.6
Rest of South-East	6.1	2.4	3.8	11.4	0.7	10.7
South-West	3.1	1.1	2.0	4.8	0.5	4.3
East Anglia	0.4	0.1	0.3	0.6	0.1	0.6
East Midlands	3.4	1.4	2.0	4.7	1.0	3.6
West Midlands	9.0	3.7	5.2	11.0	2.3	8.7
Yorkshire & Humberside	4.4	1.8	2.6	5.2	1.1	4.1
Wales	1.8	1.0	0.8	2.1	0.6	1.6
North-West	7.4	3.8	3.6	8.2	2.4	5.8
North	4.3	2.0	2.3	4.7	1.0	3.7
All sample authorities	47.0	21.3	25.7	64.7	11.1	53.6
England and Wales	109.2	49.3	60.0	158.4	25.0	133.4

[a] Adjusted by GDP deflator.
[b] Housing debt net of accumulated capital receipts (estimated using 1987/8 HRA interest receipts grossed up at average pool interest rate for region).
[c] 1975 figures include 20% of Greater London Council debt and stock.

Sources: Stock values from Table 13.2.
Debt figures from CIPFA (1975, 1989*d*).
Interest receipts from CIPFA (1989*a*).

this problem, but the figures for England and Wales as a whole and for the other regions do not appear to have any obvious bias built into them (although the East Anglian sample is clearly too small to have much weight put on it).

A further problem is that the Greater London Council existed at the start of the period, but its stock had been dispersed amongst the London boroughs by the end. Had the London sample been representative, there would have been less of a problem, as figures could have been constructed for London as a whole. As it is, this cannot be done. Instead, the figures used for the Greater London sample in 1975 (and for subsidy flows until abolition of the GLC) include 20 per cent of the GLC, as the boroughs in the sample had this proportion of its stock transferred to them.[5] The crudity of this apportionment adds another source of error into the London estimates.

For this exercise, estimates are needed for the *value* of the stock at the start and end. No such valuations exist for individual authorities. However, figures are available for the composition of the stock in terms of the type of dwelling (house, flat, or bungalow) and the number of bedrooms. A hedonic price index was constructed using data from the DoE's 5 per cent survey of building society mortgages in the first quarter of 1988, giving an estimated price for each type and size of dwelling by region (see Chapter 14 for further discussion of the issues involved in a related exercise, and Hills 1990 for more details). These estimates—strictly for the mid-point of the first quarter of 1988—were used directly as valuations for the end of March 1988, and were adjusted using the DoE's mix-adjusted regional house price indices to give the 1975 valuations (but based on 1975 stock composition).

The resulting average values are shown in Table 13.2. Note that the composition of the council stock in each region affects the valuations, so the relativities between the regions vary—as they should—from those between the prices of owner-occupied dwellings. The estimates for England and Wales as a whole are derived from the regional averages, but using the actual distribution of stock numbers by type between regions, rather than the distribution in the sample authorities.

Table 13.3 shows the estimates of the stock value, outstanding housing debt (net of accumulated but unspent capital receipts in 1988), and hence equity in 1975 and 1988 (adjusted to 1988/9 prices).

TABLE 13.4 *Real rates of return on local authority housing 1975–1988 (retrospective)*

	Growth in capital value of stock		Growth in equity			Real internal rate of return allowing for:		
	Unad-justed	Trend prices	Unad-justed	Trend capital values		Net subsidy flow	Subsidy and RTB discounts	Subsidy, RTB, and 20% lower stock value
				Debt at face value	Debt at market value			
Greater London	4.0	2.2	9.7	6.8	5.8	2.9	3.6	4.0
Rest of South-East	4.9	3.1	8.4	6.0	5.5	4.2	5.4	6.1
South-West	3.4	1.6	6.1	3.7	3.3	2.2	3.1	3.6
East Anglia	3.9	2.2	6.0	3.6	3.2	2.2	3.2	3.5
East Midlands	2.5	0.7	4.9	2.3	1.7	-0.2	0.7	0.7
West Midlands	1.6	-0.2	4.0	1.5	0.9	-0.8	-0.2	-0.2
Yorkshire & Humberside	1.3	-0.4	3.5	1.0	0.5	-1.2	-0.6	-0.7
Wales	1.5	-0.3	5.5	2.4	1.5	-1.0	-0.1	0.0
North-West	0.9	-0.9	3.7	0.8	0.0	-3.0	-2.3	-2.9
North	0.7	-1.0	3.5	0.9	0.2	-2.2	-1.6	-1.7
All sample authorities	2.5	0.7	5.8	3.2	2.6	0.5	1.3	1.5
England and Wales	2.9	1.1	6.4	3.8	3.0	0.7	1.5	1.6

Source: Author's calculations (see text).

The first point to note is that the real 'net worth' of local authority housing more than doubled over the period. Not only was the stock more valuable at the end than the start, but the real value of outstanding debt (at face value) halved. At the start, authorities in England and Wales owned 55 per cent of the equity in their stock; by the end they owned 84 per cent. The second is that there was a great variation between regions, with the value of the London and the South-East samples' equity tripling, but that in the North increasing at half that rate.

The first column of Table 13.4 shows that these figures are equivalent to an annual growth in the real capital value of the sample's stock ranging from 0.7 per cent in the North to 4.9 per cent in the South-East outside Greater London, reflecting the combined effects of capital gains (including quality changes) and changes in stock sizes and composition. However, as will be recalled from Figure 4.2, the two dates were at different points in the house price cycle, early 1975 being near the bottom of a downswing, while early 1988 was near the top of an upswing. Part of the capital growth shown thus results from this difference, rather than any long-term trend. The next column of the table shows the effects of removing variations from the underlying national trend.[6] This reduces the growth in the real value of the stock to 1.1 per cent for England and Wales as a whole, with a variation from minus 1 per cent in the North to plus 3.1 per cent in the South-East.

Looking at the growth in equity, net of outstanding debt, the same adjustment reduces the annual real growth rate from 6.4 per cent to 3.8 per cent for England and Wales, and from 9.7 per cent to 6.8 per cent for the London sample. This is, however, valuing debt at its face value. As part of local authority debt is in the form of long-term fixed-interest stocks, its market value will vary from this, if the 'coupon' interest rate on the stock does not equal current market interest rates. The next column shows the effects of adjusting (rather approximately) for this, reducing the value of debt in 1975, but increasing it in 1988.[7] With both adjustments, the growth in equity equals 3 per cent annually for England and Wales, ranging from zero in the North-West to 5.8 per cent in London.

This growth in equity does not, however, represent the return which local authorities have been achieving on their housing assets because HRAs have not been a closed system. Instead, they have received flows of subsidy from year to year, helping them to build up the equity they have at the end. The next column shows the real 'internal rate of return' which they earned over the period on the combination of their initial equity (with trend house prices and debt at market value) and the subsidies paid into HRAs each year from central government or from their own general funds (less any payments out of the HRA).[8] For England and Wales as a whole this works out at 0.7 per cent per year, with a variation from minus 3 per cent in the North-West to plus 4.2 per cent in the South-East. Note the changing order of regions as this and the next adjustments are made.

The rate of return measured in this way includes the effects of authorities having sold part of their stock at below-market prices under the Right to Buy. This will have reduced the rate of return, giving a misleading impression of what is actually being generated by rents. The next column adjusts for this, showing the real internal rate of return allowing both for subsidy flows into the HRA and for the capital loss in the years since 1980/1 as a result of Right to Buy discounts.[9] Overall, the rate of return in England and Wales is increased to 1.5 per cent, and the figures for each region are correspondingly raised, with the biggest effect, unsurprisingly, in the South-East.

This leaves two remaining issues, the adjustment to be made for the state of repair of the local authority stock, and the question of whether the values derived from sales prices of owner-occupied dwellings should be adjusted to allow for environmental and other factors which would depress the value of local authority dwellings, but would not be captured by the price indices used.

For the first, the key point is whether the state of repair of local authority housing differs from that of owner-occupied housing, and whether that differential changed over the period (as the disrepair of owner-occupied housing will be reflected in the sales prices used to derive the values used here). However, the 1986 *English House Condition Survey* found that the average value of repairs needed by local authority housing, at £670 per dwelling, was *less* than that for owner-occupied housing, £900 per dwelling (DoE 1988*d*, table 4.4).[10] Even if all the owner-occupied disrepair was concentrated in dwellings which were only infrequently bought and sold, adjusting for this would make little difference to estimates of the value of the local authority stock. Nor did the survey suggest there had been any great change in the relative condition of the local authority stock between 1981 and 1986 (ibid., p. 76). Spending on capital repairs to local authority housing in England averaged £1.4 billion per year (at 1988/9 prices) between 1976/7 and 1987/8 (Table 3.5 above), which should have been more than enough at least to counter depreciation, if not actually to reverse it. Accordingly, there seems no obvious case for adjusting the figures to reflect deterioration in stock quality over the period (on average—particular areas may, of course, have deteriorated greatly).

However, there is a case for investigating the possible effects of a general lower valuation for local authority dwellings of a given type than owner-occupied ones. The sensitivity—or rather, insensitivity—of the estimates to this is shown in the table, with the final column giving the returns generated after applying an arbitrary 20 per cent discount to the values used in both 1975 and 1988. The adjustment produces a small increase in the overall rate of return— this is because it has a greater proportionate effect on *equity* in 1975 than in 1988, but overall there is little change.

The figures in the final two columns of Table 13.4 therefore represent the best *ex post* estimate of the range of returns which local authorities obtained on their stock over the period. Note that the figures—1.5 to 1.6 per cent for England and Wales as a whole— credit the *whole* of any capital gain as part of the return. As explained above in connection with prospective returns, the landlord's return allowing for the intention that authorities will neither obtain vacant possession and sell, nor let the property in the future at economic rents, would be lower than this, with only part of the gain in vacant possession value counting towards it. The trend annual real increase in capital values allowed for in these calculations is 1.7 per cent. However, some of this will have resulted from quality improvements rather than a quality-adjusted capital gain. If the latter was indeed 1 per cent per year (with a 0.7 per cent quality improvement, therefore), the net return in England and Wales would be reduced to a range between 0.7 and 0.8 per cent (using the same way of allowing for a rising real rental stream as before).

Around these national figures, the analysis suggests that there was a very wide variation between the regions. Counting in the whole of the vacant possession capital gain, housing in the South-East, South-West, and East Anglia generated a return exceeding the long-run real interest rate, but that in the North and North-West a significant negative return. This sheds a rather different light on the lack of variation in regional rents noted in Chapter 4—despite rents being relatively high in relation to capital values in Northern regions, the relatively low rate of capital gain generated a lower total return there than in the South. Remember, however, that these are *retrospective* figures—differential rates of capital gain would have to be expected to persist systematically if they were to be taken into account in working out rents which would generate an equal return between regions in the future.

CONCLUSION

The first part of this chapter examined the *ex ante* yields on (vacant possession) capital values implied by local authority rents between 1975/6 and 1987/8, concluding that—with the final set of assumptions presented—they had averaged 0.4 per cent in real terms, reaching a maximum of 0.9 per cent in 1982/3, but falling to 0.6 per cent by 1987/8. Rents in 1987/8 would have had to about 17.5 per cent higher to generate a 1 per cent yield (which would imply equality with the average capital costs of owner-occupiers under current conditions estimated in the previous chapter). With rents as they were at the end of the 1980s, tenants had a slight—but only a slight—advantage over the average owner in terms of the effective cost of a house with an equivalent capital value.[11] (Tenants also benefit from more generous Housing Benefit treatment than owners; the effects of this are discussed in Chapter 14.)

The second part of the chapter looked at the *ex post* return on local authority housing in different regions over the same period, using balance sheet data. The best estimates here—adjusting to trend capital values, to market values of debt, for subsidy receipt, and for the effects of Right to Buy discounts—suggest that local authorities as a whole earned a 1.6 per cent annual real return on their initial equity, with a range from below minus 2 per cent in the North of England to over plus 6 per cent in the South-East. However, this credits all of the gain in vacant possession capital values to the landlord. Giving the landlord credit for the rising stream of rent payments rather than the vacant possession capital gain would reduce the overall yield in England and Wales to a little below 1 per cent. While this is well below current yields on long-term indexed gilts, it would be well *above* the equivalent—negative—costs which owners faced over the same period. However, this would only give a guide to whether *current* rents give 'tenure neutrality' if the inflation and interest rate conditions of that period were expected to recur (which does not match current market expectations). For policy purposes, the *ex ante* calculations described above would be more appropriate.

SUMMARY

- The net prospective return (calculated by deducting actual management and maintenance and CSO estimates of depreciation from gross rents) on the capital value of local authority housing as a whole in Great Britain varied from minus 0.4 per cent in 1979/80 to plus 0.4 per cent in 1982/3, with an average of about zero over 1975/6 to 1987/8 as a whole (Table 13.1).

- If one adds the whole of a trend 1 per cent real capital gain to this, the total return therefore averaged 1 per cent. However, making all of such an addition may be inappropriate where rents are intended to remain sub-economic indefinitely.

- Allowing for only part of the gain in vacant possession capital values to accrue to the landlord (and for rather slower depreciation than the CSO), the *ex ante* yield averaged 0.4 per cent over the period. Rents would have had to be 17.5 per cent higher in 1987/8 to give a yield of 1 per cent.

- The real value of local authority housing assets (net of debt) in England and Wales more than doubled between March 1975 and March 1988. Local authorities' equity share in their own housing rose from 55 per cent to 84 per cent.

- A retrospective calculation, looking at the net housing assets of individual local authorities at the beginning and end of the 1975/6 to 1987/8 period, allowing for receipt of subsidy and losses from Right to Buy discounts, suggests a total annual real return of about 1.5 per cent for England and Wales, ranging from over 5 per cent in the South-East to minus 2 per cent in the North-West (Table 13.4). Crediting only part of the vacant possession capital gain to landlords as above reduces the England and Wales yield to about 0.7 per cent.

NOTES

1. The published CSO series is for local authority dwellings 'at tenanted market value', that is, applying a discount (which fell from 62 per cent in 1975 to 50 per cent in 1987) to vacant possession market value to reflect

the presence of sitting tenants with rights to a below-market rent, the discount being derived from the private sector. For the current exercise what is relevant, however, is the return being obtained as a proportion of full capital value.

2. Note that this does not include any deduction for costs carried on the HRA which do not strictly relate to housing—for instance, where items like street lighting are charged to the HRA, but would normally be paid for from the general fund. This will lead to the estimates presented understating net returns. However, no adjustment is made for the non-inclusion of 'capitalised repairs' in the recurrent figures for management and maintenance either, an omission which has the opposite effect.

3. If the annual gross rent charged, R, the annual management and maintenance cost, M, and depreciation, D, all rise at the same rate as the real capital gain in vacant possession value, p, the net return in any subsequent year, t, will equal:

$$[R - M - D] (1 + p)^{t-1}$$

If this carries on in perpetuity (in other words, looking at it from the point of view of a landlord who never gains vacant possession), the present value of this stream of payments discounted at the general real rate of interest π comes to:

$$[R - M - D] (\pi - p)^{-1}$$

This has the same net present value as a constant real annual return of:

$$[R - M - D] \pi (\pi - p)^{-1}$$

If the real discount rate is 3.5 per cent, and the real increase in the net rental stream 1 per cent, this would mean that net rents initially equal to 2.5 per cent of capital value would give a total yield of 3.5 per cent—they would give an economic return. However, net rents which started at 1.25 per cent of capital value, again rising at 1 per cent per year, would be equivalent to a total yield of only 1.75 per cent (not the 2.25 per cent which would be reached if the whole vacant possession capital gain was included).

4. For two further authorities this information was available, but information on the subsidies going into their Housing Revenue Accounts was missing for too many years for sensible estimates to be made.

5. Up to May 1984. Figures kindly supplied by the London Research Centre.

6. Taking the average ratio of house prices to average earnings between 1970 and 1988 as representing the underlying trend, this implies that the unadjusted prices in the first quarter of 1988 were 14.2 per cent above trend, but those in 1975 were 8.8 per cent below it.

7. The value of the sample debt in 1975 was reduced by 11 per cent by this adjustment; that in 1988 increased by 2 per cent. The corresponding figures for England and Wales as a whole were a reduction of 11 per cent and an increase of 7 per cent. The adjustment was made using average interest rates for debt of the individual authorities, averaging them separately for each region, but—to minimise computation—the maturity structure of debt for England and Wales as a whole. Market interest rates were taken from CSO (1990a) and earlier equivalents, and a simple model of asset valuation used to derive market values for stock of different maturities.

8. These figures were derived for each individual authority from the annual CIPFA series of *Housing Revenue Account Statistics (Actuals)* (CIPFA 1989a and earlier equivalents), with interpolation where data were missing for isolated years.

9. The average value of discounts for England as a whole in each year was taken from HM Treasury (1990), table 8.9 (and earlier equivalents, with estimates for 1980/1 and 1981/2). Variation in discount values between regions was assumed to follow the relativities between average stock values in 1988 as shown in Table 13.2. The sample authorities were assumed to have sold the proportion corresponding to their 1988 stock share of all sales by authorities in their region each year (derived from CSO 1989a, table 5.7, and CIPFA 1988b and earlier equivalents), with 95 per cent of those sales assumed to be under the Right to Buy (in line with the national proportion between 1981 and 1987 from DoE 1989a, table 9.6).

10. A 1985 survey had estimated that there was a total of nearly £5,000 per dwelling for 84 per cent of the local authority stock in outstanding renovations and repairs needed (DoE 1985). However, this total included the costs of bringing dwellings up to a modern standard in a wide variety of respects, not just repair. The values of owner-occupied houses—used here as the basis of the hedonic prices indices—already reflect the equivalent need for renovation in the owner-occupied sector. A discount only needs to be applied to give valuations for the local authority stock if its need for renovation is *greater* than for owner-occupied dwellings, which the *English House Condition Survey* suggests is not the case. The 1985 survey was also based on local authorities' own assessments (with no defined target standard) in a situation where it was in their interests to maximise the estimates of capital work needed.

11. But as this cost is subsidised and as owners actually occupy more valuable property, this does not mean that the value of subsidies per household is greater for tenants than for owners—see Chapter 14.

14

Distributional Effects of the System

This chapter examines some of the distributional effects of the current system of subsidies, benefits, and taxation described in earlier chapters. In particular, it examines the value to local authority tenants of the difference between the actual rents they pay (gross and net of Housing Benefit) and 'economic' rents of the kind described in Chapter 5, and to owner-occupiers from a tax regime which differs considerably from one taxing the real return on their investment (as described in Chapter 11). The results presented below relate to the situation as it was in 1989/90. (For more detail on the parts of the methodology used, see Hills 1989; however, the estimates presented here supersede those presented in the earlier paper.)

The estimates are of the 'first-round' effects of the current system, that is, assuming that tenants benefit from the full amount of low rents and owners from the full amount of tax concessions. In reality there will have been a wide range of 'second-round' effects. People would have made different housing decisions without the subsidies and concessions, so that the comparison is artificial with a world in which they did not exist, but people's behaviour was unchanged. However, comparable analysis suggests that as far as distributional (but not efficiency) effects are concerned, the difference made by allowing for second-round effects is relatively minor (Brownstone, Englund, and Persson 1988; in their case examining the situation in Sweden). See also King (1983*a* and *b*) and Rosen (1987) for discussion of the effects of allowing for behavioural changes.

A probably more important limitation is that, as discussed in Chapter 11, the incidence of the subsidies and tax concessions may not in reality be on the direct recipients—tax subsidies may have been capitalised in house prices, or rent subsidies may have been 'shifted' to employers. None the less, the exercise at least provides a starting-point. The review below of previous studies—which vary widely in their results—suggests that there is scope for discussion and refinement of these comparatively straightforward measures, as well as for updating them to show the current situation.

PREVIOUS DISTRIBUTIONAL STUDIES OF ECONOMIC SUBSIDIES AND TAX CONCESSIONS

Five earlier studies also provide estimates of the first-round distributional effects of economic subsidies to local authority tenants and four of the tax advantages of owner-occupiers. The assumptions used in these studies and their results are summarised in Tables 14.1 and 14.2 and Figures 14.1 and 14.2. To give rough comparability between the studies and with the estimates provided later in this chapter, the various results are adjusted to 1989/90 prices (using the Retail Prices Index). The tables also summarise some of the key points of the estimates presented later in this chapter.

All of the studies use either published results or individual records from national household surveys (the Family Expenditure Survey, FES, or General Household Survey, GHS) to establish actual housing costs and income levels. As these surveys do not include the capital values of the individual dwellings needed to calculate economic or imputed rents, these have to be derived indirectly, in each case using the data which are in the surveys on rateable values. These are converted to capital values using relationships based on data from the Department of the Environment's annual 5 per cent survey of Building Society Mortgages (BSM), which gives both items for sales taking place each year. As discussed below, this begs a number of questions about the characteristics of the stock as a whole and those being sold each year, and in particular about values in the local authority sector as compared with the owner-occupied sector.

The most obvious point to make about the results is the very substantial variation between the different estimates. Little of this variation is caused by changes in the real level of actual rents or in the tax system between the years studied. Indeed the two estimates furthest apart (Grey *et al.* 1978, and Hughes 1981) are both for the same year, 1973, and real rents and tax rates changed comparatively little between then and 1980 (the year covered in Ermisch 1984).[1] Rather, the variation results from different specifications of the variables which determine economic subsidies or tax advantages and from widely varying levels of real house prices assumed by the authors for their calculations. Note in particular the variation from 3 to 5.5 per cent in the required real return (net of management, maintenance, and depreciation) on local authority housing, and in

TABLE 14.1 *Summary of earlier studies of distributional effects of subsidies to local authority tenants*

	Rosenthal (1977)	Grey et al. (1978)	Hughes (1981)	Robinson (1981)	Ermisch (1984)	This study
Year examined	1969	1973	1973	1977	1980	1989/90
Data source	FES (pub-lished; E&W)	FES (pub-lished; UK)	GHS (indiv-idual; GB)	FES (pub-lished; UK)	FES (indiv-idual; UK)	FES (indiv-idual; UK)
Components of economic rent (as % of capital value)						
Required return	5.5	5	3	3	3.5	3.5–4
Allowance for capital gains	—	1	—	—	1.7[a]	0.5–1
Management & maintenance	2.5	0.77	n.a.	3	2	1.7[b]
Depreciation		—	—	1		0.94[b]
TOTAL	8	4.77	n.a.	7	3.8	5.1–6.1[b]
Average capital value used (£ at 1989/90 prices)[c]						
	22,000	45,000	n.a.	26,000	40,000	26,000–33,000
Average rents and subsidy (£/week at 1989/90 prices)[c]						
Actual rent[d]	14	14	n.a.	19	14	20
Economic subsidy	19	27	7	16	15	9–19

[a] Ermisch makes this adjustment not in respect of a return anticipated to come by way of long-run real capital gains, but as a way of allowing for the advantages of favourable capital gains taxation on competing investments.
[b] For a dwelling worth £30,000 and located outside London (see text).
[c] Adjusted by Retail Price Index.
[d] See text for different authors' definitions of 'actual' rents.

assumed management and maintenance costs. If nothing else, the results serve as a warning of the great sensitivity of this kind of exercise to the assumptions made.

Perhaps remarkably in view of these wide variations, it can be seen from Tables 14.1 and 14.2 that three of the four studies which looked at both the local authority and owner-occupied sectors agree that there is rough comparability in the average value of the benefits going to households in each tenure; Hughes (1981) suggests that

TABLE 14.2 *Summary of earlier studies of distributional effects of tax advantages of owner-occupiers*

	Grey et al. (1978)	Hughes (1981)	Robinson (1981)	Ermisch (1984)	This study
Year examined	1973	1973	1977	1980	1989/90
Data source	FES (published; UK)	GHS (individual; GB)	FES (published; UK)	FES (published; UK)	FES (individual; UK)

Implicit benchmark to give tax advantages of owner-occupiers

	Grey et al.	Hughes	Robinson	Ermisch	This study
	Business investment	Real CIT (with real interest relief)	Private landlords	Business investment	Real CIT (with real interest relief)

Components of benchmark tax on owner-occupiers (% of capital value and effective tax rate for basic rate taxpayers)

	Grey et al.	Hughes	Robinson	Ermisch	This study
Imputed rents	$4 \times 30\%$	$3 \times 30\%$	$3.88 \times 34\%$	$3.5 \times 30\%$	$3.5 \times 25\%$
Capital gains	$7 \times 20\%$		$8 \times 17\text{–}30\%$	$8 \times 8.6\%$	
Mortgage interest relief	Nominal	Real	Nominal	Nominal	Real
Total benchmark tax (as % of capital value)	2.6	0.9[a]	2.7–3.7	1.74	0.875[a]

Average capital value used (£ at 1989/90 prices)[b]

	Grey et al.	Hughes	Robinson	Ermisch	This study
	50,000	n.a.	31,000	44,000	56,000

Average tax advantage (£/week at 1989/90 prices)[b]

	Grey et al.	Hughes	Robinson	Ermisch	This study
	25	11	17–23	15	14

[a] And only part of actual mortgage interest tax relief corresponding to real interest would be granted.
[b] Adjusted by Retail Price Index.

owners had the advantage. Given that the differential between the tenures is not greatly affected by the assumptions made for real house prices, these results would have been the same even if the studies had made similar assumptions about house prices.

ECONOMIC SUBSIDIES TO LOCAL AUTHORITY TENANTS

A point of difference between the five studies apparent from Figure 14.1 (apart from the sheer variation in the magnitude of the estimates) is the relationship between economic subsidy and income. In three of them—Grey *et al.* (1978), Robinson (1981), and Hughes (1981)—subsidy falls with income, but in two—Rosenthal (1977) and Ermisch (1984)—it rises. The reason for this lies in whether economic rents are being compared with gross or net actual rents (after allowing for Housing Benefit).

In the case of Rosenthal's estimates for 1969, the national rent rebate scheme was yet to be introduced, so the actual rents used were essentially gross. Ermisch's estimates for 1980 explicitly use gross rents as the point of comparison. The gradual rise in subsidy with income in these two cases thus reflects the way in which actual gross rents rise less rapidly than the capital values of the dwellings occupied by those with higher incomes.

For the other three studies the comparison is between economic rents and actual 'net rent paid' as recorded in the FES or GHS. As a result of rent rebates, this results in the greatest estimates of subsidy for those on the lowest incomes. Unfortunately, for the years before the 1982/3 reform of Housing Benefit (see Chapter 10) to which the studies relate, the measure provided by the surveys is something of a hybrid. It is indeed net of the partial rent rebates received by those with incomes above what were then Supplementary Benefit levels. However, it is a gross rent for those who would have been receiving a payment to cover all of their rent as part of Supplementary Benefit. If true net rents had been used for all cases, the subsidy estimated for the lowest income groups would have been even greater. The estimates for 1989/90 presented below show subsidies using both gross and net rents, with 100 per cent rebates taken fully into account for the latter.

TAX ADVANTAGES OF OWNER-OCCUPIERS

The results of the four studies which give estimates for owner-occupiers are shown in Figure 14.2 (the results shown for Robinson being the average of his 'maximum' and 'minimum' estimates). The data used come from the same sources and capital values are generally estimated in the same way as described above in each case.

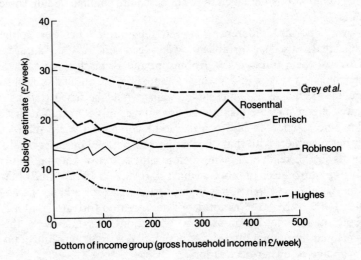

Figure 14.1 Estimates of subsidies to local authority tenants, pre-1989
Previous studies adjusted to 1989/90 prices

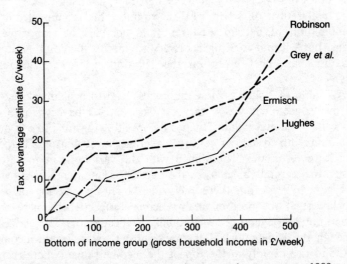

Figure 14.2 Estimates of owner-occupiers' tax advantages, pre-1989
Previous studies adjusted to 1989/90 prices

The assumptions on which they are based are summarised in Table 14.2.

An important difference between the four studies lies in the benchmark used to establish owner-occupiers' tax advantages. Three of them (Grey *et al.*, Robinson, and Ermisch) take as their benchmark a system under which imputed rents would be subject to income tax while nominal capital gains would be taxed (but at a lower effective rate reflecting the advantages of deferral of realisation, etc.). They therefore attempt to compare the taxation of owner-occupiers with that of other unincorporated business investments in the regime applying before indexation of Capital Gains Tax was introduced (a process which started from 1982/3) In Robinson's case the comparison is with private landlords and so the imputed rent to be taxed is not net of depreciation (private landlords being unable to make such a deduction). In line with this benchmark, nominal interest deductibility does not constitute a tax advantage of owner-occupation.

Hughes, by contrast, uses a benchmark of a tax system which taxes the *real* return on investments and (in his—and my—preferred measure) only allows real interest deductibility, that is, a real Comprehensive Income Tax (see Chapter 11). He therefore takes the tax advantage as being simply the lack of taxation of a real return of 3 per cent on capital value (coming from a combination of net imputed rent and accruals of real capital gains, but without it being necessary to specify the combination) plus the tax relief given on the inflationary part of interest payments.

As Table 14.2 shows, these differences lead to benchmark taxes on owner-occupiers which vary for basic-rate taxpayers from 0.9 per cent of capital value (Hughes before allowing for interest deductibility) up to 3.2 per cent (the average for Robinson's higher and lower estimates). Combined with the variations in the estimated real capital values used, these lead to the differences shown in Figure 14.2. Despite these, the studies agree that tax advantages are lowest at the bottom of the income range (where there are some non-taxpayers), rise gradually (reflecting capital values) through the wide range of incomes subject to basic-rate income tax, and rise rapidly at the top of the income range (where there are some higher-rate taxpayers and where capital values are also highest).

METHODOLOGY FOR THIS STUDY

This survey of the previous studies of the same problem suggests several lessons about promising approaches on which to build. First, there is clearly a great advantage in using survey data for individual households, rather than grouped data from published tabulations of survey results. This allows exploitation of the information within the surveys of relationships between individual household incomes, tax, and housing circumstances, rather than relying on grouped data in which these relationships have been averaged out. In addition it allows more accurate specification of the variables to be used, rather than using those which have been published.

As in Chapter 10, the results given below are drawn from simulations of tax and rent policy changes using TAXMOD (see Atkinson and Sutherland 1988). In this case, the detailed rules of the tax and benefit systems as applying in April 1989 were used (with the exception that, for consistency, the domestic rating system was assumed still to apply in Scotland) and applied to a representative sample of family units drawn from the Family Expenditure Survey.[2]

ESTIMATING CAPITAL VALUES

As mentioned above, the FES does not include direct information on capital values of dwellings occupied. It does, however, give details of the regions in which they are located, rateable values, number of rooms, date of construction (in four ranges), type of dwelling (detached house, purpose-built flat, etc.), and whether there is a garage. These variables are also included in the Department of the Environment's 5 per cent survey of new building society mortgages. A hedonic price index was constructed using these variables from the individual BSM survey records from the first quarter of 1988 (see Hills 1990). The wider range of variables than rateable value alone as used in previous studies was used not only to give improved estimates of values, but also because rateable values in England and Wales have not been reassessed since 1973, so that their relationship with capital values will have deteriorated in the intervening sixteen years. In addition, Scottish rateable values were revalued between 1982 and 1988 (so that a 1988 relationship cannot be applied to Scottish data based on the 1982 FES).

It is important to note that capital values established in this way will, of course, reflect any capitalisation which has occurred of the tax advantages of owner-occupation. For instance, Ermisch (1984) suggests that, given plausible assumptions about supply elasticities and his formulation of a 'neutral' taxation of housing, prices in 1983 were between 5 and 15 per cent higher than they would have been without the concessions. Such an effect is not adjusted for in the estimates below (as they are of short-run 'impact' effects, not of long-run effects allowing for land price adjustment), but it should be noted that it would have scaled up the estimates shown below in proportion for owner-occupiers, but *more than* in proportion for local authority tenants (as what is shown is a differential between actual and 'economic' rents).

One of the lessons from the survey of previous studies above is that the estimates are very sensitive to the date at which capital values are estimated. This is a consequence of the great instability of the UK market for owner-occupied housing, bringing wide fluctuations in real house prices (see Chapter 4). To avoid this problem, the results below are based—as one would expect any practical regime for charging economic rents or taxing owner-occupiers to be—on estimated *trend* levels of house prices. This trend is derived here using the average ratio of the Department of the Environment's 'mix-adjusted' house price series and average male earnings between 1970 and 1988 (that is, assuming a stable ratio between the two in the long run, and taking 1970 as a low point and 1988 as a high point in the cycle). On this basis prices in the first quarter of 1988 were 14.2 per cent above trend. With the assumption of a constant ratio between trend prices and earnings (growth of which was running in mid-1989 at 8.5 per cent annually), trend prices would—by complete coincidence—be 14.2 per cent higher in 1989/90 than in the first quarter of 1988. In what follows the price equation estimated for the first quarter of 1988 is therefore to be taken as representing trend prices in 1989/90.[3]

The characteristics of the stock bought and sold each year (and therefore appearing in the BSM survey) may, of course, differ from those of the stock as a whole and from year to year. Also, many of the more expensive properties are now purchased with mortgages from non-building society sources. This could bias estimates based on the BSM survey. However, given the range of indicators used in the hedonic indices described above, bias is avoided provided that the important composition differentials are reflected by these indicators. This seems a reasonable assumption—it is notable that the estimates here imply an average value for the whole stock of £50,000, compared with an average purchase price of £43,600 for the dwellings in the survey used.

A further issue is the derivation of capital values for the local authority sector from data for sales of owner-occupied property. The hedonic price indices allow for the difference between the two tenures which would be caused by differences in property types (such as the greater proportion of flats in the local authority stock), but not for any value differences which might be caused by general environmental factors or quality differences (such as state of repair). Applying the indices without correction gives an average local authority capital value of £33,000 in the first quarter of 1988. This is in line with an average undiscounted sale price of local authority dwellings in England under the Right to Buy of £30,500 in 1987/8 and £36,600 in 1988/9 (HM Treasury 1989, table 9.12). However, bearing in mind that the properties sold under the Right to Buy are more valuable and have a greater preponderance of houses as opposed to flats than the stock as a whole, this suggests that the unadjusted estimates may fail to allow for a general lower value of local authority as opposed to owner-occupied housing, even if the physical characteristics used here are the same. To allow for this— rather arbitrarily—the 'low' estimate of economic subsidies given below is based on a 20 per cent discount applied to the capital values of local authority dwellings derived from the hedonic indices. The 'high' estimate uses unadjusted capital values.

MEASURING SUBSIDIES TO LOCAL AUTHORITY TENANTS

The next problem is the specification of the economic subsidies and tax advantages to be measured. For local authority tenants, an economic rent is taken as covering three elements: actual management and maintenance costs (rather than a percentage of capital value as in the earlier studies, these are taken as £14.07 per week in London and £9.58 per week elsewhere);[4] an allowance for depreciation (0.94 per cent of capital value in London and 1.02 per cent elsewhere);[5] and a real return on capital. The two estimates shown incorporate different figures for the return on capital. The 'low' estimate uses a figure of 2.5 per cent, taken to give a 3.5 per cent real return (in line with the average yield on long-term indexed government stocks over the period February 1984 to December 1989) *less* an allowance for a long-run expected 1 per cent annual real rise in capital values and rents net of management and depreciation costs (and not due to quality improvements). The 'high' estimate uses a figure of 3.5 per cent, giving a 4 per cent real return (incorporating a small risk premium over long-term interest rates) while only allowing for a 0.5 per cent long-run annual real net rent increase. For a local authority dwelling outside London and worth £30,000, these assumptions imply an economic rent of 5.1 to 6.1 per cent of capital value, which is also the middle of the range implied by the previous studies. The value of the subsidy to tenants is simply the difference between actual and economic rents.[6]

MEASURING THE TAX ADVANTAGES OF OWNERS

In calculating the tax advantages of owner-occupiers the main benchmark comparison is with a Comprehensive Income Tax based on real returns as described in Chapter 11. As in Hughes's (1981) study, it is assumed that what would be taxed would be a total long-run real return (taken at 3.5 per cent here for the reasons explained above) on capital value, without having to make any differentiation between imputed rent and accrued capital gains. As well as estimates based on the advantage from the lack of such a tax, further estimates are given for the combined benefit from this and from the tax deductibility of nominal, rather than just real, interest payments. For 1989/90 this implies that *half* of mortgage interest tax relief is counted as a tax advantage here (given a 7 per cent inflation rate—as measured by the GDP deflator and so excluding the effects of mortgage interest rates themselves—and 14 per cent nominal mortgage rates). There would, however, be no £30,000 limit in the amount of borrowing eligible for relief in such a system, so its removal is also allowed for (increasing the relief granted by 16 per cent according to the model).

The first of these estimates therefore gives the value of the tax advantages of owner-occupation compared with a tax system which taxes real (non-interest) returns but allows (limited) nominal interest deductibility; the second gives their value against a full-blown real-based CIT allowing only real (but unlimited) interest deductibility. For comparison, the benefits of mortgage interest tax relief by itself are also given (this would give the position of owner-occupation compared with a tax system under which investment income was completely free from tax, or where housing was just treated in the way other consumption spending is treated in the UK).

RESULTS

SUBSIDIES TO LOCAL AUTHORITY TENANTS

Figure 14.3 shows the direct benefit to local authority tenants from the difference between their actual rents and the two estimates of economic rents described above. It shows the average benefit per tenant family in each 'decile group' (tenth) of all families, arranged in order of 'equivalent net resources', that is, net income after allowing for direct taxes and for housing costs and adjusted for family composition.[7] It should be remembered that local authority tenants are concentrated in the bottom half of the income distribution, where—on this basis—they represent 33 per cent of all families (including non-householders), while they only make up 11 per cent of those in the top half (and only 6 per cent in the top 20 per cent), so the results for tenants in the top decile groups are subject to wider margins of error.

The figure shows that there are two overall features. First, where the comparison is with gross rents, the cash value of the subsidy rises with income, confirming earlier findings that those with higher incomes occupy property of higher value, but the differential in value is not reflected in the rents which they pay. However, the rise with income is fairly slow, certainly much slower than the incomes themselves (so that subsidy falls as a proportion of income as income itself rises).

The second effect is shown by the comparisons with net actual rents, including the effects of Housing Benefit. These are, of course, concentrated on those with the lowest incomes, so that the combined subsidy falls between the second and fourth income decile groups. This initial fall is rather steeper than that shown in the three studies in Figure 14.1 which also look at net rent. This is because the 100 per cent rebates of those on Income Support could be allowed for here, whereas data did not permit this for earlier studies. A further effect visible in Figure 14.3 is that those with the very lowest net resources receive *less* benefit from Housing Benefit than those with slightly

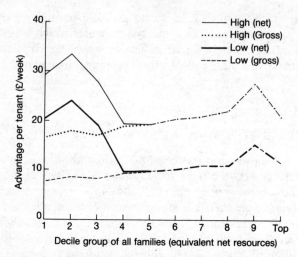

Figure 14.3 Subsidies to local authority tenants, 1989/90
Actual rents compared with economic rents

higher ones—one of the reasons that they have the lowest incomes being that they fail to claim the means-tested benefits like Housing Benefit to which they are entitled.[8]

In terms of the overall value of subsidy, that implied by the 'low' level of economic rent (giving a 3.5 per cent real return on discounted capital values and allowing for a 1 per cent per year trend rise in real rents) comes to £9.30 per week per tenant (excluding Housing Benefit), a national total of £3.1 billion per year. That implied by the 'high' estimate (giving a 4 per cent real return on undiscounted capital values and only allowing for a 0.5 per cent per year trend rise in real rents) is £18.80 per week for each tenant, a national total of £6.3 billion. These amounts compare with actual gross rents estimated at an average of £19.90 per week in the model. Rents would have had to be 47 per cent higher to equal the 'low' estimate of economic rents and 95 per cent higher to equal the 'high' estimate.

The lower of these two estimates is lower in real terms than those of the earlier studies except for that of Hughes (1981) for 1973, while the higher one implies a subsidy level as great as any of the previous studies except Grey *et al.* (1978). First, this illustrates the sensitivity of the results to the assumptions made in constructing an economic rent, in particular about expected real capital gains and about the relationship between capital values in the local authority and owner-occupied sectors. While the first of these is—by definition—almost impossible to be certain about, results from the studies currently being carried out as part of the Joseph Rowntree Foundation Housing Finance Initiative should greatly reduce uncertainty about the second.

Second, given that real local authority rents increased by more than 50 per cent between 1980/1 and 1989/90, it may seem surprising that these new subsidy estimates are not much lower. However, rents only rose by about 23 per cent in relation to earnings (and trend capital values) in the same period, and actual management and maintenance costs per dwelling have risen more rapidly than earnings growth (see Chapter 3). The excess of rents over management, maintenance, and depreciation costs has therefore not changed nearly as greatly as a percentage of capital value as might have been expected. The bulk of the difference with the earlier estimates thus results from the differences in methodology described above and in how the benchmark of 'economic' rent is calculated against which to measure the subsidy.

OWNER-OCCUPIERS' TAX ADVANTAGES

The value to owner-occupiers of tax concessions on three different bases are shown in Figure 14.4. The (mostly) lowest line shows the value of mortgage interest tax relief by itself averaged over all owner-occupiers (not just over those with mortgages). Note that non-taxpayers receive relief at the basic rate of income tax through the system of giving relief at source (also the deduction of housing costs including net mortgage interest to give net resources puts some low income mortgagers into the very lowest income group). The relief comes to £7 billion for 1989/90, or £9.05 per week for each owner (£14.05 per week for each mortgager).[9]

The middle line shows the benefit to owner-occupiers from the exclusion of imputed rents and real capital gains (taken together at 3.5 per cent of capital values per year) from income on which tax is charged. This is a slightly more valuable concession than mortgage tax relief and totals £7.5 billion for 1989/90, or £9.70 per week for each owner-occupier. The overall pattern is very similar to that of mortgage interest relief, except for the bottom and top decile groups.

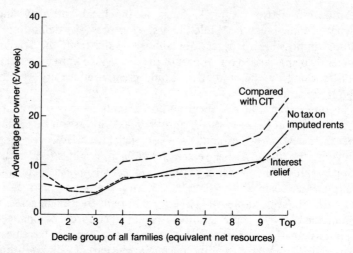

Figure 14.4 Owner-occupiers' tax advantages, 1989/90
Direct gain from tax advantage

The third line gives the total direct benefit to owner-occupiers from the difference between their actual tax treatment and that which they would receive in a real-based Comprehensive Income Tax, that is, the sum of the benefit from non-taxation of imputed rents plus the element of mortgage interest tax relief reflecting inflation rather than real interest (but with no £30,000 limit). This totals £10.7 billion for 1989/90, or £13.95/week for each owner-occupier.

By comparison with the earlier estimates of owner-occupiers' tax advantages shown in Figure 14.2, the value of the advantage against a real-based CIT is at a level very close to Ermisch's (1984) estimates for 1980. It shows the same overall change with income found by the earlier studies: that is, rather low for the lowest income groups (non-taxpayers), rising slowly with income for most of the income distribution, but rising sharply for the highest income groups (with higher tax rates and more valuable properties).

RELATIVE ADVANTAGES OF TENANTS AND OWNERS

Figure 14.5 compares the value to owners of the divergence between actual taxation and a real CIT with the benefit to tenants from the difference between actual rents and the 'low' estimate of economic

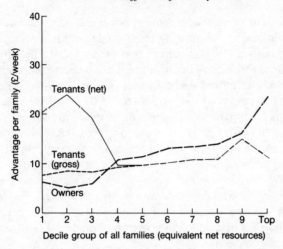

Figure 14.5 Advantages to owners and tenants
Tax advantage compared to CIT and economic subsidy ('low' estimate)

rents (preferred for this comparison as it is based on a comparable assumption of a 3.5 per cent required real return in calculating economic rents). Looking at each decile group separately, one finds the benefits to tenants (before allowing for Housing Benefit) and to owners are very similar—certainly within the margins of error of this kind of exercise—except for the top decile group, where owners have a clear advantage. The higher overall average benefit to owners than tenants (£13.95 compared to £9.30 on the basis used here) reflects the composition of the two tenures, with more owners having higher incomes. It should also be remembered that subsidies to tenants come tied to a particular property and level of service, while those to owners allow much greater choice of housing decisions. An equal—but untied—benefit will usually be more valuable to the recipient than a tied one.

Overall, the value of subsidies including Housing Benefit for local authority tenants is greatest for those at the bottom of the income distribution, while the tax advantages of owner-occupiers are greatest at the top of the distribution. Built into this system is therefore a great difference between tenures, with those on low incomes benefiting most from being tenants, but those on the highest incomes from being owners. These are obviously not the only—or even the main—reasons for tenure choice, but they will have been a factor reinforcing the growing tenure polarisation.

As a qualification, it should be remembered that a definitive conclusion as to the relative treatment of the two tenures depends on the taxation of alternative assets. Even if economic rents were charged and owners taxed according to real-based CIT principles, neutrality would only be achieved if other forms of saving were also taxed according to CIT principles. As explained in Chapter 11, not only is this not so, but also the divergences go in different directions for particular savings instruments. Only with the assumption that the alternative savings avenues open to owners and tenants are—on average—instruments like company shares which are (roughly) taxed on their real return would the conclusion definitively hold that current arrangements do give approximate overall 'neutrality' between the two tenures.

It should also be noted that for much of the income range, benefits to owners and tenants rise with income, so that the arrangements are less progressive than a system involving lump sum equal transfers to all. However, the rise is less rapid than income itself, which means that current arrangements are generally more progressive than the alternative of charging economic rents and switching to a CIT treatment of owners, using the revenue to cut the rates of income tax.

ALLOWING FOR LOCAL AUTHORITY RATES

So far these calculations ignore the impact of local authority rates. As they at least in part represented a tax on or charge for housing, they could be regarded as an offset against the subsidies going to local authority or housing association tenants and as a proxy for the taxation of owners' imputed rents (but as a straightforward penalty on the private rented sector which has no such advantage to offset).[10] Rebates of up to 80 per cent of the gross rates bill were available to those on low incomes, so the burden was lowest for the bottom 30 per cent of families. Thereafter, the net cost rose slowly, although it was significantly greater for the highest income group (see Hills 1989, figure 6).

In all, domestic rates raised £10 billion in 1989/90 after allowing for rebates. As it happens, this is almost exactly the same as the revenue which would have been raised by taxing owners' imputed

rents and raising local authority rents to the 'low' estimate of economic rents. In order to illustrate the extent to which rates acted as a
proxy for taxing owner-occupiers' imputed rents and charging economic rents to tenants, Figure 14.6 shows the effects of the combined
revenue-neutral 'reform' of making these two changes while
abolishing domestic rates (but maintaining existing mortgage interest relief). It shows the average gain or loss by decile group and the
range of gain or loss into which 80 per cent of each group falls.

While making this illustration does not imply that such a reform
would necessarily be desirable (let alone feasible), it would have
been generally progressive. In other words, rates more than
removed the advantages of subsidies at the bottom of the income
distribution, but were not enough to remove the advantages of tax
concessions at the top. This was for four main reasons. First, low-
income tenants receiving Housing Benefit would gain from the
switch from rates (where the maximum rebate was 80 per cent) to
rent (where it is 100 per cent). Second, high-income owner-occupiers
lose from the way in which imputed rents and capital gains would be
liable to tax at the higher income tax rate rather than at the same rate
as everyone else. In addition, rateable values rose rather more
slowly than capital values, so the switch in the tax base would also

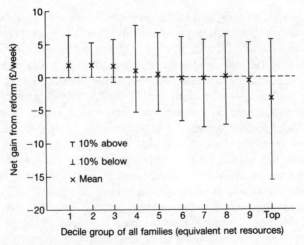

Figure 14.6 Combined reform
Net direct effect of reform, 1989/90

tend to disadvantage those with more valuable properties. Finally, private tenants (many of whom have low incomes) would gain from the abolition of rates with no offsetting loss (provided that their landlords passed the benefit on to them, a very questionable assumption). Overall, substantially more would gain—48 per cent of families—than would lose—28 per cent (the others are mainly non-householders). The balance between gainers and losers would be most favourable in the bottom half of the income distribution (see Hills 1989, table 5 for more details).

Perhaps the most striking feature of Figure 14.6 is, however, the relatively small size of the net changes illustrated. In other words, rates can be seen to have acted as a rough proxy for the taxation of imputed rents and as a contribution to raising local authority rents to economic levels not only in terms of overall revenue but also in general distributional effect—with the exceptions of the asymmetry in the Housing Benefit system and the lack of any proxy for the *higher* rate of income tax. Rates have, however, been abolished. They will thus no longer provide the offset to the other advantages of housing. As a result, housing has become substantially more privileged as a form of consumption or investment.

LIFETIME SUBSIDIES TO TENANTS AND OWNERS

The analysis above—and in the previous studies of the same subject—shows the distribution of subsidies and tax advantages on a cross-sectional basis; that is, it provides a snapshot of what was going on in 1989/90. It is, however, misleading in a very important respect. Essentially, it treats families at different points in their life cycles as if they were unconnected. Thus, the biggest 'gainers' from the current system are owner-occupiers with a recent mortgage, benefiting greatly from the tax relief on nominal, rather than real, interest payments. By contrast, elderly outright owners gain much less from the system, their advantage being only the lack of tax on imputed rents and accrued capital gains. While this is true as far as it goes, it should also be remembered that these groups are, in fact, much the same people, but at different points in their life cycles. The distribution of advantages over complete life cycles could look very different from that shown by the cross-section.

The problem is illustrated by Figure 14.7. This shows a very simple example of how a tenant and an owner might have to be

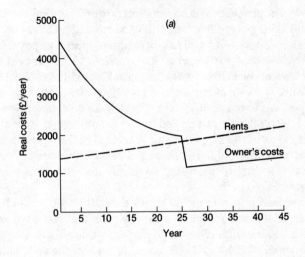

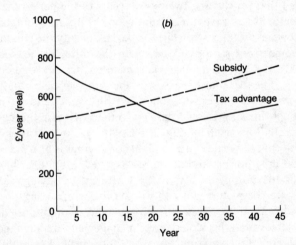

Figure 14.7 Lifetime positions of owners and tenants:
(*a*) Annual flows of rents and costs
(*b*) Owner's tax advantages and economic subsidy to tenant

treated to end up in exactly the same positions. In this case, an owner is assumed to buy a house for £40,000, financed initially entirely by a mortgage repaid over twenty-five years, and then to spend a further twenty years as an outright owner. The real value of the house rises at 1 per cent per year (with an inflation rate of 7 per cent), so that by the end of the forty-five years it is worth £62,592 (at the initial general price level). As well as conventional mortgage payments (at an interest rate of 10.745 per cent, equivalent to 3.5 per cent in real terms, and allowing for basic-rate tax relief and the £30,000 limit), the owner faces management and maintenance costs which start at £480 per year in real terms (some of which are doubtless provided in kind, but still have a value), and costs to counteract depreciation at 0.96 per cent of total capital value. Panel (*a*) of the figure shows the real value of these outgoings over the forty-five year period, showing the front-loading of mortgage payments and the drop when the mortgage is paid off.

The second line in Panel (*a*) shows the rent which would have to be charged if a tenant—making exactly the same total payments towards a combination of rent and savings—was able to accumulate the same net wealth—£62,592 in real terms—at the end. Thus it is assumed that for the first twenty-five years of the period the tenant pays rent and also saves an amount which brings total outgoings up to the owners' total costs, while for the last twenty the tenant draws on income from savings to make up the difference between the owners' outgoings on management, maintenance, and depreciation, and rent. The two thus have exactly the same net cash outgoings in each year, live in a house of equal value throughout and end up with £62,592 (at initial prices) to pass on to their heirs (in this case, it is assumed that no tenancy right is passed on). For consistency, it is assumed that the real return available on savings is also 3.5 per cent and that this return—and no more—is taxed, also at the basic rate (so that the non-neutrality of the treatment of savings does not complicate the picture; in reality some forms of savings are more favourably treated). Given these particular assumptions, the rent which achieves all this would cover management, maintenance, and depreciation and an amount equal to 1.3 per cent of capital value,[11] a total rent which starts at £1,386 per year (at initial prices), and which rises at 1 per cent per year.

The two households face identical outgoings throughout and end up in the same position. In that sense they receive equal treatment. However, Panel (b) shows the difference in the time profiles of the subsidies and tax advantages they receive, defined in the same way as above. For the tenant the economic subsidy (the shortfall from a rent which would give the full 3.5 per cent real return, allowing for the 1 per cent real capital gain each year) starts at £480 per year and rises gradually to £740 per year by the end (at initial prices). For the owner, the tax advantages start at a higher level, but end up at a lower one. Cross-sectional analysis of the kind presented earlier in this chapter would identify three groups being treated differently, in order of generosity: mortgagers in the first years of their mortgage, tenants, and older owner-occupiers. Over a life-cycle perspective, there is, however, no difference in outcome for owners and tenants.

It would clearly be rewarding to investigate further the life-cycle distribution of subsidies and tax advantages allowing for the full variety of actual circumstances, including the effects of benefit treatment, of owners moving and extending mortgage periods, and of the Right to Buy. For the present, the main point is to note the great difference which a life-cycle perspective can make.

SUMMARY

- The value of the difference between actual gross local authority rents and 'economic' rents is estimated to have averaged between £9 and £19 per week in 1989/90, equivalent to a total of between £3.1 and £6.3 billion (depending on the assumptions made in constructing economic rents).
- As earlier studies found, the value of subsidy compared with gross rents rises with income, but if Housing Benefit is allowed for, it falls.
- The value to owner-occupiers of the failure to tax the real return on their housing assets and from tax relief in excess of real interest deductibility averaged £14 per week, a total of £10.7 billion.
- Again, as earlier studies found, the value of tax advantages is low at the bottom of the income distribution, rises slowly for most of the income range, but rises sharply for the highest income group.
- The average value of owners' tax advantages is close to that of tenants' subsidies (just above or just below depending on assumptions).
- However, the relationship with income differs. If one allows for Housing Benefit, the advantages are greatest for tenants on low incomes and owner-occupiers on high incomes.
- For much of the income range benefits to both owners and tenants rise with income, but the rise is less rapid than income itself. This is more progressive than their removal used to finance a cut in income tax rates.

■ For most of the income distribution, rates provided an approximate offset to the lack of taxation of imputed rents for owner-
occupiers and the shortfall of actual local authority rents from
economic rents. Their abolition has decisively improved the relative position of housing compared with other forms of consumption or individual investment.

■ Cross-sectional results can give a misleading impression of the
distribution of benefits over the whole life cycle. The different
time profiles of advantages mean that some owners appear to be
doing better than tenants and others worse, even if the eventual
outcomes are identical.

NOTES

1. Robinson's estimates are based on a sample average for actual rents
   which is substantially above the average gross rents reported by local
   authorities at the time (which was still about £14 per week at 1989/90
   prices). This probably reflects the inclusion of other costs as well as
   rents in the data used.
2. The incomes and other characteristics of families ('family' here including a single person) from the 1982 Family Expenditure Survey have
   been adjusted to 1989/90 levels and the results from individual observa-
   tions have been differentially grossed up to give results which are representative of the population as a whole as known from other sources,
   allowing for differential response rates to the survey as well as com-
   positional changes since 1982 (see Atkinson, Gomulka, and Sutherland
   1988 for an account of this process).
3. This does not, however, adjust for *relative* price changes between regions
   over the period. There are indications, for instance, that the ratio of
   London prices to those elsewhere was above trend in the first quarter of
   1988, but this has not been adjusted for. It should also be noted that the
   1989 house price: earnings ratio (not available when the exercise reported here was carried out) was higher than in 1988 (see Figure 4.2).
   Using 1988 as the peak of the cycle will therefore tend to understate the
   estimates of trend prices used in this chapter.
4. These figures were arrived at by taking actual average spending figures
   for London and the rest of England and Wales for 1987/8 and adjusting
   by the DoE's assumptions for increases in management and maintenance costs up to 1989/90 built into its Housing Subsidy formula, combined with the assumed level of spending in Scotland built into the
   Housing Support Grant formula for 1989/90.
5. The percentages allowed for depreciation have been calculated to
   approximate 1.2 per cent of rebuilding costs in the different regions,

adjusting for the relatively greater importance of land as a component of capital value in London.

6. In the earlier version of these results (in Hills 1989), these estimates were adjusted upwards to give the constant real annual payments which would have the same net present value as the expected rising stream of differences between economic and actual rents. This was incorrect. While the value of economic subsidy may well be rising in real terms, the concern here is with subsidies accruing now, not their potential future value. The author is very grateful to Glen Bramley and Mark Kleinman for having pointed this out.

7. Giving a weight of 1.0 for a single person, 1.6 to a married couple and 0.4 for each child.

8. The model assumes that roughly 75 per cent of those entitled to Income Support receive it, while 50 per cent of those in full-time employment (or self-employment) who are entitled to Housing Benefit receive it, and 87.5 per cent of others entitled to Housing Benefit.

9. The results from the model have been adjusted from those originally presented in Hills (1989) to allow for higher interest rates in 1989/90 than originally expected.

10. As rates were an indirect tax, it could be argued that if their effects are taken into account, so should the exemption of housing from VAT. A rough estimate of the VAT which would be due at 15 per cent on owner-occupiers' imputed rents (at 2.5 per cent of capital value), on the 'low' estimate of economic local authority rents, and on private rents would be about £5.5 billion at 1989/90 prices. More than half of the net yield of rates could thus be seen as having been a proxy for VAT, significantly reducing the amount to be allocated as an offset to the other advantages of housing.

11. This matches the capital cost of housing services to basic-rate owner-occupiers shown in Table 12.3, relating to the column with alternative investments taxed on their real return, with a 7 per cent inflation rate, and a weighting towards a higher equity element over the whole forty-five year period than there is for the current group of owners as a whole, with its weighting towards those at early stages of their ownership careers.

15

Subsidies to Local Authorities and Housing Associations: Patterns of Incentives

The previous chapter looked at distributional effects of subsidies and tax concessions. This looks at another aspect of the subsidies described in earlier chapters for associations and authorities—the reaction of subsidy to changes in actual rents and spending, and hence the implications for incentives to the organisations and for the risks they carry.

As an example of the issue, under the pre-1989 subsidies to housing associations, a rent officer would have set a fair rent for a new dwelling, bearing no particular relationship to its value or cost of provision. Thanks to Housing Association Grant (HAG), the association's finances would have been insulated from any variations in the initial rent or (by and large) in the capital cost. Furthermore, if the association was receiving Revenue Deficit Grant (RDG), the same could have been true of recurrent costs: extra spending (up to the allowances) was met pound for pound by RDG. For those associations liable to Grant Redemption Funds (GRF), any benefit to the association from future rent increases would also be removed—again, pound for pound. Finally, if the tenant had been receiving Supplementary Benefit, he or she would not have been materially affected by the rent charged or future increases in it either.

In effect someone was being provided with somewhere to live by the state. The 'rent' charged was immaterial to both landlord and tenant, its level simply determining how much of the cost was borne by one part of government through benefit and how much by another, through subsidy. The effect of cost variations on the landlord was minimal. The combination of cost and price pressures which operates in much of the rest of the economy was almost entirely absent. This did not, of course, mean that the association was completely unconstrained. If its spending went above the management and maintenance allowances, it would have to use up reserves. If capital costs were too far above 'Total Indicative Cost', they might be disallowed, or the association might lose future grant allocations. If its aim was to maximise its number of units, a fixed allocation would give an incentive to control capital costs. However, its position was more like that of a government department, operating within a departmental budget, than of an independent agent making its own decisions in a market.

CHANGES IN RENT LEVELS

HOUSING ASSOCIATIONS

Under the pre-1989 system, associations were unaffected by the initial rent on new properties: a higher fair rent simply meant that they could service a higher residual loan and would receive less HAG. In effect, they faced a 100 per cent marginal tax on the initial rent. The same was true for subsequent rent levels once associations became liable to GRF: any rent increase on HAG-funded property would then increase GRF pound for pound. Whilst only a minority of associations were liable to GRF in the 1980s, their numbers would have increased rapidly through the 1990s if it had continued. Associations entitled to RDG were similarly unaffected by changes in rent levels (in this case on all of their properties); higher rent levels simply meant a smaller deficit and lower RDG.[1]

All this has now changed. For new dwellings, actual rents (now set by the association) do not affect subsidy. HAG is predetermined and new schemes are neither liable to Rent Surplus Fund (replacing GRF) nor eligible for RDG. Associations are, essentially, on their own. For existing dwellings, associations keep 15 per cent of any increase in the surplus calculated for the new RSF, 15 per cent goes to the Housing Corporation, and 70 per cent towards a sinking fund for major repairs on existing property, substituting for the major repairs grant which would otherwise be needed. If such grant had been available, the change from GRF to RSF would have cut the 'tax rate' on rents for existing properties from 100 per cent to 85 per cent (if grant would not in fact have been available, the cut is to 15 per cent).

For an association still receiving RDG, any increase in fair rents (for pre-1989 tenants) is fully reflected in lower grant, but half of the excess of assured tenancy rents on pre-1989 stock over their average fair rents can be retained. The 'tax rate' on assured-tenancy rents is thus 50 per cent. However, the higher average fair rents, the less the relevant excess: associations receiving RDG actually benefit (in the short run) from *lower* fair rents: the 'tax rate' here is now above 100 per cent (however, it is RSF which is more important in the long run).

LOCAL AUTHORITIES

Actual rent levels set by local authorities had no effect on Housing Subsidy in the 1980s, as subsidy was set on the assumption that rents were increased each year in line with the central guidelines. Transfers to and from the general fund complicated the picture. For instance, if lower rents were financed by increasing a Rate Fund Contribution, this increased the authority's 'total expenditure' for Block Grant purposes (see Chapter 6), which would have an impact depending on the authority's marginal Block Grant rate. As Figure 6.2 shows, by the second half of the 1980s these were negative for most authorities in England and Wales (in Scotland, RFCs did not affect the equivalent grant). Most authorities *gained* Block Grant if they used higher rents to cut RFCs—there was a 'negative tax'.

If, however, the effects of rent variations were kept within the HRA (for instance, matching changes in management and maintenance spending), there would have been no effect on subsidy or grant. This feature has been carried over to the new HRA Subsidy system in England and Wales from April 1990, under which ring fencing rules out transfers between the HRA and general fund altogether. There is no longer any option but for rent changes to have a full impact on the HRA (except to the extent that HRA Subsidy varies with the cost of actual rent rebates). The rules of the Housing Support Grant in Scotland have the same effect.

A curiosity of the change is that the subsidy will, for some years, depend on the actual rents authorities were charging in 1989/90. The lower these were, the lower the initial rent guideline. For some authorities (constrained by the maximum or minimum rent increase guidelines), rents £1 higher in 1989/90, meant £1 less subsidy in 1990/1, and possibly in subsequent years—a 'tax rate' on rents in that year of over 100 per cent! However, when some authorities responded to this by cutting their rents early in 1990 (to reduce the 1989/90 average), the Government excluded any rent changes made after 12 January 1990 from the calculations.

RECURRENT SPENDING

HOUSING ASSOCIATIONS

Under both old and new housing association subsidy systems, actual management and maintenance spending has had no effect on HAG or GRF/RSF. These depend on standard allowances, not actual spending. It is only for RDG that there would there be any effect on subsidy from actual spending. In this case, RDG would give a marginal subsidy rate of 100 per cent on spending up to the allowances (but with no effect beyond that). Apart from this, there has been no marginal incentive to spend at allowance levels, but they appear, none the less, to have been used as targets (see Hills 1987c, figure 6)—they acted as limits to the spending which could be carried out without dipping into reserves.

LOCAL AUTHORITIES

For local authorities, the effects of changes in management and maintenance spending have mirrored those of changes in rents. Housing Subsidy was generally unaffected by actual spending, but Block Grant in England and Wales would have been affected (generally adversely) by higher RFCs. Ring fencing now rules out the latter effect. However, for a minority of authorities from December 1986, Housing Subsidy depended on the *lower* of actual management and maintenance spending and what would otherwise have been calculated as 'reckonable' for subsidy purposes. This reduced the advantages of 'capitalising' repairs spending (capital spending receiving positive subsidy as described below, and also evading constraints like rate capping). The effect was that those authorities which were in subsidy and were also spending less than would otherwise have been reckonable received Housing Subsidy at 100 per cent rate on extra management and maintenance spending. This feature has not been carried forward to the new HRA Subsidy.

The initial allowances built into the new formula depend for most authorities on actual spending between 1986/7 and 1988/9.

Until explicit allowances depending on stock composition are brought in, subsidy will be higher pound for pound for extra spending (adjusted for inflation) on average over those three years. This rule also hits those authorities which had capitalised much of their repairs spending in those years (although there are floors to this effect—see Chapter 7). This effect is, of course, retrospective, so it can only affect actual spending by example: the history of central subsidies to local government suggests that higher actual spending in one year may turn up as the base for some future subsidy (although relying on this would be a gamble).

An important—but unquantifiable—effect of ring fencing is that any efficiency gains or savings within the housing department now stay within the HRA, without the possibility of their being effectively siphoned off through lower RFCs (or higher contributions to the general fund).

CAPITAL COSTS

The effects of capital spending on subsidy depend on whether a new dwelling enters the stock. This section describes what happens when there are no extra dwellings, that is, the effects of *variations* in the costs of new dwellings or of renovations to existing ones.

HOUSING ASSOCIATIONS

Under the old system, variations in capital costs on a new dwelling were met pound for pound by additional HAG (unless unacceptably far above TIC levels or deemed 'non-qualifying'). A main aim of the new system was to remove this 100 per cent marginal subsidy. 'Tariff' associations now receive a fixed grant—variations in capital cost have a full impact on the associations' finances. Other associations receive a grant which (within certain limits) varies by the predetermined grant percentage (less than 100 per cent).

LOCAL AUTHORITIES

The combined effects of the old Housing Subsidy and Block Grant on marginal subsidy rates for additional capital spending were very involved (see Hills 1987*a* and *b* for detailed discussion). Indeed, they were almost certainly too involved to have any discernable effect on behaviour (see Kleinman, Eastall, and Roberts 1989), capital controls being of much greater importance.

The minority of authorities in receipt would have 75 per cent of additional loan charges met by Housing Subsidy, provided that costs were within Admissible Cost Limits (ACL). However, if the balance of costs came from the general fund, Block Grant would be affected, mostly adversely in the short run, so the combined subsidy rate was below 75 per cent (but positive). For those not receiving Housing Subsidy, the only effect would be on Block Grant, so there would generally be a negative subsidy if additional costs were met from RFCs. In the longer term, however, a minority of authorities (those whose Grant Related Expenditure included an element reflecting a notional RFC—see Chapter 6) would have had the *whole* of any additional costs met from increased Block Grant (as GRE would eventually have been adjusted for the extra loan charges). For these authorities, the long-run marginal grant rate was 100 per cent.

Under the new HRA Subsidy and the ring fence, all this is a great deal simpler. HRA Subsidy adjusts by the full amount of any loan charges provided that total capital spending is within the HRA capital spending guideline. All authorities thus now face a 100 per cent marginal subsidy rate up to the guideline, above which it falls to zero. In Scotland, Housing Support Grant already had the same feature.

Whereas the old system gave most authorities a direct interest (of varying strength) in their capital costs, the new one removes the direct financial effects of variations in costs. The pressure on authorities comes not through the revenue effects of their capital spending, but through the 'credit approval' system (see Chapter 6) which controls the total of capital spending (and the limit on HRA capital spending which can result in increased HRA Subsidy). If costs are high, fewer units can be built or improved.

BUILDING A NEW DWELLING

The subsidy effect of a new dwelling has generally differed from that of additional capital spending in general, as the number of dwellings affects subsidy as well as the resultant capital costs.

HOUSING ASSOCIATIONS

Until 1989, associations would break even if they charged the fair rent on a new dwelling and spent no more on management and maintenance than the allowances. Initial HAG levels could as a result be very high. Receipt of HAG implied, however, that an association would probably have to make Grant Redemption Fund payments in subsequent years. The true level of grant, subtracting this later liability, depended on later movements in rents and costs (see Hills 1987c, appendix I). For instance, HAG would cover 86 per cent of capital cost for a new-build project if the nominal interest rate was 10.745 per cent (3.5 per cent in real terms with 7 per cent inflation) and the initial fair rent, net of management and maintenance, equalled 1.5 per cent of capital cost. If rent and costs rose by 8 per cent in nominal terms each year, the later GRF payments would reduce the true value of the grant to only 52 per cent. However, the old system also included the promise of future major repairs grant—with a present value roughly equal to that of the GRF payments (on the basis of currently recommended provisions for major repairs).

Under the new system, capital grant levels vary across the country (they were intended to average 75 per cent in England and Wales in 1989/90). As there is no subsequent grant redemption or major repairs grant, these levels also represent the true capital grant. Allowing for the lack of major repairs grant, this is less generous than previous arrangements and new association rents have to be correspondingly higher, especially if one takes account of the less favourable terms on which private finance is available than on-lending from the government used to be. Break-even rents thus depend on a combination of actual capital costs and actual management and maintenance spending (see Table 8.2).

LOCAL AUTHORITIES

As with variations in capital costs, the effect of a new dwelling on an authority's finances in the 1980s depended on its Housing Subsidy and Block Grant position. For authorities receiving Housing Subsidy, the net effect was that the authority would break even on a new dwelling if it spent the amount allowed as 'reckonable' management and maintenance per dwelling and charged rents which started off equal to 25 per cent of the loan charges on it plus—in theory—a provision towards the 25 per cent of later major repairs which would not have been paid for from subsidy (giving a total approaching 3 per cent of capital cost; see Hills 1988*a*, appendix 4), but rose in line with the Department of the Environment's flat rate rent guidelines each year. By contrast, an authority out of subsidy would have to cover not only actual management and maintenance spending and full loan charges, but also in most cases make up for any lost Block Grant if any part of this was financed from the general fund. Once again, regardless of Housing Subsidy, for authorities whose GRE included an element for notional RFCs the dominant effect in the longer term would be adjustments in Block Grant. Such authorities would have broken even if rents had been set in line with what had been regional average rents in 1980/1, uprated by the annual subsidy guidelines (see Hills 1987*a* and *b*).

The new system simplifies all this. For a new dwelling, as for any other, all that matters are the authority's rent guideline and the allowance for management and maintenance built into the subsidy formula. These imply that initial break-even rents should be set in proportion to the authority's recent Right to Buy valuations, regardless of the actual cost or value of new dwellings. The average rent guideline for England for 1990/1 is just under £1,200 per year, perhaps 2.8 per cent of the capital cost of new dwellings (allowing for 20 per cent inflation from the 1988 figure of £51,000 from DoE 1989*a*, table 6.19). If Right to Buy valuations and the costs of new dwellings are in proportion across the country, this implies break-even rents for new dwellings very similar to those which used to apply for authorities receiving the old Housing Subsidy (but with new—and higher—allowances for management and maintenance spending). This now applies to virtually all authorities (as they receive HRA Subsidy) and there is no longer any effect from Block Grant.

The implied break-even rents for new local authority dwellings under the old Housing Subsidy system (for those receiving it) and under the new HRA Subsidy system (in so far as there are any new local authority dwellings) are very similar on average—at 1990/1 rent levels—to the fair rents supported by the old housing association finance system, so the effective capital grant rates are also much the same as calculated above for housing associations until 1989. The new housing association system is less generous; it remains to be seen what the average rent guidelines for local authorities in later years will imply.

APPRAISAL: INCENTIVES AND RISKS

These features of the subsidy systems before and after the changes in 1989 and 1990 are summarised in Tables 15.1 and 15.2. The immediately striking feature is the difference in the patterns of incentives facing the two kinds of organisation. Not only that, but recent changes have not moved in a consistent direction. In some cases they have amounted to a somersault. As one might have expected from a government keen to introduce 'market' disciplines, the changes to housing association finance removed the 100 per cent marginal subsidy rates on additional capital costs, increasing pressures on associations towards cost-effectiveness. However, the change to local authority subsidies went in the precisely opposite direction, with the new system incorporating 100 per cent marginal subsidy rates and relying only on the constraints of the capital control system.

Nor have the changes produced consistent signals for appropriate rents on new property. For associations the move has been from fair rents (varying relatively little over the country) to higher rents which depend partly on capital costs and partly on actual management and maintenance spending. For authorities, break-even rents on *new* dwellings (as opposed to existing ones) are rather similar under HRA Subsidy to those under Housing Subsidy, varying roughly in direct proportion to capital costs.

There is greater consistency between the two systems in the general absence of features which react to levels of actual rents or recurrent spending, although associations still face the effects of Rent Surplus Fund and Revenue Deficit Grant for their pre-1989 stock, which can largely remove financial incentives. For authorities such effects are absent—unless they exercise 'grantsmanship' and decide that as changes to subsidy formulae generally favour those authorities which have had low rents or high spending in the past, they might benefit from such effects in some possible future change.

While the recent changes—particularly for housing associations—have had the aim of increasing cost-effectiveness, there are two ways in which they have had the opposite effect. The first is that while the new system has not changed the pattern of marginal incentives for associations' recurrent spending, it has changed the constraints on them. Under the old system, rents were set externally, so associations were constrained directly. In a functioning rental

TABLE 15.1 *Summary of marginal effects of subsidy systems in the 1980s*

	Housing associations	*Local authorities*
Changes in rent levels	100% tax on higher initial rents from HAG calculation.	No effect on Housing Subsidy.
	100% tax on higher subsequent rents if liable to GRF or receiving RDG.	Block Grant increased for most authorities if rents raised and RFCs reduced.
Changes in spending on management and maintenance	No effect for most associations.	No effect on Housing Subsidy for most authorities, but 100% subsidy at margin for those in subsidy and spending below otherwise reckonable level (after December 1986).
	100% subsidy at margin for associations receiving RDG (up to allowances).	
		Block Grant reduced for most authorities if spending financed by higher RFCs.
Variations in capital costs	100% subsidy at margin from HAG.	(a) For authorities receiving Housing Subsidy, positive subsidy at rate up to 75%. (b) For other authorities, subsidy at marginal Block Grant rate (generally negative). (c) In long run, for authorities with notional HRA deficit in GRE, these effects dominated by 100% subsidy via Block Grant.
Building a new dwelling	Association breaks even if it charges fair rents and spends at M&M allowance level.	(a) For authorities receiving Housing Subsidy, break-even if M&M spending equals 'reckonable' level and initial rents equal percentage of capital costs.

table continued overleaf

TABLE15.1 (*contd.*)

	Housing associations	Local authorities
		(b) For other authorities, rents would have to cover actual costs, any subsidy from RFCs leading to loss of Block Grant.
		(c) In long run, for authorities with notional HRA deficit in GRE, these effects dominated by break-even rents depending on regional average rents in 1980/1.

market, rents cannot be set far above the market rent, so there would be an indirect constraint. Associations now face something in between—they receive enough subsidy to set rents well below market levels, but can choose that level themselves. While the majority appear to be striving to keep rents down as much as possible, an association could exploit the situation, with its management setting high (but still below market) rents, using the revenue to pay itself high salaries or to cover inefficiency. Preventing this will put a new load on Housing Corporation monitors, and creeping cost inflation could occur, even if blatant abuses are stopped. Ironically, the switch to the new system has *weakened* one of the constraints on association costs.

Secondly, one reason for avoiding subsidy systems with 100 per cent rates of subsidy at the margin is that they have the undesirable effect that much weight has to be put on administrative—possibly bureaucratic—controls, rather than leaving people and organisations free to make decentralised choices in the light of the costs and benefits about which they have much better knowledge than the centre. However, the corollary is that risks are borne by the subsidy system, rather than by organisations which might not be able to carry them. This effective 'pooling' of risk may have substantial cost advantages.

For instance, part of the change since 1989 has been to leave associations to raise 'private finance' to supplement HAG. In order

TABLE 15.2 *Summary of marginal effects of new subsidy systems*

	Housing associations	*Local authorities*
Changes in rent levels	Actual rents on new dwellings do not affect subsidy.	Actual rent variations do not affect HRA subsidy (except to cover rent rebates).
	For old-HAG funded property: 85% tax on rents via RSF; if receiving RDG, 50% tax on assured tenancy rents and more than 100% tax on higher fair rents.	Subsidy in initial years of new system higher, the lower actual rents were in 1989/90.
Changes in spending on management and maintenance	No effect for most associations.	Actual variations in spending do not affect HRA subsidy.
	100% subsidy at margin for associations receiving RDG (up to allowances).	Efficiency gains stay within HRA. Subsidy in first year at least of new system higher, the higher actual spending over 1986/7 to 1988/9 for most authorities.
Variations in capital costs	No change in fixed HAG for 'tariff' associations. Subsidy at pre-determined percentage for other associations (within limits).	100% subsidy at margin via HRA Subsidy.
Building a new dwelling	Break-even rents on new dwellings depend on combination of actual capital costs and actual M&M spending.	Break-even rents and spending equal DoE guidelines for authority with rents eventually in proportion to local capital values.

for this money to evade Treasury accounting conventions which would otherwise drag it back within public spending controls, there can be no government guarantee for this borrowing, not even the fall-back of possible RDG. As a result, private lenders charge a risk premium to what they see as small and unusual organisations. This premium can add up to 2 per cent to borrowing costs above those which the government would have to pay for its own borrowing. In the context of real interest rates below 5 per cent, this is a very substantial addition to costs indeed. For instance, increasing the real interest rate from 3.5 to 5 per cent would raise the servicing costs of a twenty-five-year indexed loan by 17 per cent. While part of this cost does represent a genuine valuation of the risk involved, much of it is a deadweight loss which has to be set beside any gains in cost-effectiveness which may result from the changed pattern of incentives.

The pattern of development may also be affected by changes in risk bearing. The intention of the removal of the 100 per cent marginal subsidy on capital cost from the HAG system was to increase pressures on associations to control capital costs (including the speed of development). This has had a corresponding effect on development period risk, all or part of which is now carried by the association, whereas little was before. This makes rehabilitation of existing property less attractive to associations than it was before, as the risks involved are much greater than with, for instance, a new-build project on a green-field site, for which a fixed-price contract may be negotiable. In the first year of the system there was indeed a marked decline in rehabilitation projects (*Housing Associations Weekly*, 23 February 1990, p. 1).

At a wider level, associations and local authorities are now open to very different levels of long-term risk. To a very large extent, authorities do not have to worry unduly about long-term risks, as unexpected movements in interest rates or recurrent costs would largely be absorbed by changes in HRA subsidy, while future rent levels lie largely in the hands of the Department of the Environment.

By contrast, associations are now far more exposed, particularly on new developments (in the past GRF absorbed a substantial amount of risk). Subsidy for new developments is intended to be on a 'fund and forget' basis: the right amount of HAG will be put in to start with, after which associations are on their own. The difficulty is that it is very hard to set the correct level of grant to give at the start to cope with the balance between rents and costs over thirty years or more. Even if grant is 'right' on average, it will almost certainly turn out to have been too generous in some cases, not generous enough in others.

Associations are now taking on considerable risks. What happens if an association has a sinking fund for major repairs earning interest at a rate which falls behind the escalation of building costs at a crucial moment? There is also the relationship between loan-servicing costs—on a low-start basis—and the rents which have to be (or can be) charged. What happens, for instance, to an association which funds its programme using deferred-interest loans with a pre-determined rate of escalation which turns out to be higher than the rate of inflation? Much discussion of the risks of low-start finance concentrates on the risk with indexed loans that inflation may be unexpectedly high; with deferred interest loans, the risk is that in-flation—and the growth of 'affordable' or even chargeable rents—may be unexpectedly low (if, for instance, full membership of the European Monetary System brings British inflation down to Ger-man levels). This problem is greatest with fixed-rate loans; if loans are at variable interest rates, a fall in inflation may generate a fall in interest rates. However, variable-rate loans are, of course, exposed to any movement in short-term interest rates.

Some risks can be hedged. Building costs for major repairs may be linked to property prices, so planning to fund major repairs in part from future borrowing against equity may reduce exposure. Borrowing at least partly on indexed rather than deferred-interest terms may lead to debt-servicing costs which move more closely in line with incomes and 'affordable' rents. None the less, sole reliance on initial capital grants has significant shortcomings as a way of subsidising housing to be provided over several decades, an issue returned to in Chapter 17.

SUMMARY

- The subsidy systems to associations and authorities differ in the patterns of incentives given to the two kinds of organisation, and the recent changes to them have not been in a consistent direction.
- Some of the changes—notably to association capital finance and the effect of ring fencing in keeping cost savings within the HRA—have increased the pressures for cost control, but

others—for instance the removal of constraints on association rents and the reaction of HRA Subsidy to capital costs—have weakened them.

■ Both systems still incorporate some features which imply 100 per cent marginal rates of subsidy or 100 per cent 'taxes' on income, increasing the need for administrative controls.

■ The corollary of increasing incentives is that risks are also increased. The cost of risk premiums in private finance for associations has offset some of the gains from increased pressures for cost control. Increased risks also make rehabilitation projects look less attractive than new-build projects.

■ The sole use of initial capital grants to subsidise new association developments without any mechanism for later adjustment is fundamentally more exposed to risk than a recurrent-grant system of the kind used for local authorities. 'Fund and forget' financing has significant drawbacks as a way of providing housing subsidies.

NOTE

1. This discussion relates to rent *levels*—associations retained a powerful interest in letting property and collecting rent revenue once rent levels had been set: HAG, GRF, and RDG were all calculated using a standard allowance for voids (unlet property). Any improvement on this standard benefited the associations; anything worse drained reserves.

PART VI

Reform

16

The Reform Agenda

Proposing housing finance reform is a popular armchair sport. This chapter surveys nineteen sets of reform proposals published (or in one case republished) during the 1980s as a prelude to my own, put forward in the final chapter, which will doubtless contribute to a similar pile in the 1990s. Further reform proposals can be found in the *Evidence* and *Supplement* to the Inquiry into British Housing (1985*a* and 1986).

Yates (1989) makes a useful distinction between 'rational economic' and 'rational political' approaches to housing policy reform. The former aim to improve both horizontal equity between tenures and vertical equity, usually with reforms to reduce the tax advantages of owner-occupation, to produce a more market-related structure of rents, and to improve housing benefits (or allowances) for those with low incomes in all tenures. By contrast, 'rational political' approaches acknowledge the political popularity of policies favouring owner-occupation, and either defend the status quo or favour increasing other subsidies to match those for owners.

Most of the proposals surveyed below fall into the 'rational economic' category. Where they differ is in the size of the role which they want the market to play, and in the extent to which the reforms proposed are tempered by political constraints. Four groups are distinguished: a wholly market-orientated group; a group with similar long-term objectives for market-like rent structures, but with proposals more influenced by distributional equity concerns; a group with a central concern to achieve 'tenure neutrality' within perceived political constraints; and a group which puts little weight on market signals. The key points of the proposals are summarised in Table 16.1, which lists the studies in very approximate order in the political spectrum, running from right to left. It should, however, be stressed immediately that this grouping and ordering is approximate and for ease of exposition only, and that it creates bedfellows from people whose views differ in many important respects.

TABLE 16.1 *Housing finance reform proposals*

	Owner-occupiers	Local authorities	Private sector	Housing Benefit
Minford, Peel, and Ashton (1987)	Abolition of MITR[a] 'unlikely to be a priority'.	Market rents phased in over five years.	Market rents phased in over five years.	Ceiling on benefits to unemployed (at 70% of net income in work).
Coleman (1989)		Preferably market rents, with subsidy through benefits.	Market rents. Tax equivalence with owner-occupiers.	Ceiling on Housing Benefit equal to median market rent in region.
Black and Stafford (1988)	Retain MITR, reintroduce taxation of imputed rents (and capital gains, unless landlords exempted).	Market rents.	Market rents.	Abolition of Housing Benefit, but compensation through general income maintenance system.
Ermisch (1986)		Gradual move towards economic rents.	Gradual deregulation. Partial exemption of rent received from income tax.	'Rent-proportional' Housing Benefit depending on lump sum plus 75% of rents.
Ermisch (1984)	Remove MITR ceiling. Tax imputed rents and capital gains.	Economic rents giving competitive real return.	Remove rent controls.	Housing allowance based on income and cost of 'minimum standard' dwelling for household type (not actual costs).

Berthoud and Ermisch (1985)	Remove MITR ceiling. Tax imputed rents (with relief for insurance, depreciation and maintenance).	Move towards economic rents in long term.	Gradual deregulation.	'Rent-proportional' housing allowance based on mixture of actual and standard costs (standard costs only for owners).
Grey, Hepworth, and Odling-Smee (1978)	Keep MITR. Tax imputed rents and capital gains.	Economic rents (3% of capital value plus management and maintenance).	Economic rents as legal maximum?	Universal Housing Allowance (up to 90% of gross economic rent at lowest incomes; to all tenures).
Inquiry into British Housing (1985b)	Phase out MITR over 10 years. No tax on imputed rents or capital gains.	Capital value rents (4% of capital value plus management and maintenance).	Capital value rents.	Replace Housing Benefit with 'needs related housing allowance' (based on lower of flat-rate and actual costs).
Fender (1986)	Tax owners' imputed rents on *equity* share. Abolish existing MITR. Replace domestic rates with Local Income Tax.			

TABLE 16.1 (*contd.*)

	Owner-occupiers	Local authorities	Private sector	Housing Benefit
Walker (1986)	'Housing income tax' (on real interest rate multiplied by capital value). MITR retained with regional limits.			Extend housing benefits (including allowance for repairs) to owner-occupiers (based on economic cost of housing, not cash flow).
Atkinson and King (1980)	Tax *nominal* return to owner-occupiers (or phase out MITR).	Rents which yield 'target rate of return' equivalent to cost of capital to owners.		
Yates (1989)	MITR retained (without limit). 'Housing costs insurance scheme' (combining taxation of real return and housing allowance). 'Housing bonds' (linked to return on equity shares) available to owners and tenants.			Housing allowance to owners and tenants based on standard costs. 'Topping up' if actual costs to owners exceed 20% of income *but* paid for through surrender of equity share.

Warburton (1983)	Phase out MITR. Introduce a 'housing wealth tax' (based on a percentage of capital values).	Move towards economic rents.		Non-means-tested universal housing allowance (taxable through reformed tax system).
Goss and Lansley (1981)	Abolish higher rate MITR. Retain ceiling in cash. Phase out MITR in some way, e.g. over 15 years. Extend capital gains tax to owners or reduce CTT[b] exemption?	Increase subsidies to tenants to give equivalence to owners (*or* reduce subsidies to owners). National rent pooling between authorities.	Bring private and housing association rents into line with local authorities.	Non means-tested but taxable universal housing allowance (with graduated income tax) extended to mortgages (but not outright owners).
Griffiths and Holmes (1985)	End higher-rate MITR. Progressively reduce basic-rate MITR but increase for some groups. Encourage index-linked mortgages (backed by index-linked savings). Abolish stamp duty. CGT[c] at end of 'housing career'?	Subsidies to give 'broad parity' with owner-occupiers. National rent pooling. HRAs to exclude non-housing costs.		Extend to meet costs of low-income owners.

TABLE 16.1 (*contd.*)

	Owner-occupiers	Local authorities	Private sector	Housing Benefit
Labour Housing Group (1989)	Maintain £30,000 limit in cash. Fixed-rate 'Housing Interest Subsidy'. No increase in HIS for movers. New entrants receive HIS tapered over 10 years. Lower CTT threshold?	National rent pooling. Notional rents based on 10% of regional average manual earnings. Loss of subsidy if rents above certain limits.	Recurrent subsidy to housing associations, not capital grants.	Housing Benefit replaced by 'Housing Costs Relief' with 33% taper on gross income. Extended to mortgagers, but not for first year and limit related to initial payments.
Kelly (1986)	Withdrawal of MITR over 10 years. Encouragement of index-linked mortgages.	'National cost pooling'. Indexed loans to local authorities.	Stronger controls on private rents.	More generous system, extended to owners' mortgage interest and repair & maintenance costs.
Malpass (1988)		'Consumption expenditure pricing' (i.e. rents cover management and maintenance only).		
Association of Metropolitan Authorities (1987)	Abolish MITR.			Universal housing allowance extended to mortgage payments and owners' repair & maintenance costs. Universal flat-rate payment plus means-tested 'top-up' based on actual costs.

a Mortgage interest tax relief.   b Capital Transfer Tax.   c Capital Gains Tax.

MARKET-ORIENTATED APPROACHES

This group starts from the basic belief that both the housing market and the whole economy would benefit if rents were set by a free market. For Minford, Peel, and Ashton (1987) the central problem is the labour immobility caused by the current pattern of subsidies and rent controls. They propose a five-year period over which all private-sector rent controls would be removed (for existing tenants as well as new ones, whose rents were in fact decontrolled by the 1988 Housing Act) and local authority rents raised to market levels. This would, they argue, increase labour mobility amongst the employed, substantially improving the operation of the labour market.

They are, however, worried that this increase in rents combined with the current Housing Benefit system, covering 100 per cent of rents for those with the lowest incomes, would actually reduce incentives for the unemployed to take a job (as net resources in work will have been reduced by the increased rents, but not those out of work). To avoid this, they propose that benefits for the unemployed should be subject to a ceiling (that is, in some cases reduced) equal to 70 per cent of previous net income when in work. This 'wages stop' would mean that rent increases would hit the employed and unemployed equally, and the incentive to take a job would not be reduced.

At first sight the distributional consequences of this combination seem highly regressive, particularly as the authors argue that 'it is unlikely to be a high priority to abolish mortgage tax relief. Its economic cost is small, the political cost of abolition too high' (p. 120). They argue (p. 121) that these consequences might be offset by raising tax thresholds and reducing the basic rate of income tax to 25 per cent (actually carried out in 1988). While such tax changes (if on a larger scale) might offset the *average* loss to tenants (which they put at £13 per week at 1986 prices), it seems highly unlikely that they could counter the inherent tilt against those on low incomes. Meanwhile, owner-occupiers would gain from tax cuts without any offsetting loss, reinforcing the regressive effect.

Coleman (1989) shares the aim of establishing an unfettered private rental market, but recognises the barriers to this caused by the relative tax advantages of owner-occupation (see Chapter 12). He therefore combines his proposal for market rents (preferably in all tenures) with 'tax equivalence' with owner-occupiers for private landlords. He does not spell out what form this would take, but suggests that, assuming that tax concessions to owner-occupiers remain, private landlords should either receive grants or Corporation Tax exemption (preferring this to the advantages weighted towards short-term renting given by the Business Expansion Scheme). He also would like to see a reduction in the 100 per cent marginal subsidies offered by Housing Benefit in its current form through the imposition of regional limits related to median rents— intended to affect a larger proportion of tenancies, not just the minority of high rents ruled out under current limits set by rent officers.

At the end of Black and Stafford's (1988) book, they suggest a radical move towards zero housing subsidy to all tenures. This would involve retention of mortgage tax relief (apparently in nominal terms), but taxation of owners' imputed rents and—if private landlords had not been exempted—their capital gains. Rent control would be abolished and local authority rents raised to market levels at the same time as Housing Benefit was abolished, but other benefits improved. In their view this would result in such an increase in overall economic efficiency that 'Gainers could easily compensate losers from this set of changes with a social gain left over' (p. 133). First, some of the reasons why this free-market nirvana might not, in fact, achieve the optimal distribution of resources which they suppose have been discussed in Chapter 2. Second, the authors' view that the 'Political repercussions of such radical changes may not be as considerable as individual tinkering with particular parts of the subsidy apparatus' (p. 133) seems overoptimistic in the extreme.

MARKET SIGNALS WITH EQUITY

While Ermisch (1984; 1986) and Berthoud and Ermisch (1985) share the aim of establishing market rents in the private sector and economic rents for local authority housing, they are more concerned than the previous group with the distributional effects and with the pace of change. They therefore include proposals for the reform of housing benefits, intended simultaneously to produce greater help on average for those with low incomes and to remove the 'up-marketing problem' described in Chapter 10.

The three sets of proposals neatly illustrate Yates's classification of reforms. Ermisch's (1984) proposals are the closest to the 'rational economic' approach: 'Merely tinkering with the present pattern will not take us much closer to a system based on taxpayer preferences' (p. 17). Owner-occupiers would be taxed on their imputed rents and capital gains, but with full tax relief for interest. Local authorities would charge rents which gave a competitive real return on their assets. Rent controls would be removed from the private sector. Income-related housing allowances—which would extend across all tenures—would not depend on actual housing costs but on the cost of a 'minimum standard' dwelling for that family type in that area. Aside from the question of whether tax relief should be given on real or nominal interest (see Chapter 11), these proposals would indeed produce 'tenure neutrality' (with zero subsidy in economic terms to each tenure), and would give benefits in a way which did not affect the marginal cost of housing.

The later adaptation of these proposals in Berthoud and Ermisch (1985) makes rather more concessions to the 'rational political' approach. In particular they stress that economic and market rents are a 'long solution' rather than one to be achieved overnight. They also propose a hybrid housing allowance scheme. Rather than being based only on standard costs, it would be based partly on actual costs and would have the general 'rent-proportional' form described in Chapter 10. For those on the lowest incomes the allowance would equal 75 per cent of actual costs and 25 per cent of 'standard' costs. The proportion of this total paid would fall with income to zero at a fixed level depending on household type. This combination would insulate those on the lowest incomes from most (but not all) of the changes in rents, but would still avoid the up-marketing problem for those with higher incomes.

Ermisch's (1986) proposals to the Inquiry into British Housing are more influenced by political constraints. Rather than propose removing tax concessions to owner-occupiers, he suggests partial exemption of rent received by landlords from income tax as an alternative way of giving more tax equivalence, but at a positive level of subsidy. As with the earlier proposals, he suggests a gradual move towards economic local authority rents and deregulated private rents, with the rent-proportional housing benefit described above, but in this case not extended to owners, presumably because they retain their tax advantages.

Grey, Hepworth, and Odling-Smee (1978) propose a 'rational economic' solution along much the same lines as Ermisch (1984) for owner-occupiers and local authority rents. They suggest, however, that 'economic' rents should also be calculated for the private sector and that 'These might become legal maximum rents' (p. 46), a departure from the proposals described so far, which aim at a de-regulated private sector. To replace existing housing subsidies they propose an 'explicit subsidy system', or universal housing allow-ance. The proposed formula for this is somewhat involved (technically, it is a quadratic function of rent and income), designed to rebate up to 90 per cent of gross economic rent for those with the lowest incomes, but a smaller proportion as income rises. Their calculations suggest that the effects of such a change would be very progressive between income groups taken as a whole (this would remain true even if one adjusted the results to more realistic esti-mates of capital values and hence of economic rents; see Tables 14.1 and 14.2 above).

Given this overall progressivity, the authors may have been sur-prised by the hostility which their proposals generated from the housing world (see, for instance, Aughton 1978). Part of the prob-lem—shared with many other proposals for reform—is that while a reform may have effects which are progressive overall, there may still be substantial variation within income groups, creating hardship for some on low incomes. In an earlier analysis of these proposals using individual data from the Family Expenditure Survey (Hills 1980), I found that if one allows for take-up of the proposed universal allowance to be a relatively optimistic 80 per cent, the majority of those in the lowest decile group of gross house-hold income (net of the appropriate 'needs allowance' for that household type) would be losers, albeit to a fairly small extent. Nearly all local authority tenants in the lowest income group would have lost.

The key aims of the Inquiry into British Housing chaired by the Duke of Edinburgh were to 'create fairness between tenants and owner-occupiers, between home owners with mortgages and those without, and between all tenants' and 'to stimulate housing invest-ment in all sectors' (1985b, p. vii). To this end, they propose that mortgage interest tax relief, subsidies to tenants, and Housing Benefit should be replaced by a 'needs-related housing allowance', which would apply across all tenures. They also suggest that rents in both social and private sectors should be set according to the same principles, giving landlords (and hence potential new investors) a competitive real return, which they suggest means setting rents equal to 4 per cent of capital value, plus management and maintenance and any service charge.

The Inquiry's *Report* presents these proposals as meeting both 'rational economic' and 'rational political' aims. Whether they really achieve this is debatable. First, as will have been evident from Chapters Eleven and Twelve, withdrawal of mortgage interest tax relief does *not* create the equity between tenures and within owner-occupation claimed. The report concedes that taxation of imputed rents and owners' capital gains would be necessary for 'true fiscal neutrality', but rejects these on grounds of political practicality (1985*b*, p. 18). While it is fair enough to decide that political rationality outweighs the economic, it seems wrong then to claim—as the Inquiry does—that economic rationality is still achieved.

Perhaps more seriously in terms of the effects of the package, the *Report* seems seriously to underestimate the capital value of local authority housing. This is crucial, because its proposals rest on the idea that rents could simultaneously give private investors a competitive return and give the same return to social landlords (ensuring equity between tenants), but only result in a modest rise in local authority rents—14 per cent according to the example given for 1983/4 (p. 21). This rests on a valuation of local authority dwellings in England at an average of £12,750 in that year (equivalent to £17,350 in 1989/90, adjusting by the RPI). This seems far too low, partly for reasons of methodology (see Whitehead 1987, and Whitehead and Kleinman 1988), and partly because the year chosen happened to be near the bottom of the house price cycle. Also, the issue of depreciation seems to have been ignored. The suggestion that rents giving a return on capital of 4 per cent would only entail a rise in local authority rents of 14 per cent can be contrasted with the estimate in Chapter Fourteen that rents in 1989/90 would have had to have been between 47 and 95 per cent higher to give a return of between 3.5 and 4 per cent.

The Inquiry's housing allowance, with a limit placed on eligible costs (to avoid the up-marketing problem) could also cause significant losses for some low-income households which are masked in the broad income groups presented in the *Report* (p. 18). This would be worsened if the rents implied by the 4 per cent return had been more realistically estimated.

As with the proposals for owner-occupiers, political accept-ability (and other reasons) may rule out a substantial rise in local authority rents, but the consequence of this is to lose the 'economic rationality' of equivalent treatment to different tenants, if private landlords really are to receive a competitive return.

TENURE NEUTRALITY WITHIN POLITICAL CONSTRAINTS

The next group of proposals is less concerned with establishing market (or equivalent) rents than with creating some kind of equity between owners and local authority tenants, allowing in varying degrees for the 'political rationality' of the popularity of tax conces-sions to owners. They differ in their perceptions of what would be needed to achieve this, some of the differences going back to contrast-ing views of an appropriate 'neutral' benchmark for taxing owner-occupiers (see Chapter 11).

Fender's (1986) proposal is a rare example of simultaneous thought being given to housing finance and local taxation (most considerations of one of the issues ignoring the implications for the other). He focuses on the taxation of owner-occupiers, without specifying what would happen to other tenures. Here he puts for-ward a very neat solution to achieving something close to a real Comprehensive Income Tax treatment of owner-occupation, namely that owners should be taxed on the imputed rent they receive from the *equity* they have in their property. Existing mortgage inter-est tax relief would be abolished, but taxing only the equity share would come close to giving real interest relief, without the compli-cations of calculating it. Part of his aim in making this proposal is to offset the great increase in the tax advantages of housing otherwise caused by the abolition of domestic rates. He also suggests a local income tax (LIT) as a fairer alternative to the Poll Tax. In effect, his proposal would switch from a system of local property taxation to national property taxation and local income taxation.

Walker (1986) also focuses on owner-occupiers. His proposal is to introduce a 'housing income tax', including in owners' taxable income an amount equal to the long-term real interest rate (as given by the yield on gilts) multiplied by the capital value of their dwellings. This would effectively give taxation of imputed rents and capital gains, but with the advantage that 'a housing income tax need not be as difficult a concept to communicate as imputed rent' (p. 67). He would retain nominal interest tax relief, but with the limit varying in proportion to regional house prices. He also gives a careful account of what would be needed to bring benefits for owners into line with those for tenants, pointing out that to achieve this it is the economic cost of owners' housing, not the cash flow interest costs, which should be counted as owners' costs, and that owners' housing income should be included in their income assessment.

Atkinson and King (1980) are concerned with equity between tenures, but also with the distorting effects which the current tax system has on the cost of capital to owner-occupiers (see Table 12.3). One of their proposals is that local authority rents should be set so that the rate of return generated equals the capital cost of housing services for owner-occupiers, a proposal which is returned to in the next chapter. They are also concerned, however, to end the way in which this cost varies between owner-occupiers and with the inflation rate. Writing in 1980, before Capital Gains Tax had been indexed, they argue that neutrality with the treatment of other assets required the *nominal* return on owner-occupied property to be taxed (and nominal interest payments to be deductible). This would have had quite considerable effects—nominal returns being generally in double figures, rather than the 3–5 per cent range for real returns. Note that if this was done, the relevant target rate of return for local authority housing—and hence rents—would also be substantially higher. These changes would, of course, generate substantial revenue which could be used to establish a more generous system of housing allowances and to cut personal tax rates.

These are very dramatic proposals (although the authors give in passing the alternative of simply phasing out mortgage interest tax relief, without discussing the relative merits of this). They also have an element of letting the tail wag the dog, in this case reforming the taxation of owner-occupiers to equate with the treatment of nominal interest. As was shown in Table 11.1, there is a great range of benchmarks to choose from in the British tax system. Their proposal would give neutrality with one of them, but it is not a very satisfactory one (being highly sensitive to inflation and leading to tax bills which could more than wipe out real returns); it would not bring owner-occupation into line with other important forms of saving, such as pension funds or—now that Capital Gains Tax is indexed— even with equity investment or private landlords. The authors argue that 'there will be those who dismiss the proposals discussed here as unrealistic. To them we would reply that it is no less unrealistic to suppose that one can reasonably continue with a system of housing finance which is greatly distorted by taxation and inflation and which leads both to patent inequities and to a bizarre pattern of incentives' (p. 15). Reasonably or not, that system has in most aspects continued for the ten years since that comment was written.

Yates's (1989) proposals include a number of very interesting innovations. First, she shares with other reformers the aim of taxing the real return on owner-occupation and of extending some kind of housing allowance to owners. However, to make the proposal more saleable politically she combines the two into what she calls a 'housing costs insurance scheme'. Some people—with low in- comes—would receive payments out of the scheme, others would make payments in, the packaging being designed to show that its purpose was to iron out fluctuations in circumstances, not to penal- ise owner-occupation.

Second, while the basic part of the housing allowance—what she calls the 'by right' element—would be based on standard, rather than actual, costs. Owners would have the option of receiving a larger amount—a 'by choice' element—if their actual costs exceeded 20 per cent of income (for instance because of front- loaded mortgage interest). However, this optional addition would be given in return for surrendering an equivalent equity share. This neatly permits the allowance to cope with the cash flow problems which result from flat-rate allowances, while avoiding the up- marketing problem usually caused by linking allowances to actual costs.

These equity-sharing arrangements then allow her third innova- tion, the introduction of 'housing bonds'—essentially buying part of the pool of equity shares resulting from the housing allow- ances—which could be purchased by tenants wanting a stake in the housing market or by owners wanting to diversify their risk. The combination of equity sharing and housing bonds would break down the current rigidity of consumption and investment patterns in the housing market. At the moment people are constrained to make a joint purchase of a house to live in and the same amount of housing to invest in; given the choice they might prefer a different mix, an option which would be opened up by these proposals.

Warburton's (1983) proposals would both withdraw mortgage interest tax relief and levy a 'housing wealth tax' on owner-occupiers, with the rate of return subject to tax chosen to approximate imputed rents plus annual *real* capital gains. In terms of the analysis in Chapter 11, this would be a more severe treatment for owners than a real Comprehensive Income Tax, thanks to the lack of any interest deductibility. He proposes a move (which he stresses should also be gradual) towards economic rents for local authority dwellings. More radically, he favours a proposal described in Goss and Lansley (1981) for a universal housing allowance which would not be means-tested, but which would be taxable. For this to achieve the distributional effect desired, he and they envisage that the income tax system would also have been reformed so that taxpayers faced a more graduated structure of marginal tax rates (otherwise, with 95 per cent of taxpayers paying at the basic rate, taxation of the allowance would achieve little in the way of targeting).

For Goss and Lansley (1981) the relative balance of subsidies between tenures and within the owner-occupied sector had been regressive in the 1970s and became more so in the early 1980s. Their proposals—like the measures they use to assess this balance—focus on conventional, rather than on economic measures. Thus their main proposals for owner-occupation are the withdrawal of mortgage interest tax relief through a combination of abolishing higher rate relief, maintaining the limit (then £25,000) in cash, and finding some way of phasing out the relief altogether over less than fifteen years. For local authority tenants their aim is equivalence with owners (apparently on the basis of subsidies calculated in historic terms, as for public expenditure), but a system of national pooling would be required to bring equal treatment to tenants of authorities with varying levels of historic debt. Housing association and private rents would then be brought into line with these levels. Finally they propose the system of universal housing allowances which would be non-means-tested but taxable through a reformed income tax structure described above as part of Warburton's package. However, in their case this would not extend to outright owners (as they do not propose any tax on imputed rents).

Griffiths and Holmes (1985), from a similar political perspective, put forward a related set of proposals but with some important differences. Notably they are sceptical about universal housing allowances:

First, the call for integrated reform can turn into a recipe for stalemate, since the problems of simultaneous reform of housing finance, social security and taxation threaten to become intellectually and politically unmanageable. Second, no-one has yet designed a UHA scheme which is less than formidably expensive, precisely because it is a universal benefit targeted—unlike, say, child benefit—on virtually the entire population. (p. 33)

They do, however, argue that Housing Benefit should extend to the 'housing costs' of low-income owners (but do not define these).

They also argue that a tax on imputed rents or 'housing wealth tax' would not be politically viable, and while they support some form of tax on owners' capital gains, they suggest it should be collected 'at the end of an owner's "career" in owner-occupied housing, perhaps through some form of supplement to capital transfer tax [now Inheritance Tax]' (p. 33). They propose the end of higher-rate interest relief and progressive reduction and restructuring of the remaining relief, perhaps with more for first-time buyers. They suggest the encouragement of index-linked mortgages, evening out payments in real terms, backed by index-linked savings accounts (although they do not address the crucial question of how such accounts would be taxed). Like Goss and Lansley, they propose that subsidies to local authorities should give 'broad parity' with owner-occupiers, and that national rent pooling should even out differences between individual authorities. While individual rent setting would remain with the authorities, they argue that the tradition of 'flat' differentials in rents is not egalitarian, as those in the worst housing receive the least subsidy, and it means that allocations have to be made 'with no assistance from market signals of consumer preferences' (p. 32).

The Labour Housing Group (1989) makes similar proposals for restructuring interest relief into a 'Housing Interest Subsidy', without higher-rate relief and with the limit fixed in cash. They add that for existing borrowers, relief should not increase when they move and take out a larger mortgage, and that for new borrowers relief (perhaps at a higher initial rate than now) should be tapered to zero over ten years. Rather than taxing capital gains, they suggest that the capital transfer tax threshold be reduced, so that tax is payable at the point of inheritance.

Their proposals for 'national rent pooling' are more explicit than those of earlier authors. They argue that the payments into or receipts from the pool should depend on the calculation of a notional HRA (as is, in fact, done for the new HRA Subsidy), with the notional rents varying not according to capital values, but in proportion to—they suggest 10 per cent of—manual workers' earnings in each region. They also suggest that these guideline rents should only be exceeded if tenants agree after consultation, and that above certain limits, higher rents should result in loss of subsidy (and presumably even higher rents). They also suggest that subsidies to housing associations should be brought into an equivalent system of recurrent subsidy, replacing the existing capital grants.

They suggest that the taper in Housing Benefit (renamed 'Housing Costs Relief') be cut from 65 per cent on net income to 33 per cent on gross income, and that entitlement should be extended in a limited way to mortgage interest. In an attempt to minimise the extension of the up-marketing problem which this could involve, they suggest that benefit for home-buyers would not be available in the first year of a mortgage and that thereafter it would be available according to the same taper calculations as for tenants, but limited so that it brought down interest payments to no less than the proportion of gross income (less Income Support) which was absorbed in the first year. While the motivation for this proposal is clear, some of its effects might prove difficult to explain: for instance, two people in otherwise identical circumstances might receive different amounts of benefit simply because one had purchased in a year when interest rates were relatively low.

NON-MARKET APPROACHES

The final group put least weight on Griffiths and Holmes's 'market signals of consumer preferences'. Kelly (1986) suggests that for a variety of reasons the idea of reviving the private rented sector is a mirage, arguing that protection for existing private tenants and rent controls should be made more effective and that it is only through the social rented sector that the necessary supply of homes will come. He suggests that mortgage interest relief be phased out over ten years, combined with the extension of Housing Benefit both up the income scale through lower tapers, and to the mortgage repayments and repair and maintenance costs of owner-occupiers. He does not address the problems of extended benefit at a marginal rate of 100 per cent to owners' purchase costs, or of the general extension of the up-marketing problem to higher income levels. He also endorses the idea of indexed mortgages and of national rent pooling, describing it (more accurately) as 'national cost pooling'.

As an alternative to ideas of economic rents or national rent pooling, Malpass (1988) suggests what he calls 'consumption expenditure rents' for local authorities. Under this, rents would simply cover management and maintenance costs, while all capital costs would be subsidised in full, the justification given being that tenants never acquire the houses in which they live (although this ignores the opportunity cost of the capital tied up in them). This would imply rents significantly lower than they have been historically. It is hard to see what objectives this pricing system would meet, other than making a generalised transfer to local authority tenants. It could be pointed out that in the past real interest rates to owners have been zero or negative—so that tenure neutrality would support rents excluding any return on capital at all; this does not, however, seem particularly pertinent, given the level to which real interest rates have risen over the 1980s.

Finally, the Association of Metropolitan Authorities (1987) puts forward a package for a 'new deal for home owners and tenants'. It says little about the rented sector, but concentrates on abolition of mortgage tax relief combined with the introduction of a 'two tier' housing allowance to replace all existing housing benefits. The first part of this would be a universal flat-rate payment to all households—they suggest £10 per week in 1986 prices. On top of this about a quarter of households would receive a means-tested 'top-up' payment to cover the difference between this and actual housing costs, including rents, rates, water rates, a notional amount for owners' maintenance, and mortgage payments.

It estimates that this package would cost—at 1986 prices—about £4 billion, but that 30 per cent of households would still lose as a result. This proportion would obviously be higher if one allowed for the offsetting measures necessary to raise the lost revenue; for full assessment of this kind of package, its consequences on a 'revenue neutral' basis would be much more helpful than the results which the AMA presents. The proposed housing allowance would substantially widen the poverty trap and worsen the up-marketing problem. In effect—in the reverse of the Inquiry into British Housing's proposed allowance—people would receive the *higher* of actual costs and the flat-rate element. Once someone was receiving the 'top-up' element (which would extend to almost anyone whose costs were high enough), the marginal cost of housing would be zero, and the state would pick up all the costs of—for instance—buying a much larger house. Allowing for this, the £4 billion per year price tag is probably a severe underestimate.

CONCLUSION

The various proposals surveyed in this chapter are summarised in Table 16.1. There is clearly no shortage of proposals—with a range of objectives and of varying degrees of practicality—on which to draw. The next chapter attempts to synthesise some of these ideas, with the aim of minimising some of the undesirable effects of the current system which have been described in earlier chapters.

17

Untangling Housing Finance

This chapter presents a synthesis of what seem the most promising parts of the proposals surveyed in the last chapter, together with some additions, chosen to address the key problems identified in the book. While this could be called a package, it does not come with the usual caveat that it should be considered only as a whole, with its careful balance ruling out separate consideration of its components. This is always a forlorn injunction—readers and policymakers are bound to look at the parts they like best and to think of other ways in which they could be combined. Second, as Griffiths and Holmes (1985) argued, it is a recipe for stalemate, since simultaneous reform of all the relevant areas, while not impossible—as witnessed by the changes between 1988 and 1990—does present immense political and operational problems (as witnessed by the same changes). Instead, a series of steps is presented which, while not producing a completely coherent and balanced system of housing finance (the constraints of 'political rationality' discussed in the last chapter effectively rule that out), would at least produce a much less tangled structure than we have now.

TEN KEY PROBLEMS

1. EQUITY BETWEEN TENURES

Some believe that council and housing association tenants, paying well below market rents, have been 'feather-bedded' by comparison with owner-occupiers. Others believe that tax concessions to owners have the opposite result, particularly after the real rent increases of the early 1980s.

The analysis in earlier chapters supports neither characterisation of the overall balance between the main tenures. Simple comparisons between cash flows to local authority Housing Revenue Accounts (HRAs) and through mortgage interest tax relief have very limited value. Making a more meaningful comparison is more difficult, but on one key comparison—between the average 'capital cost of housing services' to owners and the *ex ante* rate of return on assets implied by gross local authority rents—tenants had a slight advantage at the end of the 1980s (see Chapters 12 and 13). Similarly, the average value of tax concessions to owners (compared with the situation if the real return on housing was taxed) and of the economic subsidy to local authority tenants (measured by comparing gross rents with rents giving an economic return) in 1989/90 gave something between a small advantage to owners and a small advantage to tenants, depending on the assumptions made (see Chapter 14).

This does not mean that there are no problems of equity between the tenures. First, these findings are for averages, while the patterns of advantage *within* the tenures are very different, as discussed below. Second, the rents which housing associations are now having to charge 'assured tenants' put this group in a decidedly worse position than owners. As the same catch-phrase about rents being 'within the means of those in low-paid employment' has been used to describe both these and the Government's intentions for overall local authority rents in the future, the same could eventually apply to council tenants as well. Third, the private rented sector is clearly in a worse position, not only than the two main tenures, but also than other businesses.

2. EQUITY WITHIN TENURES

The value of tax concessions varies substantially between owner-occupiers (see Table 12.3), with the greatest advantages going to higher rate taxpayers and those with the largest mortgages. This contributes to a distributionally perverse pattern of advantages by income (see Chapter 14)—those with the highest incomes benefiting most and those at the bottom least (although, as the advantages generally rise less rapidly than income itself, it would be regressive to remove them to finance a simple cut in income tax rates). Notably, low-income owners receive no help with regular repair and maintenance costs, in contrast to the help which low-income tenants receive with the rents covering equivalent costs.

For local authority tenants the relationship between subsidy and income is more logical, although marred by the failure of Housing Benefit to achieve full take-up. The key issue here is the variation of gross rents—and hence subsidy—between different dwellings and across the country. In the past there was relatively little variation— people have paid the same amount for different things, which some may see as an equity problem. By contrast, the new HRA Subsidy system appears designed to result in *more* variation than there is either in costs or in what tenants can afford.

However, while the recent pattern has been of rents which are lowest in relation to costs in high-cost regions, Chapter 13 shows that the same regions have, *ex post*, shown the greatest return on local authority housing assets. If the differential rates of capital gain which caused this were expected to persist indefinitely, relatively little variation in rents between regions could be defended on the grounds that economic rents would also vary less than costs (working through the construction of an economic rent given in Chapter 5). However, while there appears to be a popular expectation that capital gains will continue to be systematically faster in some areas than others, it is hard to see what the grounds for this are, other than simple extrapolation from the past.

For housing associations the key questions are the disparity between the fair rents paid by pre-1989 tenants and those paid by new ones, and the relativity between association and council rents. Given the similarity between council and association tenants, it is unclear why subsidy systems should continue to be structured to produce different results.

3. THE OVERALL LEVEL OF HOUSING SUBSIDIES AND TAX ADVANTAGES

Domestic rates provided an approximate offset to the lack of tax on owners' imputed rents and real capital gains and to the economic subsidies going to local authority tenants, although not at the bottom and top of the income distribution (see Chapter 14). A side-effect of the replacement of domestic rates by the Poll Tax has been a substantial improvement in the position of housing relative to other forms of consumption or investment with no obvious gain in either distributional or housing production terms, and with what are argued to be damaging effects on the economy as a whole (Muellbauer 1990). At present, this shift may not irrevocably have entered expectations or the constraints of 'political rationality'.

4. POLARISATION OF HOUSING CHOICES

Housing can be what economists call a 'joint product'. Owner-occupiers purchase not only somewhere to live for a period, but also invest in a particular asset, with the size of investment fixed by the house in which they live. Tenants purchase only the former. Such limited choices are inefficient—given a free choice, some might choose a different mix of housing consumption and investment than that institutionalised by the current system. Those who cannot afford to purchase an entire dwelling might still like some stake in the housing market. Others might want to hedge between property in different regions—one constraint on mobility of labour is the worry of some potential movers that relative price movements might prevent return. There are good reasons of risk aversion, given the volatility of house prices, for people to want to own the whole of a property (giving them indefinite occupation rights), but there may also be those who would prefer a somewhat different housing investment than this implies.

5. MISMATCH BETWEEN THE ECONOMIC COSTS OF HOUSING AND CASH FLOWS

Throughout the book, the differences between economic costs of housing and the cash flow costs of management and maintenance and debt servicing have recurred as a source both of difficulty in understanding the current system and of some of its problems. As well as the problems for subsidy design caused by the front-loading of conventional debt servicing (see Chapter 5), there are the 'hidden' costs of depreciation and of the 'opportunity cost' of capital tied up in a dwelling. In all three areas—subsidies, benefits, and taxation— it is the cash flows which receive attention. This results in the greatest benefits going to those with the greatest cash flow rather than underlying costs, for instance those with large mortgages rather than low-income outright owners.

6. THE STRUCTURES OF SUBSIDY TO HOUSING PROVIDERS

Several shortcomings in the structures of subsidy for local authorities and housing associations have not been remedied by the 1989 and 1990 changes (see Chapters 6 to 9 and 15). First, while there may be good reasons for retaining separate systems of subsidy to the two kinds of organisation, there seems little reason why they should be structured to produce such different results, in terms not only of rents, but also of the incentives (or lack of them) which they embody. For instance, grants to housing associations have been reformed to give them a direct interest in their capital costs just as an equivalent incentive has been removed from local authority housing.

A second common problem is the complete lack of clarity in meaning in the Government's formulation that rents should be 'within the reach of those in low paid employment'. For council tenants the lack of any clear definition leaves great uncertainty about future rents, denying them the information needed to make choices about savings levels, the Right to Buy, or how to vote on a proposed change of landlord. While the political reasons for this are unsurprising, the cruel result is that people have to make important decisions in the dark. Similarly, the Housing Corporation's Tenants Guarantee puts associations under an 'overriding requirement' to charge rents which are 'affordable', but what this means is undefined.

The dragging of rent rebates into calculation of the new HRA Subsidy for authorities negates the advertised advantage of 'ring fencing'—clear separation of the *landlord* function from local authorities' roles as housing 'enablers' and regulators (and as convenient channels for administering part of the benefit system). Second, while the heavy reliance on whatever 'damping' formula the Department of the Environment decides on each year continues, the system will not offer the clear relationship between management effectiveness and rents which it was supposed to. Instead, for some time to come, it will be impossible for people to work out whether changes in rent and service levels result from landlord effectiveness, the unravelling of previous arrangements, or even political favouritism.

Problems arise from the 'fund and forget' philosophy of the new system for associations, without any later 'in-course correction' from variable recurrent subsidy or removal of surpluses. This does give a strong incentive—associations have to live with mistakes indefinitely—but it also introduces a high degree of risk on the balance between costs and rents over a long period. Setting the right level of grant to equate the two over a thirty-year or more future is not only difficult, but also increases risk margins, the costs of which are substantial. The new association system also gives little recognition for the area improvement effects of the rehabilitation work which associations used to carry out, giving benefits beyond the housing directly provided. Further, borrowing using low-start 'deferred interest' finance while building up explicit major repairs funds, as has been encouraged in the first years of the system, may not offer the best protection against uncertain future costs.

7. LACK OF CONSUMER POWER IN A RATIONED SYSTEM

In a competitive market, if a producer offers poor value for money, consumers can switch to an alternative supplier, choosing the mix of price and quality or quantity which suits them best. Within a rationed system with below-market prices, choices may be more limited, or entirely absent. Most authority and association tenants have little choice about the rent-service mix which they receive, and only limited—often prohibitively expensive—options to take their custom elsewhere. For instance, the removal of the right of new association tenants to a fair rent means that associations now set their own rents with only distant limits given by market rents in the free-entry private sector. While most associations are working hard to keep rent levels down, some tenants could end up captive to inefficient or extravagant managements.

The free-market solutions proposed by the first group of would-be reformers surveyed in Chapter 16 might solve this kind of problem. However, if as argued below the combination of 'political rationality' and the need for equity between the main tenures rules these out, tenants need to be given improved ways both of judging the service which they receive and of exercising control, where they are dissatisfied with the combination of rent and service provided.

8. THE STRUCTURE OF HOUSING BENEFIT

The virtual inevitability of some of the problems with Housing Benefit discussed in Chapter 10—the contribution to some form of poverty trap and lack of complete take-up—provides an important rationale for some use of general rather than just income-related subsidies. More particular problems with the current system are: the failure to keep 'affordability ratios' down to acceptable levels for people with incomes around the point where entitlement ends; the 'up-marketing' problem of benefit rising pound for pound with any increase in costs; and differences between the treatment of low-

income owners and tenants. The analogous structure now introduced for improvement grants embodies similar poverty trap and
up-marketing problems—if anything, on a larger scale.

9. THE PENALTIES IMPOSED ON THE PRIVATE RENTED SECTOR

One does not have to be an enthusiast for the free market or unaware
of the problems of the relationship between private landlords and
tenants to see an important role—albeit limited—for a sector
offering free access to those without the capital or borrowing power
to become owners but who also fail to qualify under the rationing
conditions of authorities and associations, and others wanting to
make a relatively short-term move. It is not just that the private
rented sector is disadvantaged relative to owner-occupation and
subsidised renting, but its costs are *higher* than they would be if it
was 'unsubsidised'. As Nevitt (1966) pointed out a quarter of a
century ago, British tax law assumes houses to have infinite lives.
The tax concessions now offered through the Business Expansion
Scheme are not an appropriate offset, as the main advantage goes to
those intending to rent property for short periods, and it has a very
high cost to government compared with alternative subsidies to
tenants.

The lack of political consensus about the future of rent control
has a very damaging effect. With the Government having withdrawn
virtually all safeguards for new tenants, but the Opposition discussing the possibility of reimposing controls, potential landlords face
great uncertainty about future rents and market values of properties
with sitting tenants. Given such uncertainty they can demand a far
higher short-term rate of return than they could if others were prepared to enter the sector for the rates of return available on other
kinds of investment. This increases rents and reduces services to
some of those already in the worst housing positions.

10. SEPARATE DECISION-MAKING ON SUBSIDIES, BENEFITS, AND TAX CONCESSIONS

Housing is a classic example of different constraints being placed on
'public spending' and on 'tax expenditures', even if the two have the
same net effect on public finances. In the last decade increasingly
draconian measures have been taken to limit 'public spending' on

housing, but the cost of mortgage interest tax relief has soared. If they had been within the same budget constraints, a different mix could have been chosen. Misconceptions also result from the presentation of public spending only in terms of flows of current and capital spending, without any information on movements in the stock of assets and debt (as is attempted in Chapter 13). There are also problems with the co-ordination of policy towards Housing Benefit and housing subsidies. Some of the decisions taken by what is now the Department of Social Security on Housing Benefit have been unhelpful towards housing policies being pursued by the Department of Environment, while much of the saving to the housing budget from lower subsidies has re-emerged directly as higher social security costs. However, when the DoE ran rent rebates and allowances, the system meshed poorly with the rest of social security, so it is not entirely clear that reversing the 1982/3 switch of responsibilities would be desirable. There is a distinction between housing provision and income maintenance, even if they need careful co-ordination.

TEN AIMS FOR REFORM

Starting from a blank sheet, the most convincing arguments for intervention in the housing market (see Chapter 2) would be those concerned with raising the quality of housing available to those on low incomes, recognising the shortcomings of purely income-related benefits, and with improving the worst of the stock, with 'external' area benefits. The pages preceding this have not, however, been blank. While rejecting the implied argument of the 1977 Green Paper that nothing should ever change, people's expectations and factors like capitalisation of tax concessions in house prices do put severe limits on the speed of change. With the addition of 'political rationality' arguments limiting generalised assaults on the tax advantages of owner-occupiers, together with the difficulty of imposing taxes if there are no flows of cash (like imputed rents and accrued capital gains), the room for manoeuvre becomes limited, although it seems premature to accept that the case for a general property tax is lost, particularly given the unpopularity of the Poll Tax.

These arguments together suggest the first three of ten aims for reform:

1. A 'big-bang' reform of housing finance, with all existing subsidies subsumed into a single integrated and rational housing allowance, is not a realistic option. Reform has to be gradual.
2. Tax concessions for owner-occupiers cannot be withdrawn overnight, but should be gradually restructured to tilt their benefits in favour of those on lower incomes. The feasible field for operation is mortgage interest tax relief.
3. It is more feasible and (in macroeconomic terms) more important to restore a general tax on housing—either through a restoration of domestic rates in some form, or through a national property tax—than to attempt to reintroduce 'Schedule A' taxation or impose tax on owners' accrued capital gains.

Equity between the two main tenures and the limitations of Housing Benefit then imply that:

4. Gross local authority and housing association rents should be sub- economic, but give in broad terms a return on capital equivalent to the capital costs of owners, allowing for their tax advantages.

Equity within the rented sector and the need for a 'level playing field' in which tenants could judge the performance of their landlord then suggest:

5. Local authority and association subsidy systems should allow equivalent results in terms of the rent required by a particular level of service. The system should be based on explicit principles and should incorporate incentives for cost control, but without exposing providers—and their tenants—to high degrees of risk.

The aim of keeping some kind of open-access sector functioning, and of attracting some new investment, suggests:

6. Private landlords should be able to earn a reasonable long-term return on new investment, with rent control used only to rule out rents which would give a return substantially above that available elsewhere, without tax disadvantages compared with other businesses (but not owner-occupiers).

Private rents would remain above those charged by local authorities and housing associations. The circle of consistent rents in all tenures at a level giving a competitive return, without large rent increases for council tenants, cannot therefore be squared in the way in which the Duke of Edinburgh's Inquiry hoped. People will continue to pay different amounts for the same thing. This implies that:

7. Housing Benefit should continue to cover 100 per cent of the actual rents of those on the lowest incomes, but its structure should be adapted to minimise up-marketing, to reduce the need for direct controls, to allow increases in its overall generosity, and to allow extension to certain costs of low-income owner-occupiers.

Widening the range of choices people can make for the relationship between their housing consumption and housing investment suggests:

8. Arrangements which introduce a 'fuzzier' distinction between tenures should be encouraged.

This, in combination with the advantages of bringing cash flow housing costs closer to underlying economic costs suggests:

9. Borrowing forms which are less front-loaded in real terms, equity sharing arrangements (and 'housing bonds' to match them) should be encouraged.

Constraints on public resources also imply that tax and subsidy structures should give rough equivalence across and within tenures (otherwise more is being spent to achieve a given result in one area than another), and that:

10. Planning of public spending and taxation should impose similar constraints on explicit subsidies and on tax concessions.

SPECIFIC POLICY MEASURES

The following suggestions are designed to meet these aims, at least in part. More detailed arguments for and against some of them can be found elsewhere in the book.

TAXATION OF OWNER-OCCUPIERS

In terms of 'economic rationality' it would undoubtedly be better to restore taxation on owners' imputed rents and tax their real capital gains than to restrict relief for interest. However, political practicality strongly suggests that, if concessions to owners are to be restructured, it is only interest relief which is a feasible target. As a first part of such a 'second best' reform, higher rate mortgage interest tax relief should be abolished. This would leave all relief channelled through the Mortgage Interest Relief at Source (MIRAS) system, with equal relief for all and no necessary connection with the tax system. The relief could then be reclassified as part of the housing budget, coming under the same constraints as the rest of public spending, and its structure could—if desired—be changed from a constant percentage of interest to something which focused help on those who needed it most. At the same time the £30,000 limit should be frozen, until the gradual effects of inflation have brought the overall cost of relief under control. With no other change in structure, this alone would have changed the relief's nature from one of greatest help to the richest owners to something closer to a flat-rate allowance towards mortgage costs.

To help reduce the problems caused by the front-loading of mortgage payments, index-linked mortgages should be encouraged. MIRAS relief would only be given on the real interest payments on these, but simultaneous changes to tax rules could allow banks and building societies to offer indexed accounts (like 'Granny bonds'), on which only the real return would be taxable for the majority of taxpayers, provided that they were backed by matching mortgages.[1]

Secondly, equity-sharing should be promoted, financed through a system of regional housing bonds, as suggested by Yates (1989). For instance, first-time buyers could be offered an optional 'by choice' addition to MIRAS relief, in return for surrendering an equity share on their property, repayable on sale and requiring an annual payment in the interim, the size of which would be linked to regional house prices (without the annual payment, there would be a 'lock-in' effect, with advantages to equity sharers from staying put). Similarly, elderly owners could be offered the chance to sell part of their equity to help unlock part of their wealth, under similar conditions.

TAXATION IN GENERAL

Stamp duty on residential property should be abolished. The only justification for this tax—recent in its importance, but archaic in its form—is that it offsets the other tax advantages of owner-occupation. Provided—here there is a 'package'—that the tax advantages of owner-occupation were restructured, it should go, with benefits to those moving and leading to some improvement in stock utilisation. Failing that, the structure of the duty could at least be reformed to look more like a 'slice' system, both improving its progressivity and removing the current jump in liability at the threshold.

Second, a general tax on housing should be restored to fill the gap in the tax system left by the abolition of domestic rates. The obvious option would be to replace the Poll Tax with a modernised version of domestic rates, but if some alternative local tax was used, such as Local Income Tax, a national property tax—a 'National Domestic Rate'—could perform much the same role in housing policy terms (see Fabian Society Taxation Review Committee 1990 for a more detailed discussion of local taxation).

LOCAL AUTHORITY AND HOUSING ASSOCIATION RENTS

Both for equity between tenants and in order to allow fair comparison between their effectiveness, the subsidy systems for local authorities and housing associations should be structured so that the two subsidy systems would allow organisations with the same level of efficiency to deliver comparable combinations of rent and management and maintenance services.

The consistency and transparency of the systems is perhaps more important than their exact form, but I would suggest that, in broad terms, the return generated by gross rents should equal the capital cost of housing services to owner-occupiers (as suggested by Atkinson and King 1980). Elsewhere, I have described a system of 'target rents' which could be adapted to achieve this (Hills 1988*a* and *c*). The qualification 'in broad terms' is important. Given fluctuations in house prices and the uncertainties around other key elements, it is *not* suggested that rents be defined by an unvarying percentage of current capital value plus an allowance for other costs. Instead, such a calculation should be carried out initially, but the system then adjusted each year to keep average target rents in line with a measure of incomes. If the capital value of housing continues to move with incomes in the long term, this would keep rents in line with both trend capital values and 'affordability'. If, after several years, this assumption proved incorrect, some adjustment would be needed.

The initial average target rent would be chosen to cover three elements: an average allowance for management and maintenance; a percentage of average rebuilding cost covering full depreciation; and a percentage of trend capital value. The subsidy compared with an economic rent would thus be contained in the final element, with the percentage set being *below* the long-run real interest rate minus the expected real capital gain (which the percentage would be for an economic rent). For instance, calculations in earlier chapters suggest a figure of about 0.7 per cent to match the tax treatment of owners as it was in 1989/90 if house prices were on trend.[2]

Subsidies would allow individual providers to break even while charging rents covering a management and maintenance allowance for their region, an estimate of full depreciation based on rebuilding cost, and the standard national percentage of its trend capital value (capital values would have to be estimated anyway to run the reintroduced local or national property tax). The rents underlying subsidy would thus vary between properties and regions, but much less than market or economic rents.[3]

These 'target rents' would be used to calculate subsidy, but providers would be free to charge different rent levels. For instance, higher rents could support greater management and maintenance spending than the allowances, or savings in costs could allow lower rents. In this way incentives towards 'good husbandry' would be preserved.

This approach is based on equity in treatment between owner-occupiers and authority and association tenants. An alternative would be to set the initial average target rent directly on the basis of 'affordability', with a measure of income chosen and a percentage set on other grounds (which was the starting point for the earlier version of this proposal). This initial level might not generate equal treatment with owners, but movements in subsidy from year to year, and the relative treatment of different providers could follow a similar pattern to 'target rents'.

INFLUENCE FOR CONSUMERS IN A RATIONED SYSTEM

Any structure which leaves their average rents well below market levels would perpetuate the limits on the power of 'exit' which tenants have to discipline ineffective landlords, given the high cost of moving into the free-entry market sector. Alternative ways of

preventing abuse of the 'local monopoly' power of landlords need
to be strengthened, including:

- mechanisms giving tenants direct control of parts of the service,
  running through the spectrum of locally accessible management,
  Estate Management Boards, tenant management and ownership
  co-operatives;
- subsidy systems which give clear signals and guidelines about
  financial constraints, for instance for the level of management
  and maintenance spending supported by particular rents;
- a wide range of providers, operating on a 'level-subsidy playing
  field', offering a range of possibilities for the rent-service mix;
- formal monitoring of landlords by the Audit Commission and
  the Housing Corporation, with clear guidelines for rents as well
  as service standards built into the process (for associations at
  present, the meaning of 'affordable rents' is too vague for this
  purpose).

The Right to Buy and 'Choice of Landlord' do provide some powers
of 'exit' for local authority tenants, but with the former only open to
those with the resources to exercise it (in which case, discounts tilt
the choice heavily in favour of doing so), and the latter subject to a
highly contentious voting system and, at present, offering a choice
between unknown rents. If transfer terms were based on the same
rent guidelines as subsidies, tenants would be offered a clearer and
fairer choice.

LOCAL AUTHORITY SUBSIDIES

A corollary of some of these aims—and a move which could have
advantages in its own right (see Power 1987*b* and 1988)—would be a
financial system involving complete separation of the local
authority landlord function. 'Ring fencing' has not, in fact, achieved
this. First, the grants for rent rebates should be separated from HRA
Subsidy, disentangling social security and housing subsidies.
Second, the possibility of transfers out of the HRA should be withdrawn.

Such separation has the important advantage of allowing efficiency savings within the housing department to stay within it. Those
who remain enthusiasts for restoring Rate Fund Contributions are
referred to Chapter 6 and the citations there on the sheer complication of the interactions between RFCs and the old Block Grant

system, and should consider what would have happened if housing had not been isolated from the whole ghastly business of the introduction of the Poll Tax (the abolition of which will not be without problems, either). This should not rule out the ability of authorities, as part of their wider responsibilities, to make payments for defined purposes into the HRA on the same conditions as they would to housing owned by others, or for services which it is most efficient for the housing department to provide, but which would normally be paid for from the general fund for other residents.

With the extrication of rent rebates from its calculation, HRA Subsidy would become negative in some cases. Low-debt authorities would make a payment out of their HRA into a pool, while others would receive payments from it. There is no reason to expect the pool to exactly balance overall at target (or otherwise 'affordable') rents, any more than an individual authority's HRA would (witness the changes in the real value of debt servicing carried on the national HRA since the mid-1970s shown in Chapter 3). In general, particularly if building programmes were restarted, central government would have to contribute into the pool, but there are circumstances in which it would take a net payment out of it.

Apart from this major change, much of the new HRA Subsidy system could be preserved, but with differences in calculation of some key elements:

- replacement of rent guidelines based solely on relative Right to Buy valuations with guidelines derived as described above;
- the use of explicit allowances for management and maintenance spending (rather than past spending) as soon as possible, with allowances matching those given to housing associations (but reflecting different stock conditions); and
- rapid phasing out of *ad hoc* 'damping formulae' (which would be less important with the rent structure suggested above).

Note that the rents implicit in the subsidy system would depend on average regional allowances for management and maintenance spending, but the subsidy paid would channel most help to those individual authorities with the greatest repair problems.

The remaining problem with HRA Subsidy is the 100 per cent subsidy which it gives to new capital spending at the margin. This could be removed by ensuring that the measure of capital value used to determine guideline rents reacted—in the short term, at least—to capital spending. In other words, for new capital spending it would be *cost* rather than *value* which would matter (say, for a period of five years, after which an explicit valuation would be made). Authorities would then see their aggregate rent guidelines increasing to reflect the 'target rent' resulting from actual costs per unit for new units. The more costs per unit were kept under control, the lower the rent which could be delivered. Under current arrangements rent guidelines are unaffected by new spending, and the pressure for cost control—and 'good husbandry' of capital resources—is much less.

Finally, to bring the cash flows of subsidy to authorities closer to the underlying economic costs, a proportion of new local authority borrowing could be on indexed terms, either directly or through central government on-lending.

HOUSING ASSOCIATION SUBSIDIES

Most dramatically there could be a switch from capital grants to recurrent subsidies. Apart from making it much easier to put local authorities and housing associations on to an equal footing, this would also end the problem of trying to set the correct level of grant to equate costs and rents over several decades. The subsidy system would then carry many of the risks and uncertainties involved, effectively pooling them, rather than leaving them to add to the costs of small organisations. Such a switch would also end the need for Rent Surplus Funds or Revenue Deficit Grant—they would be subsumed in calculation of need for subsidy (based on a notional income and expenditure account) in the same way as happens for local authorities. There might also be cash flow advantages to government from giving subsidy over a period of years rather than as an initial grant (depending on the definition and control of public spending). A disadvantage from the point of view of associations is that it might be felt that 'up-front' grants are safer than those depending on the whims of later Governments (although this kind of argument did not prevent the introduction of Grant Redemption funds in the early 1980s).

Short of this, the existing capital grant system could be modified, notably with calculation of grant percentages to allow associations to charge 'target rents' on new developments. With current interest rates and capital costs, this would require a higher level of grant than is currently being offered (although at other times it might be lower). Also, urgent attention is needed to the way in which associations provide for major repairs. Explicit major repairs funds may be inefficient, as the rate of interest on deposits is usually below that on outstanding borrowing, which it would be better to repay. They may also be unnecessary, as there may be scope for associations to remortgage property when major repairs are needed—current provisions may raise rents unnecessarily. Instead, associations could be set a target for the total liability from the combination of net outstanding debt and accumulated depreciation (or need for major repairs) in relation to stock value. The association could then choose the debt/asset structure to achieve this, but it—and its monitors—would know that the target ratio had been chosen to be consistent with an explicit rent structure.

This ratio could also be used to control an 'in-course correction' mechanism if—as a result of changed circumstances like dramatic changes in inflation, interest rates, or building costs, but no fault of the association—the initial capital grant turned out not to have been generous enough. Such a safety net would allow associations to build less of a risk margin into rents and those lending to them to charge less of a risk premium.[4] To further spread the risks being taken on by housing associations, there could be wider use of equity sharing as a way of raising capital (see Best 1990 for an innovative scheme of this kind), for instance, through developing the market for 'regional housing bonds' suggested above in connection with equity sharing arrangements for owners.

Finally, if rehabilitation of existing housing is seen as having benefits going beyond the housing directly provided, there should be specific additional grants for rehabilitation projects in designated areas.

THE PRIVATE RENTED SECTOR

More than in any other, the private rented sector would benefit from consensus about its role (however limited that was seen to be). This would require concessions from both sides of the political spectrum:

- on the right, acceptance that there is a need for safeguards against tenants being exploited by the 'local monopoly' which the costs of moving give a private landlord;
- on the left, acceptance that such safeguards should leave private landlords able to receive a long-term return on new investment which is competitive with that on other business investments.

This was a key aim of the Inquiry into British Housing (1985*b*). It proposed a new kind of 'approved' landlord, which could mobilise long-term funds from building societies, pension funds, insurance companies, and so on. These would be monitored and regulated in a way which allowed a reasonable long-term return (rather than a gamble on short-term speculative profits), so that a new sector could grow up free of the disreputable past of private renting in Britain. There is much to be said for these arguments, although remarkably little sign of any such consensus emerging. As far as the financial underpinnings are concerned, agreement could be sought for the following:

1. New lettings of property above a certain value—say the median regional price in the owner-occupied sector—would continue outside rent control.
2. For other property, control would be of a form which ruled out excessive returns on capital value, but which was not a binding constraint in most cases. This could involve allowing a clearly competitive return—such as 5 per cent in real terms—or using a reference to other parts of the housing market (as in West Germany).
3. The Business Expansion Scheme would be scrapped, but depreciation allowed as a tax deduction. This would move closer to neutrality with other businesses, and remove the short-term bias of the BES.

HOUSING BENEFIT AND IMPROVEMENT GRANTS

The current system of Housing Benefit and alternatives to it are discussed in detail in Chapter 10. For the reasons given there, and to support moves towards a situation where rents in general vary somewhat more with quality of accommodation and service, the following moves to establish a more generous benefit formula could be taken (see Figure 10.6):

- retain the current formula based on 100 per cent of rent for those with income at IS level, but cut the taper from 65 to 60 per cent;
- introduce a second part of the formula based on 60 per cent of rent with a taper of only 20 per cent;
- pay benefit at the higher of these two amounts, the switch to the second occurring in all cases where the excess of income over the IS rate equals the actual rent.

This allows benefit to extend to a higher income level—producing a substantial reduction in maximum 'affordability ratios'—while *reducing* the up-marketing problem. Two further moves would then be possible: reliance on administrative limits on eligible rent and size of accommodation could be reduced, and eligibility could be extended to some repair and maintenance costs of low-income owners, for instance, through encouraging local authorities and housing associations (and other organisations approved and monitored by the local authority) to offer 'care and repair' contracts to elderly owners, the regular payments for which would count as 'rent' for benefit purposes,

The new means test for improvement grants has similar problems. Here one could build on some of Yates's (1989) proposals in a different context: ·

- retain the new unified structure for improvement grants;
- abolish the means test;
- cut the 'by right' rate of grant from 100 per cent to, say, 75 per cent (to restore an incentive for cost control without detailed and expensive local authority supervision); and
- offer a 'by choice' addition of up to 25 per cent, in return for surrendering an equity share (with payments and the link to regional housing bonds as described above).

THE DEVELOPMENT OF 'FUZZY TENURES'

The combination of measures described above already blurs some of the sharp distinction between tenures, for instance through:

- tenants having more control over the housing in which they live;
- equity sharing arrangements for first-time buyers, elderly owners wanting to 'staircase down' by releasing some of their equity, or those choosing a full improvement grant 'by choice' addition, all breaking the link between housing consumption and investment;
- regional housing bonds to allow others—including tenants—to vary their stake in the housing market;
- promotion of care and repair contracts for owners through Housing Benefit eligibility.

In addition to these—which would require an institutional system to back the equity share/regional housing bonds market—it would be useful to promote: further 'staircasing' arrangements under which purchasers can buy part of a dwelling but rent the rest (with an option to purchase more—to 'staircase up'), extending them so that those who would otherwise lose their homes through mortgage default could 'staircase down'; 'flexible tenure' arrangements, which offer a choice of equity shares, for instance, to those moving into sheltered housing (Ayrton *et al.* 1990); or 'rent to mortgage' schemes (under which tenants can purchase an equity share in their house through adding an extra amount to the rent they pay).

PUBLIC EXPENDITURE PLANNING

Finally, in addition to the major change of bringing mortgage interest relief within the housing budget, it would be helpful if the presentation and planning of public spending distinguished more clearly between current flows of subsidy and capital investment and gave attention to the 'balance sheet' aspects of public housing (as explored in Chapter 13), in particular the changing values of the assets in use, of outstanding debt in relation to those assets, and of accumulated depreciation.

LAST WORDS

The kinds of changes outlined above cannot by themselves mobilise the extra resources needed to provide more housing and to improve the existing stock, but they would help to ensure that extra resources were used as efficiently and as fairly as political constraints allow. The various threads of housing finance can be untangled—but it will take care and patience.

SUMMARY

■ Ten key problem areas:
- equity between tenures;
- equity within tenures;
- the overall level of subsidies and tax advantages to housing;
- polarisation of housing choices;
- mismatch between the economic costs of housing and cash flows;
- structures of subsidy to housing providers;
- lack of consumer power in a rationed system;
- the structure of Housing Benefit;
- penalties imposed on the private rented sector; and
- separation of decision-making on subsidies, benefits, and tax.

■ Ten overall policy aims:

1. A 'big-bang' reform, with all subsidies subsumed into a single integrated housing allowance, is not realistic. Reform has to be gradual.
2. Taxation of owner-occupiers should be gradually restructured in favour of those on lower incomes, mainly by reforming mortgage interest relief.
3. It is more important and feasible to restore a general tax on housing than to tax owners' imputed rents and capital gains.
4. Local authority and housing association rents should be subeconomic, broadly giving a return on capital equivalent to owners' costs.
5. Subsidy systems for different providers should allow equivalent results, based on explicit principles, and incorporating incentives for cost control, but not high degrees of risk.
6. Private landlords should be able to earn a reasonable return on new investment, with equivalent taxation to other businesses.
7. Housing Benefit should cover 100 per cent of actual rents at the bottom, but be adapted to minimise up-marketing and the need for direct controls, to extend to somewhat higher income levels and to certain costs of low-income owners.
8. 'Fuzzier' distinctions between tenures should be encouraged.
9. Less front-loaded forms of borrowing are needed, with equity sharing arrangements, and with 'housing bonds' to match them.
10. Similar constraints should apply to explicit subsidies and tax concessions.

Specific changes which would be consistent with these aims include:

■ For owner-occupiers: abolition of higher-rate tax relief; inclusion of mortgage relief in the housing budget; freezing the £30,000 limit; and encouraging index-linked mortgages and equity-sharing backed by regional housing bonds.
■ For housing as a whole: abolition of stamp duty; and restoration of a general tax on housing.
■ Subsidies to local authorities and housing associations should be comparable, with gross rents generating a return equal to the capital cost of housing services to owner-occupiers.
■ The power of tenants to prevent abuse of the 'local monopoly' power of landlords within a rationed system should be strengthened.

- Local authorities: complete financial separation of the landlord function; rent rebate costs should be taken out of HRA Subsidy; the possibility of transfers out of the HRA should be ended; authorities should be able to make payments for defined purposes into the HRA as for other housing; rent guidelines should be based on 'target rents' as described above; explicit allowances for management and maintenance should be introduced; 'damping formulae' should be phased out quickly; the subsidy system should give an incentive to control capital costs.

- For housing associations there are good arguments for a switch from a capital grant to recurrent subsidies. If capital grants are retained: the grant percentage should give equivalence with local authorities; major repairs provisions should be reviewed; an 'in-course correction' mechanism is needed; equity sharing and 'regional housing bonds' could be more widely used to raise capital; area improvement effects of rehabilitation projects should be recognised by the grant system.

- Private rented sector: new lettings of property above a certain value should not be controlled; otherwise, control should be designed only to rule out excessive returns on capital value; the BES should be scrapped; depreciation should be tax-deductible.

- Housing benefit: add a second taper to the existing formula in the way described above and in Chapter 10; reduce reliance on administrative limits on eligible rent and size of accommodation; extend eligibility to certain repair and maintenance costs of low-income owners.

- Improvement grants: retain the new unified structure; abolish the means test; limit the 'by right' grant to 75 per cent of costs; offer a 'by choice' addition of up to 25 per cent, in return for an equity share.

- Establish institutions to run the equity share/regional housing bonds market; promote further 'staircasing' and 'flexible tenure' arrangements.

- Make a clearer distinction between current and capital flows of public spending and give more attention to 'balance sheet' aspects.

NOTES

1. There are two problems to be avoided here. First, there would be a major revenue loss if banks and building societies could offer indexed

accounts, with only real interest taxable, which were matched by lending on which nominal interest was deductible. The second is that taxation of real interest only would be of different value to taxpayers facing different tax rates—the result would be that higher-rate taxpayers would specialise in such accounts. To avoid this, the lack of taxation of inflationary uplift should be limited to a single rate (the basic rate under the current system or the general withholding rate under a rate structure involving more graduation), with those liable at higher rates taxed partially on the uplift.

2. To give a return of 0.94 per cent—the average capital cost of housing services to owners calculated at the end of Chapter 12—rents net of management, maintenance, and depreciation would have to remain equal to 0.67 per cent of current capital values, if these were expected to increase annually by 1 per cent in real terms (with a real interest rate of 3.5 per cent).

3. If this limited variation between regions was deemed to be too great, the standard percentage applied to capital values could be varied regionally, although this would be a further compromise away from 'neutrality' and would produce some oddities at the edges of regions. It would also mean that subsidies in areas like the South-East would continue to be of greatest value, and that tenants in the North would be receiving relatively little subsidy in economic terms, a rather perverse result in terms of the different incomes in the regions.

4. Under current definitions this might be interpreted by the Treasury as a 'guarantee' for the borrowing, the whole of which would then come within public spending limits. A more appropriate response would be for a calculation to be made of the expected cost of any such arrangement, and for the—much smaller—value of this to be included within public spending.

References

Aaron, H. J., Galper, H., and Pechman, J. A. (eds.) (1988), *Uneasy Compromise*. Washington DC: Brookings Institution.

Ayrton, R., Best, R., Bettesworth, R., *et al.* (1990), *Flexible Tenure: Lessons Learned from an Innovative Housing Project for Elderly People*. York: Joseph Rowntree Memorial Trust.

Association of Metropolitan Authorities (1987), *A New Deal for Home Owners and Tenants*. London: AMA.

Atkinson, A. B., Gomulka, J., and Sutherland, H. (1988), 'Grossing-up FES Data for Tax-Benefit Models', in A. B. Atkinson and H. Sutherland (eds.), *Tax Benefit Models*, Suntory Toyota International Centre for Economics and Related Disciplines [STICERD] Occasional Paper 10. London: London School of Economics.

—— and King, M. A. (1980), 'Housing Policy, Taxation and Reform', *Midland Bank Review*, Spring, 7–15.

—— and Sutherland, H. (1988), 'TAXMOD', in A. B. Atkinson, and H. Sutherland (eds.), *Tax Benefit Models*, STICERD Occasional Paper 10. London: London School of Economics.

Aughton, H. (1978), 'New Subsidy Proposals Leave Much to Discuss', *Roof*, July, 121–2.

Baker, C. V. (1976), *Housing Associations*. London: Estates Gazette.

Berthoud, R. (1989*a*), 'Social Security and the Economics of Housing', in A. Dilnot and I. Walker (eds.), *The Economics of Social Security*. Oxford: Oxford University Press.

—— (1989*b*), 'Issues for Housing Support', in J. Hills, R. Berthoud, and P. Kemp, *The Future of Housing Allowances*. London: Policy Studies Institute.

—— and Casey, B. (1988), *The Cost of Care in Hostels*, Policy Studies Institute Research Report 680. London: PSI.

—— and Ermisch, J. (1984), 'Policy Studies Institute [Evidence to the Housing Benefit Review]', in P. Kemp and N. Raynsford (eds.), *Housing Benefit: the Evidence*. London: Housing Centre Trust.

—— —— (1985), *Reshaping Benefits: the Political Arithmetic*, Policy Studies Institute, Studies of the Social Security System 10. London: PSI.

Best, R. (1990), 'New Funding Package for Rented Housing', *Search*, 4, 19–21.

Beveridge, W. H. (1942), *Report on Social Insurance and Allied Services*, Cmnd. 6404. London: HMSO.

Black, J., and Stafford, D. C. (1988), *Housing Policy and Finance*. London: Routledge.

Board of Inland Revenue (1985), *Inland Revenue Statistics 1985*. London: HMSO.

—— (1989), *Inland Revenue Statistics 1989*. London: HMSO.

Bradshaw, J., and Deacon A. (1983), *Reserved for the Poor*. Oxford: Martin Robertson.

Bramley, G., Le Grand, J., and Low, W. (1989), 'How Far Is the Poll Tax a "Community Charge"? The Implications of Service Usage Evidence', *Policy and Politics*, 17. 3, 187–205.

Brownstone, D., Englund, P., and Persson, M. (1988), 'Tax Reform and Housing Demand: The Distribution of Welfare Gains and Losses', *European Economic Review*, 32, 819–40.

Bucknall, B. (1984), *Housing Finance*. London: Chartered Institute of Public Finance and Accountancy.

Central Housing Advisory Committee (1961), *Homes for Today and Tomorrow* (Parker Morris Report). London: HMSO.

Centre for Housing Research (1989), *The Nature and Effectiveness of Housing Management in England* (Maclennan Report). London: HMSO.

CIPFA [Chartered Institute of Public Finance and Accountancy] (1975), *Return of Outstanding Debt (England and Wales) as at 31st March 1975*. London: CIPFA.

—— (1979), *Financial, General and Rating Statistics 1979/80*. London: CIPFA.

—— (1981), *Financial, General and Rating Statistics 1981/82*. London: CIPFA.

—— (1987*a*), *Housing Revenue Account Statistics 1987–88 (Estimates)*. London: CIPFA.

—— (1987*b*), *Block Grant Statistics 1987–88*. London: CIPFA.

—— (1988*a*), *Block Grant Statistics 1988–89*. London: CIPFA.

—— (1988*b*), *Housing Rents Statistics at April 1988*. London: CIPFA.

—— (1989*a*), *Housing Revenue Account Statistics 1987–88 (Actuals)*. London: CIPFA.

—— (1989*b*), *Financial and General Statistics 1989–90*. London: CIPFA.

—— (1989*c*), *Rate Collection Statistics 1987–88 (Actuals)*. London: CIPFA.

—— (1989*d*), *Capital Expenditure and Debt Financing Statistics 1987–88*. London: CIPFA.

Coleman, D. C. (1989), 'The New Housing Policy—A Critique', *Housing Studies*, 4. 1, 44–57.

Coles, A. (1989), 'How Often Do People Move House?', *Housing Finance*, 4, 15–16.

CPAG [Child Poverty Action Group] (1981), *Back to the Drawing Board: A Response to the Consultative Document 'Assistance with Housing Costs'.* London: CPAG.

CSO [Central Statistical Office] (1989a), *Regional Trends 24.* London: HMSO.

—— (1989b), *United Kingdom National Accounts 1989 Edition* (the CSO Blue Book). London: HMSO.

—— (1990a), *Financial Statistics*, Feb. London: HMSO.

—— (1990b), *Economic Trends*, Feb. London: HMSO.

DE [Department of Employment] (1987), *Family Expenditure Survey 1986.* London: HMSO.

—— (1989a), *New Earnings Survey 1989.* London: HMSO.

—— (1989b), *Family Expenditure Survey 1987.* London: HMSO.

—— (1990), *Employment Gazette*, Feb. London: HMSO.

Department of the Environment (Northern Ireland) (1988), *Housing Statistics 1987.* Belfast: HMSO.

DHSS [Department of Health and Social Security] (1985a), *Housing Benefit Review: Report of the Review Team*, Cmnd. 9520. London: HMSO.

—— (1985b), *Reform of Social Security*, i, Cmnd. 9517. London: HMSO.

—— (1985c), *Reform of Social Security: Programme for Change*, ii, Cmnd. 9518. London: HMSO.

—— (1985d), *Reform of Social Security: Programme for Action*, Cmnd. 9691. London: HMSO.

DoE [Department of the Environment] (1977a), *Housing Policy: A Consultative Document*, Cmnd 6851. London: HMSO.

—— (1977b), *Housing Policy Technical Volume.* London: HMSO.

—— (1979), *Housing Association Subsidies and Rents: A Consultation Paper.* London: DoE.

—— (1980), *Appraisal of the Financial Effects of Council House Sales.* London: DoE.

—— (1981), *Assistance with Housing Costs.* London: DoE.

—— (1985), *An Inquiry into the Condition of the Local Authority Housing Stock in England 1985.* London: DoE.

—— (1986), *Paying for Local Government*, Cmnd. 9714. London: HMSO.

—— (1987a), *Housing: The Government's Proposals*, Cm. 214. London: HMSO.

—— (1987b), *Finance for Housing Associations: The Government's Proposals.* London: DoE.

—— (1987c), *Home Improvement Policy: The Government's Proposals.* London: DoE.

—— (1988a), *Capital Expenditure and Finance: A Consultation Paper.* London: DoE.

—— (1988b), *New Financial Regime for Local Authority Housing in England and Wales: A Consultation Paper.* London: DoE.

DoE [Department of the Environment] (*contd.*)
—— (1988*c*), *New Financial Regime for Local Authority Housing: Note by the Department of the Environment*, Oct. London: DoE.
—— (1988*d*), *English House Condition Survey 1986*. London: HMSO.
—— (1989*a*), *Housing and Construction Statistics 1978–1988 Great Britain*. London: HMSO.
—— (1989*b*), *The Specification of Guideline Rent Increases for HRA Subsidy: A Paper by the Department of the Environment*. London: DoE.
—— (1989*c*), *The Housing Revenue Account Subsidy Determination 1989*. London: DoE.
—— (1989*d*), *HRA Subsidy: M & M Allowances*. London: DoE.
—— (1989*e*), 'Autumn Statement: Chris Patten Announces Environment Department's Future Spending Plans', Press Release, 15 Nov. London: DoE (mimeo).
—— (1989*f*), *Renovations Grants: Proposed Test of Resources*; Home Improvement Policy: Consultation Paper. London: DoE.
—— (1990*a*), *Housing and Construction Statistics September Quarter 1989*. London: HMSO.
—— (1990*b*), *Housing Subsidy and Accounting Manual 1990*. London: DoE.
Doling, J., and Davies, M. (1984), *Public Control of Privately Rented Housing*. Aldershot: Gower.
Donnison, D. (1982), *The Politics of Poverty*. Oxford: Martin Robertson.
Duckworth, S. (1989*a*), 'Rent Surplus Fund—How It Will Work', *Housing Associations Weekly*, 10 Mar., 9–11.
—— (1989*b*), 'Revenue Deficit Grant—How it Now Applies', *Housing Associations Weekly*, 30 June, 10–13.
Duncan, S. (1990), 'Do House Prices Rise that Much? A Dissenting View', *Housing Studies*, 5. 4, 195–208.
Ermisch, J. (1984), *Housing Finance: Who Gains?*, Policy Studies Institute Studies of the Social Security System 5. London: PSI.
—— (1986), 'The Economics of British Housing: Present Subsidies and Options for Reform', in Inquiry into British Housing, *Supplement*. London: National Federation of Housing Associations.
Esam, P., and Oppenheim, C. (1989), *A Charge on the Community: The Poll Tax, Benefits and the Poor*. London: Child Poverty Action Group Ltd. and Local Government Information Unit.
Fabian Society Taxation Review Committee (1990), *The Reform of Direct Taxation*. London: Fabian Society.
Fender, J. (1986), 'Local Taxation and Housing Finance: A Proposal for Reform', *Lloyds Bank Review*, Oct., 17–30.
Forrest, R., and Murie, A. (1984), 'Right to Buy? Issues of Need, Equity and Polarisation in the Sale of Council Houses', School of Advanced Urban Studies Working Paper 39. Bristol: SAUS.

Foster, C. D, Jackman, R., and Perlman, M. (1980), *Local Government Finance in a Unitary State*. London: Allen & Unwin.

Foster, J. (1975), 'The Redistributive Effect of the Composite Income Tax Arrangement', *The Manchester School*, 43. 2, 144–57.

Fry, V., and Stark, G. (1987), 'The Take-up of Supplementary Benefit: Gaps in the "Safety Net" ', *Fiscal Studies*, 8. 4, 1–14.

Garnett, D., Reid, B., and Riley, H. (1990), *Housing Finance*. Coventry: Institute of Housing (Services)/Longman.

Gibson, J. (1981), *The New Housing Subsidy System and its Interaction with Block Grant*. Birmingham: Institute of Local Government Studies.

Glennerster, H. (1985), *Paying for Welfare*. Oxford: Basil Blackwell.

Goode, R. (1980), 'The Superiority of the Income Tax', in J. A. Pechman (ed.), *What Should Be Taxed: Income or Expenditure?*. Washington DC: Brookings Institution.

Goss, S., and Lansley, S. (1981), *What Price Housing? A Review of Housing Subsidies and Proposals for Reform*. London: SHAC.

Greve, J. (1990), *Homelessness in Britain*. York: Joseph Rowntree Memorial Trust.

Grey, A., Hepworth, N. P., and Odling-Smee, J. (1978), *Housing Rents Costs and Subsidies: A Discussion Document*. London: Chartered Institute of Public Finance and Accountancy.

Griffiths, D. and Holmes, C. (1985), *A New Housing Policy for Labour*, Fabian Tract 505. London: Fabian Society.

Hemming, R. and Hills, J. (1983), 'The Reform of Housing Benefits', *Fiscal Studies*, 4. 1, 48–65.

Henney, A. (1985), *Trust the Tenant: Devolving Municipal Housing*, Policy Study 68. London: Centre for Policy Studies.

Hills, J. (1980), 'UK Housing Taxation, Subsidies and the Distributional Consequences of Reform', University of Birmingham M.Soc.Sc. thesis (mimeo).

—— (1983), 'Stamp Duty on Housing: A Modern Tax', *Fiscal Studies*, 14. 3, 75–80.

—— (1987*a*), 'Subsidies to Social Housing in England: Their Behavioural Implications', London School of Economics Welfare State Programme Discussion Paper 24. London: LSE.

—— (1987*b*), 'Subsidies to English Local Authority Housing since 1981', London School of Economics Welfare State Programme Research Note 6. London: LSE.

—— (1987*c*), 'When Is a Grant not a Grant? The Current System of Housing Association Finance', London School of Economics Welfare State Programme Discussion Paper 13. London: LSE.

—— (1988*a*), 'Twenty-First Century Housing Subsidies: Durable Rent-Fixing and Subsidy Arrangements for Social Housing', London School of Economics Welfare State Programme Discussion Paper No.33. London: LSE.

References

Hills, J. (*contd.*)

—— (1988*b*), *Changing Tax: How the Tax System Works and How to Change It*. London: Child Poverty Action Group Ltd.

—— (1988*c*), 'Hitting the Target', *Roof*, Sept./Oct., 22–5.

—— (1989), 'Distributional Effects of Housing Subsidies in the United Kingdom', London School of Economics Welfare State Programme Discussion Paper 44. London: LSE.

—— (1990), 'Hedonic Price Indices for Housing Derived from the 1988 5 per cent Survey of Building Society Mortgages', London School of Economics Welfare State Programme Research Note 21. London: LSE.

—— Hubert, F., Tomann, H., and Whitehead, C. (1990), 'Shifting Subsidies from Bricks and Mortar to People', *Housing Studies*, 5.

—— and Mullings, B. (1990), 'Housing: A Decent Home for All at a Price within their Means?', in J. Hills (ed.), *The State of Welfare: The Welfare State in Britain since 1974*. Oxford: Oxford University Press.

HM Treasury (1979), *The Government's Expenditure Plans 1979–80 to 1982–83*, Cmnd. 7439. London: HMSO.

—— (1987), *Accounting for Economic Costs and Changing Prices* (Byatt Report). London: HMSO.

—— (1989), *The Government's Expenditure Plans 1989–90 to 1991–92*, Cm. 601–21. London: HMSO.

—— (1990), *The Government's Expenditure Plans 1990–91 to 1992–93*, Cm. 1001–21. London: HMSO.

Holmans, A. E. (1987), *Housing Policy in Britain*. London: Croom Helm.

—— (1990), *House Prices: Changes Through Time at National and Sub-National Level*, Government Economic Service Working Paper 110. London: Department of the Environment.

House of Commons Environment Committee (1981), *Council House Sales*, Second Report Session 1980/81, HC 366-I. London: HMSO.

Housing Corporation (1988), *Tenants Guarantee: Guidance on Housing Management Practice for Registered Housing Associations*. London: Housing Corporation.

—— (1989*a*), *Rent Policy and Principles*, Circular HC 60/89. London: Housing Corporation.

—— (1989*b*), *The Future of Special Needs Housing: Consultation Paper*. London: Housing Corporation.

—— (1990), *Housing Associations in 1989: An Analysis of the HAR 10/1 Statistical Returns*. London: Housing Corporation.

Hughes, G. A. (1981), 'The Distributional Effects of Housing Taxation and Subsidies in Britain', in L.-J. Waldén (ed.), *Housing Policy: The Just Price and the Role of the Public Housing Sector*. Gavle: National Swedish Institute for Building Research.

Inquiry into British Housing (1985*a*), *Evidence*. London: National Federation of Housing Associations [NFHA].

—— (1985*b*), *Report* (Duke of Edinburgh's Report). London: NFHA.

—— (1986), *Supplement*. London: NFHA.

Kay, J. A. and King, M. A. (1990), *The British Tax System* (5th edition). Oxford: Oxford University Press.

Kelly, I. (1986), *Heading for Rubble*. London: Catholic Housing Aid Society.

Kemp, P. (1984), *The Cost of Chaos: A Survey of the Housing Benefit Scheme*. London: SHAC.

—— (ed.) (1986), *The Future of Housing Benefits*, Centre for Housing Research Studies in Housing 1. Glasgow: CHR.

—— (1987), 'The Reform of Housing Benefit', *Social Policy and Administration*, 21, 171–85.

—— (1989), 'Alternatives to Housing Benefit', in J. Hills, R. Berthoud, and P. Kemp, *The Future of Housing Allowances*. London: Policy Studies Institute.

—— and Raynsford, N. (eds.) (1984), *Housing Benefit: The Evidence*. London: Housing Centre Trust.

Kilroy, B. (1975), 'Housing Associations' in *Housing Finance*, Institute for Fiscal Studies Publication 12. London: IFS.

—— (1978), *Housing Finance: Organic Reform?*. London: Labour Economic Finance and Taxation Association.

King, M. A. (1983*a*), 'Welfare Analysis of Tax Reforms Using Household Data', *Journal of Public Economics*, 21. 2, 183–214.

—— (1983*b*), 'The Distribution of Gains and Losses from Changes in the Tax Treatment of Housing' in M. Feldstein (ed.), *Behavioural Simulation Methods in Tax Policy Analysis*. Chicago: University of Chicago Press.

Kleinman, M. (1987), 'Private Finance for Rented Housing: An Analytical Framework', Cambridge University Department of Land Economy Discussion Paper 18. Cambridge: Department of Land Economy.

—— Eastall, R., and Roberts, E. (1989), 'Local Choices or Central Constraints? Modelling Capital Expenditure on Local Authority Housing', Cambridge University Department of Land Economy Discussion Paper 23. Cambridge: Department of Land Economy.

Labour Housing Group (1989), *Housing Finance: Interim Policy Statement*. Sheffield: LHG.

Lakhani, B., Read, J., and Wood, P. (1989), *National Welfare Benefits Handbook*. London: Child Poverty Action Group Ltd.

Layfield Committee (1976), *Local Government Finance*, Cmnd. 6453. London: HMSO.

Leather, P. (1983), 'Housing (Dis?)Investment Programmes', *Policy and Politics*, 11. 2, 215–29.

—— and Murie, A. (1986), 'The Decline in Public Expenditure', in Malpass (ed.), *The Housing Crisis*. London: Croom Helm.

Likierman, A. (1988), *Public Expenditure: Who Really Controls It and How*. Harmondsworth: Penguin Books.

Maclennan, D. (1986), 'The Pricing of Public Housing in the United Kingdom', in Inquiry into British Housing, *Supplement*. London: National Federation of Housing Associations.

Malpass, P. (1988), 'Pricing and Subsidy Systems in British Social Rented Housing: Assessing the Policy Options', *Housing Studies*, 3. 1, 31–9.

—— (1990*a*), *Reshaping Housing Policy: Subsidies, Rents and Residualisation*. London: Routledge.

—— (1990*b*), 'Rents within Reach', *Roof*, Jan./Feb., 38–41.

—— and Murie, A. (1987), *Housing Policy and Practice* (2nd edition). Basingstoke: Macmillan Education.

Meade Committee (1978), *The Structure and Reform of Direct Taxation*. London: Allen and Unwin.

Minford, P., Peel, M., and Ashton, P. (1987), *The Housing Morass*, Hobart Paper 25. London: Institute of Economic Affairs.

Muellbauer, J. (1990), 'The Great British Housing Disaster', *Roof*, May/June, 16–20.

Mullings, B. (1989), 'The Relationship between Housing Subsidy, Rent Guidelines, and Changes in Local Authority Rents between 1980 and 1988', London School of Economics Welfare State Programme Research Note 17. London: LSE.

Nevitt, A. A. (1966), *Housing, Taxation and Subsidies*. London: Nelson.

OPCS [Office of Population Censuses and Surveys] (1989), *General Household Survey 1987*. London: HMSO.

Pechman, J. A. (ed.) (1977), *Comprehensive Income Taxation*. Washington DC: Brookings Institution.

Pollitt, N. (1989), 'To the Lifeboats', *Roof*, Nov./Dec., 30–1.

Power, A. (1987*a*), *Property before People: The Management of Twentieth-Century Council Housing*. London: Allen & Unwin.

—— (1987*b*), 'The Crisis in Council Housing: Is Public Housing Manageable?', London School of Economics Welfare State Programme Discussion Paper 21. London: LSE.

—— (1988), 'Council Housing: Conflict, Change and Decision Making', London School of Economics Welfare State Programme Discussion Paper No.27. London: LSE.

Public Accounts Committee (1978), *Ninth Report 1977–78*, HC 622. London: HMSO.

Robinson, R. (1981), 'Housing Tax-Expenditures, Subsidies and the Distribution of Income', *The Manchester School*, 49. 2, 91–110.

Rosen, H. S. (1987), 'Housing Subsidies: Effects on Housing Decisions, Efficiency and Equity', in A. J. Auerbach and M. Feldstein (eds.), *Handbook of Public Economics*, i. Amsterdam: North Holland.

Rosenthal, L. (1977), 'The Regional and Income Distribution of the Council House Subsidy in the United Kingdom', *The Manchester School*, 45. 2, 127–40.

Scottish Development Department (1987), *Scottish Housing Statistics 1987*. Edinburgh: HMSO.

—— (1989), *Public Expenditure to 1991 92: A Commentary on the Scottish Programme*. Edinburgh: SDD.

—— (1990), *Public Expenditure to 1992–93: A Commentary on the Scottish Programme*. Edinburgh: SDD.

Shelter (1975), *Reform of Housing Finance* (Evidence to the Housing Policy Review). London: Shelter.

Society of County Treasurers (1981), *Block Grant Indicators 1981–82*. Beverley: SCT.

—— (1987), *Block Grant Indicators 1987–88*. Beverley: SCT.

Stafford, D. C. (1978), *Economics of Housing Policy*. London: Croom Helm.

Travers, T. (1986), *The Politics of Local Government Finance*. London: Allen & Unwin.

Walentowicz, P. (1988), *Room for Improvement: Renovation Policies for Older Private Housing*. London: SHAC.

Walker, A. (1986), *Housing Taxation: Owner-Occupation and the Reform of Housing Finance*, Catholic Housing Aid Society Occasional Paper 9. London: CHAS.

Walker, R. (1985), *Housing Benefit: The Experience of Implementation*. London: SHAC.

Warburton, M. (1983), *Housing Finance: The Case for Reform*, Catholic Housing Aid Society Occasional Paper 8. London: CHAS.

—— (1989), 'Receipts—a Chance for Redistribution', *Housing*, Mar., 14–17.

Welsh Office (1989), *Welsh Housing Statistics 1989*. Cardiff: Welsh Office.

White, M. I. (1977), 'Comment [on "Homeowner Preferences"]', in J. A. Pechman, (ed.), *Comprehensive Income Taxation*. Washington DC: Brookings Institution.

Whitehead, C. M. E. (1978), 'The £25,000 Limit', *CES Review*, 4, 12–15.

—— (1980), 'Stamp Duty', *CES Review*, 8, 5–8.

—— (1987), 'Capital Value Rents in Social Housing', paper presented to ESRC/Rowntree Housing Studies Group, Cambridge, Mar. (mimeo).

—— and Kleinman, M. (1988), 'Capital Value Rents: An Evaluation', in P. Kemp (ed.), *The Private Provision of Rented Housing*. Aldershot: Avebury.

—— Yates, J. (1989), 'Housing Policy Reform: A Constructive Critique', *Urban Studies*, 26, 419–33.

Index